Somatics in Dance, Ecology, and Ethics

Somatics in Dance, Ecology, and Ethics

The Flowing Live Present

Essays by
Sondra Fraleigh

Bristol, UK / Chicago, USA

First published in the UK in 2023 by
Intellect, The Mill, Parnall Road, Fishponds, Bristol, BS16 3JG, UK

First published in the USA in 2023 by
Intellect, The University of Chicago Press, 1427 E. 60th Street,
Chicago, IL 60637, USA

Copyright © 2023 Intellect Ltd
All rights reserved. No part of this publication may be reproduced,
stored in a retrieval system, or transmitted, in any form or by
any means, electronic, mechanical, photocopying, recording, or
otherwise, without written permission.

A catalogue record for this book is available from
the British Library.

Copy editor: MPS Limited
Cover designer: Aleksandra Szumlas
Cover image: *Ashley Meeder gazing at a misty-red sea star on
Holbox Island in Mexico*. Photograph © Rames Xelhuantzi, 2016.
Production manager: Debora Nicosia
Typesetter: MPS Limited

Hardback ISBN 978-1-78938-719-3
ePDF ISBN 978-1-78938-720-9
ePUB ISBN 978-1-78938-721-6

To find out about all our publications, please visit our website.
There you can subscribe to our e-newsletter, browse or download our current
catalogue and buy any titles that are in print.

www.intellectbooks.com
This is a peer-reviewed publication.

Contents

List of Figures	vii
Acknowledgements	xiii
Introducing Scripts and Dances	1
1. Ethical World Gaze	6
2. Body and Nature: Quest for Somatic Values, East, and West	26
3. Mind Matters: Mind as Portal and Precarity in Somatic Experience	37
4. A Future Worth Having: Somatic Ethics of Flow and Curiosity	59
5. Walking Well: A Play of Touch and Restoration in Three Acts	85
6. Everyone Needs to Breathe	106
7. Talking to Tremors: Somatics in Dance, Dialogics, and Silence	127
8. Back to the Dance Itself: In Three Acts	142
9. Phenomenologies in The Flowing Live Present	165
10. On Dance and Phenomenology: Interview with Sondra Fraleigh *Amanda Williamson*	185
11. Enacting Embodiment and Blue Muffins	207
12. Attunement and Evanescence	225
Postscript Notes to Self	245

Figures

Figure 1.1:	Ashley Meeder. Gazing at a misty-red sea star on Holbox Island in Mexico. Photograph © Rames Xelhuantzi, 2016.	9
Figure 1.2:	Ashley Meeder. Dancing to match beached driftwood on Holbox Island in Mexico. Photograph © Rames Xelhuantzi, 2016.	10
Figure 1.3:	'Blue Muffins in Snow Canyon', dancing into the soft sandstone. Left to right: Sarah Gallo, Denise Purvis and Meghan Brunsvold. Photograph © Tom Gallo, 2015.	14
Figure 1.4:	Sondra Fraleigh. Photograph © Tom Gallo, 2015.	15
Figure 1.5:	Kimerer LaMothe's charcoal drawing of a white-lined sphinx moth of Colorado and Utah, also called 'hummingbird'. Photograph © Kimerer LaMothe, 2017.	22
Figure 2.1:	Amber Watkins walking the Desert Rose Labyrinth in Kayenta, Utah. Photograph © Kay Nelson, 2015, used with permission.	27
Figure 2.2:	In 'Sounding Earth', Robert Bingham explores voice with dance in Snow Canyon, Utah. Photograph of Robert Bingham by Sondra Fraleigh, 2018.	28
Figure 2.3:	*Florentis*, a film on ageing and loneliness by Ruth Way, a performance and somatics professor in the United Kingdom and a graduate of Eastwest Somatics. Video still of *Florentis* by Ruth Way, 2018.	29

SOMATICS IN DANCE, ECOLOGY, AND ETHICS

Figure 4.1:   Cave improvisation in *Mukuntuweap* (Zion Canyon, Utah). 60
Photograph © Sarah Jeffreys, 2019.

Figure 4.2:   Tree Reflection in Water. Oak Creek in *Mukuntuweap*   73
(Zion Canyon, Utah). Photograph © Sarah Jeffreys, 2019.

Figure 5.1:   Philip Barr in Somatics Class with Sondra Fraleigh and   89
Kelly Ferris Lester at the State University of New York,
Brockport in the early 2000s.

Figure 5.2:   Eastwest Graduate Alaina Deaver lifting and cradling   92
the leg from side-lying. Photograph by Sondra
Fraleigh, 2017.

Figure 5.3:   Eastwest Graduate Alaina Deaver lifting slowly with   93
attention to movement potentials from under her
partner's elbow and wrist. Photograph by
Sondra Fraleigh 2017.

Figure 5.4:   Eastwest Graduate Alaina Deaver lifting the arm   94
slowly and a little higher. Photograph by Sondra
Fraleigh, 2017.

Figure 5.5:   Eastwest Graduate Alaina Deaver waiting for   94
Denise Purvis's arm to settle into her hands.
Photograph by Sondra Fraleigh, 2017.

Figure 5.6:   Eastwest Graduate Alaina Deaver settling the head   95
gently on its horizon. Photograph by
Sondra Fraleigh, 2017.

Figure 5.7:   Eastwest Somatics Graduates practice in class, with   96
Darby Sheridan and Ruth Way. Photograph by
Sondra Fraleigh, 2015.

Figure 5.8:   Sondra Fraleigh's hands finding breath in the neck.   97
Photograph courtesy of Sondra Fraleigh, 2015.

Figure 5.9:   Eastwest students in classwork. Photograph by   98
Sondra Fraleigh, 2012.

Figure 5.10:   Eastwest students assisting each other. Photograph   99
by Eastwest Graduate, Michelle Ikle, 2010.

Figure 5.11:   Amber Watkins-Olpin practices Mountain Stride in   100
walking the Desert Rose Labyrinth in Kayenta, Utah.
Photograph by Sondra Fraleigh, 2015.

Figure 5.12:	Michelle Akane Sugimoto assists Ann Guhman. Assistance in standing tall, balancing the head on top of the spine, and walking well. Photograph by Sondra Fraleigh, 2012.	102
Figure 5.13:	Classwork with Sondra Fraleigh: checking in with each other at the end of a hands-on therapy session. Photograph by Sondra Fraleigh, 2006.	104
Figure 6.1:	Warren Fraleigh in 1944, a veteran of the Second World War and 95 years old in 2020.	110
Figure 6.2:	Photograph of Sondra in 'Cow Face' from Hatha Yoga. Photograph by Kelly Ferris, 2002.	112
Figure 6.3:	Annabella with Warren. Photograph by Sondra Fraleigh, 2020.	114
Figure 6.4:	Annabella with Christina. Photograph by Sondra Fraleigh, 2020.	114
Figure 6.5:	Annabella on her way to the park. Photograph by Sondra Fraleigh, 2020.	115
Figure 6.6:	Nathalie Guillaume, an Eastwest Somatics graduate, with Joan Englander at the Eastwest Retreat in Santa Barbara in 2012. 'Seahorse', music and video by Sondra Fraleigh. Photograph by Sondra Fraleigh, 2012.	121
Figure 6.7:	SIMBI, Nathalie Guillaume. Photograph courtesy of Nathalie Guillaume, 2020.	122
Figure 6.8:	Ashley Meeder, Dancing Back the World. Selfie photograph by Ashley Meeder in 2020.	124
Figure 8.1:	Squishy Toes in Reciprocal Play. 'Selfie', 2017. Copyright Ashley Meeder. Courtesy: Eastwest Somatics Mexico, principal teacher, Ashley Meeder.	148
Figure 8.2:	Sondra Fraleigh dancing in Snow Canyon, 2015. Copyright Robert Bingham.	154
Figure 8.3:	Three Blue Muffins in Snow Canyon, 2017. Dancers: Megan Brunsvold, Sara Gallo, and Denise Purvis. Photograph © Tom Gallo.	155
Figure 8.4:	Matching Hands, 2017. Photograph © Ashley Meeder and Eastwest Somatics Messico.	156

Figure 9.1:	The Flowing Live Present, a somatic improvisation directed by Sondra Fraleigh at Southern Utah University in Cedar City, Utah. Dancers: Megan Brunsvold (top) and Denise Purvis (bottom). Photograph © Sondra Fraleigh, 2015.	166
Figure 9.2:	The Flowing Live Present, a somatic improvisation directed by Sondra Fraleigh at Southern Utah University in Cedar City, Utah. Dancers: Devise Purvis (top), Megan Brunsvold (middle), Robert Bingham (bottom). Photograph by Sondra Fraleigh, 2015.	168
Figure 9.3:	The Flowing Live Present. Dancers left to right, Denise Purvis, Robert Bingham, Megan Brunsvold. Photograph by Sondra Fraleigh, 2015.	173
Figure 9.4:	Photograph of Sondra Fraleigh in the furrowed potato fields of Circleville Utah. Photograph © Robert Bingham.	177
Figure 10.1:	Sondra Fraleigh leading discussion at an Eastwest Somatics workshop in Saint George, Utah, 2014. Photograph © Richard Biehl (Eastwest student).	186
Figure 10.2:	Sondra Fraleigh teaching a Bodywork section of an Eastwest Somatics workshop in Auckland, New Zealand in 2011. Photograph © Karen Smith (Eastwest student).	192
Figure 11.1:	Robert Bingham in Blue Muffins, a work in process. Photograph by Sondra Fraleigh, 2015.	211
Figure 11.2:	Lesly Chamberlain and Roman Morris in 'Magic Egg Butoh', a metamorphic Place-Dance by Sondra Fraleigh. Photograph by Sondra Fraleigh, 2015.	211
Figure 11.3:	Other Stories (2007). Photographed by Devon Cody. Dancer Inka Juslin.	215
Figure 11.4:	Other Stories (2007). Photographed by Devon Cody. Dancer Susan Kozel.	216
Figure 11.5:	Whispers (2004). Photographed by Elisa Gonzalez. Co-directed by Thecla Schiphorst, Susan Kozel, and Sang Mah.	217

Figure 11.6:	Sondra Fraleigh in 'Visiting Butch Cassidy's Cabin'. Place-Performance collaboration with Robert Bingham. Video and computer-generated music by Sondra Fraleigh, 2015.	221
Figure 12.1:	Sondra Fraleigh at age 75 near her home in Southwest (Color Country) Utah. Photo by Kay Nelson © 2014, used with permission.	226
Figure 12.2:	Ohno Kazuo in his 90s, photographed by Koko Kiyama, in 2001 in Tokyo's Shinjuku Park Tower Hall. Used with permission of Ohno Kazuo archives.	230
Figure 12.3:	Sondra Fraleigh in *Ancient Body Butoh* (2014), Snow Canyon, Utah. Photo by Kay Nelson © 2014, used with permission.	239
Figure 12.4:	Sondra Fraleigh dances *Ancient Body Butoh* (2014) in a burned out trailer home. Photo by Kay Nelson © 2014, used with permission.	242

Acknowledgements

I wish to acknowledge several wonderful authors, editors, friends, and advisors in the United Kingdom who have supported my somatic work over the years. The essays in this book have been edited or reviewed by them and first published through Intellect Press journals.

Amanda Williamson is first among them, having edited several essays in this book and encouraged more. She also elicited my explanations of phenomenology and its growth in dance studies through her interview in this book. Sarah Whatley, who I met through our shared interests in dance scholarship, subsequently reviewed and edited work on my behalf, for which I am also grateful. Vida Midgelow edited 'Blue Muffins' and dedicated an entire issue of *Choreographic Practices* to my curation of ecosomatic work with Robert Bingham and others. What can I say? My associations with the publishing community for somatics in the United Kingdom have brought me many friends and colleagues, including Juliet Chambers-Coe and Lily Hayward-Smith. They edited the most recent work in this book.

I became acquainted with the poetic style of Canadian, Celeste Snowber, through Intellect journal interactions and appreciated our work together on the board of *Dance, Movement & Spiritualities*. Ruth Way, who teaches at Plymouth University, is a graduate of my program at Eastwest Somatics Institute. She continues to contribute her eloquent intergenerational somatics and films to my outlook on dance in its performative possibilities.

Americans, Karen Bond, Shannon Rose Riley, Sara Gallo, and Robert Bingham, have all furthered my perspectives on ecosomatics and practice as research. Karen Barbour and Alison East from New Zealand have been a source of inspiration for my work on performing nature. I am also greatly indebted to Maxine Sheets-Johnstone and Susan Kozel, my longtime associates and friends in 'the flowing live present' of phenomenology.

These creative, critical influencers keep me on my toes, and I feel them dancing beside me.

As always, my students, several of whom you will meet on these pages, enrich my life and writing. As the author of these essays, my name appears everywhere,

xiii

but I am keenly aware that I don't write alone. This book is a work of 'we-life', as the founder of phenomenology Edmund Husserl writes of it. I feel the presence of my teachers, students, and colleagues come to life in the discoveries of these essays.

NOTE

1. Fraleigh, Sondra and Bingham, Robert (eds) (2018), *Performing Ecologies in a World in Crisis, special edition of Choreographic Practices*: 9/1.

Introducing Scripts and Dances

Writing and Dancing: are these not incompatible? I love to dance and write. Both carry me to the edge of precarity and align me impossibly with gravity. The live materials of movement and language stir my curiosity. These pages offer quests for readers who thrive on such creative curiosity in the thinking, knowing body. I trust themes to unwind in ways I can't predict, since I have learned through scripts and dances that bodily life is not a stable biological essence; instead, it is evanescent and ethically emergent. Accordingly, my studies in this book of essays expand a personal voice through philosophy, language and the felt truth of somatic experience. Navigating incompatibilities of language and somatic experience prefigures *poiesis*, a connective aesthetic doing, similar to the merging of material minds with larger environments. Forging planetary health begins with such doings through the connective tissue of care.

When writing *Dance and the Lived Body*, begun in 1970 and finished in 1987, I was immersed in a state of dance as a choreographer and performer, even as I also studied yoga and meditation. Alongside this in the 1980s, I began somatic studies in the Alexander Technique and the Feldenkrais Method, eventually becoming a Feldenkrais teacher and practitioner of hands-on methods of touch. The somatic work I teach today started to take shape in 1990. It took me the next 25 years to understand the transformative potentials of somatic movement arts and for these to mature textually in *Moving Consciously* (2015). I amplified this effort with other authors in *Back to the Dance Itself: Phenomenologies of the Body in Performance* (2018). This book explores the relevance of several strands of phenomenology in quests of dance and performance.

In 1986, I became acquainted with butoh, the postmodern and often surreal form of dance coming out of Japan after the Second World War. Eventually, I studied butoh and Zen meditation in Japan, Canada and the USA. As a result, and with the help of my journal, I wrote *Dancing into Darkness: Butoh, Zen, and Japan* (1999). During the 1990s and still later over several trips, I renewed my associations with Japanese culture and students as a guest teacher at Ochanomizu University in Tokyo. At the dawn of 2000, I traveled to India to further my studies of yoga and lecture on dance and philosophy. During my stay in India, I began to develop a somatic practice that I now teach as *Land to Water Yoga* (2006). Gradually, the global reach of butoh became apparent to me. Its somatic basis, imagistic ethos and expressions of ecological and social crisis appear in *Butoh: Metamorphic Dance and Global Alchemy* (2010).

I risked a deeply related venture in 1990, the evolution of Eastwest Somatics Institute: For Dance, Movement, and Yoga. This initiative developed modestly during my tenure as a professor of dance at the State University of New York in Brockport. After that, the institute's programs developed for twenty-plus years in various international locations where I taught as a guest and independently. Eventually, I added other teachers and adopted the term *Shin Somatics* to characterize our methods of movement and therapy. *Shin* comes from my study of butoh and is also from the calligraphy of my Zen teacher Shodo Akane-sensei. It means unity at one with difference: *body and mind are one.*

As I write this in 2022, Eastwest Somatics is celebrating 32 years as an institute for somatic arts. Many of our graduates teach through unity principles and values, which I explain further in 'Mind Matters', a new essay in the present book. Our students come from different walks of life, but many identify as dancers. Some people find their dance through music, visual art or performance art, and some associate deeply with environmental nature. There is no one way to dance. We teach that everyone can dance. At Eastwest, we give attention to the healing potentials of intuitive dance, somatic yoga and hands-on restorative therapies. Through the unity of *shin*, we seek a reference point and agreement around which community might take shape through responsive improvised dances. This also, when we attune our dances with the environment or in restorative bodywork with others. Habits of pain and traumatic memories held in the body morph in trust through finely tuned touch when we are patient enough for this to happen.

Dancing Identity: Metaphysics in Motion (2004) updates my philosophy of dance and somatics in the twenty-first century. This work's revaluing of darkness contains a somatic perspective maturing in my practice and thought for many years. I hoped to sew a poetics of somatics into the writing while elaborating a post-metaphysical phenomenology, culture-nature continuum and inclusive feminism. Simone de Beauvoir is the hero of the book. It travels forward from her work in France, *Ethics of Ambiguity* (1948) and *The Second Sex* ([1949] 1972), towards the contemporary American feminism and phenomenology of Judith Butler (1999) – also including Maurice Merleau-Ponty, Jean-Paul Sartre, Martin Heidegger, my colleague Maxine Sheets Johnstone and other post-metaphysical figures of phenomenology. *Dancing Identity* is not about identity politics; it studies identity through the lens of dance and embodiment, tempering identity further in the telling of ecosomatic life stories. Untangling ecological crisis, then and now, I remain close to my body and the body of others.

The art of walking backwards

I invite you to balance between precarity and gravity in a backward step – the spirit in which this book is written. Like most of us, I was raised in hopes of endless progress and learned to fear indeterminacy. Yet, today we face precarity head-on as we find that we humans are at fault in destroying forests and verdant vales, deep green seas and blue skies. In this, we hazard our human bodies and risk the bodies of all others. We blunder and stagger on because we have learned to walk toward progress. What if we could empty ourselves of controlling overdrives so that life might flood in with its present-time gifts? Somatic intersections with environ-mentality speak to this, just as this book does, not to detail ecological crisis from a science standpoint, important as this is, but to explore it from 'bodily lived entangled materiality' first investigated in the material feminisms of Karen Barad and others (2008).

I like to walk backwards. I do it every day to remind myself that a backward step aids my understanding of the future and that each day is as young and old as I am. I want to renew my sense of what forward means in a better world that welcomes unpredictable encounters in conditions of vulnerability – not in repression of others but in respect of fairness. Walking back, we might welcome a future of care – not simply for ourselves but for a multiethnic and more-than-human world. Moving back towards *lack* rather than forward toward *art* suggests suspension of dominant goal-setting, that the world-sense of our collective somas might get a new start. Somatic projects in dance, leadership and psychology step into such open potentiality, where everything is not already written or known. Somatic studies offer opportunities to cultivate interactive futures of care, admitting lack of control through existential trust and not-knowing. These possibilities do not ensue from flat answers but grow from lived experiences of mind and listening, a perspective this book hopes to enable.

I seek to remain open to the fairness expressed in somatic listening and to explain more about this in these pages; indeed, somatic arts cultivate a full range of feeling in embodied life, precarious as it is. Thus, I write for those who dare to enter the unplanned character of time, chancing the intrinsic values of present-centered attention in the art of walking backwards. The somatic ethos I hope to define invites patience, not progress – that industrial word from the nineteenth century still with us and stomping on sacred ground. As I explain in this book, I am not decrying excellence and foresight but I question the overreach of mastery – mastery of nature in particular, which implicates pollution and threatens life continuities. Similarly, mastery is an endpoint in the annals of art and education, not a springboard.

Written over the last eight years, these essays constitute some of my experiences and commitments in the emerging field of somatic studies, mainly as these essays collect both practice and research. The studies are self-study in large measure, not abstract but of *shared embodiments*, that most elusive and fascinating autoethnographic topic. I might be studying my experience of a city, like New York or London, but I'm not. I gather my words from the closeness of my own body, teaching in community through the intimacy of dance-for-everyone, not to mention teaching through touch with all this implies ethically. My creative impetus comes from movement, not distant or thrown away and forgotten, but as near as pain and trauma. In this book, I seek to lift dance and movement out of the formal and send it towards the living. At the same time, I hope to weave formal sources of research and philosophy into the essays. I trust that a broad understanding of somatic phenomena might emerge.

Most of the pieces have been previously published by Intellect Press and are collected here with abstracts introducing them. I place the introductory essays, 'Ethical World Gaze' (2017) and 'Body and Nature' (2022) at the beginning because they broach all of the main themes of the collection. Three new works that follow: 'Mind Matters', 'A Future Worth Having' and 'Walking Well' are published here for the first time. After that, the essays descend backwards toward the earliest one, 'Attunement and Evanescence' (2015). This essay develops a Zen ethos of 'just dancing' to entreat the present and awkwardness, rejecting norms of perfection and the immoral separations of humans from nature. *The Flowing Live Present* in the subtitle comes from one of my early essays (2016) and Edmund Husserl, the founder of phenomenology. His phrase captures a poiesis of embodied presence central to an understanding of *soma*. I trust that readers will make their own connections through this temporal opening.

The collected essays explore somatic practices in dance as they draw upon ecology and ethics; all of them speak to creativity in somatics and nonbinary wholebody consciousness. Unity of bodymind and natureculture is the central subject of one of the new essays, 'Mind Matters: Mind as Portal and Precarity in Somatic Experience'. This can be read as an extension of 'Consciousness Matters' (2000), published twenty years earlier. The present book includes two of my case studies that embed somatic approaches to restorative hands-on work: (1) 'Talking to Tremors' and (2) 'Walking Well'. The latter is a new essay with several illustrative images.

Taken as a whole, this collection makes existing and new essays available in one place. Of note, the sixth essay, 'Everyone Needs to Breathe' (2020), is written as an ode to home and family during the first wave of COVID-19; it also develops political nuance and accessible performance practices for readers to do. All of the chapters engage dance from a dancer's voice and somatic commitment, which doesn't mean they are exclusive. The book's aim is pragmatic and theoretic at once. In its pages, I invite somatics-identified readers into an ethos of resilience and an aesthetics of care, intoning subtexts of phenomenology that ring throughout in readiness for surprise.

The new essays, 'A Future Worth Having' and 'Mind Matters', finish with springboards and storyboards to encourage students and teachers in the somatics field toward story assemblages of their own. There is no one way to read this book. It is not linear but more a spiral. Read any part that interests you first and then move on, walking forward or backward from there. All of the essays are creatively threaded through phenomenology, research in neuroscience and autotelic dance practices done for intrinsic benefits, not for the gaze of an audience. The entwinement of ethics with somatics is intended to provoke thoughtful engagement with theory and practice. Ethics extends towards ecology and somatic practice in these pages.

REFERENCES

Barad, Karen (2008), 'Posthumanist performativity: Toward an understanding of how matter comes to matter', in S. Alaimo and S. Heckman (eds), *Material Feminisms*, Bloomington: Indiana University Press, pp. 120–54.

Beauvoir, Simone ([1948] 1992), *The Ethics of Ambiguity* (trans. B. Frechtman), New York: Philosophical Library.

Beauvoir, Simone (1957), *The Second Sex* (ed. and trans. H. M. Parshley), New York: Knopf.

Butler, Judith (1999), *Gender Trouble: Feminism and the Subversion of Identity*, New York: Routledge.

Fraleigh, Sondra ([1987] 1996), *Dance and the Lived Body*, Pittsburgh: University of Pittsburgh Press.

Fraleigh, Sondra (1999), *Dancing into Darkness: Butoh, Zen, and Japan*, Pittsburgh: University of Pittsburgh Press.

Fraleigh, Sondra (2000), 'Consciousness matters', *Dance Research Journal*, 32:1, Summer, pp. 54–62.

Fraleigh, Sondra (2004), *Dancing Identity: Metaphysics in Motion*, Pittsburgh: University of Pittsburgh Press.

Fraleigh, Sondra (2006), *Land to Water Yoga*, Chicago: iUniverse Press.

Fraleigh, Sondra (2010), *BUTOH: Metamorphic Dance and Global Alchemy*, Urbana: University of Illinois Press.

Fraleigh, Sondra (ed.) (2015), *Moving Consciously: Somatic Transformations through Dance, Yoga, and Touch*, Urbana: University of Illinois Press.

Fraleigh, Sondra (ed.) (2018), *Back to the Dance Itself: Phenomenologies of the Body in Performance*, Urbana: University of Illinois Press.

1

Ethical World Gaze

EARTH SPINNING IN space grounds our world-sense of belonging, as do our spinning dances. This essay explores self-world-earth relationships, particularly how direction of attention (intentionality) becomes formative in dancing. More widely, it develops a philosophy of an ethical world gaze, promising to enliven the senses. Somewhere between untenable extremes of optimism and pessimism, actions born of joy and hope draw me towards this possibility. Earth, world and nature entwine in language and perception, but they also have divergent aspects to be theorized. These imprecise terms become increasingly more discrete in the course of this essay, textured through perspectives of Buddhism, eco-phenomenology and butoh. Examinations of ethics in dance and attendant relationships of morality build from there. I explore all of this in four sections of this work: 'Stargazing', 'Faces of joy and evanescence', 'Texturing world and nature', and 'As the moth'.

When I was 5 years old, my father read a book to me about the travels of Marco Polo. What joy! I asked him to read it over and over again, and imagined myself a world traveller. Over the years, this has come true; I have travelled the world. Many places have taught me how to pay attention to the new, the novel, the historically grand or simply grounding. Navigating the unknown draws one's attention to small and overlooked details of place, tastes of food never imagined and faces never glanced. Chancing the unknown widens one's world gaze, and at best engenders empathy for those who are bereft and have little. This gaze is contemplative attunement that takes the form of wonder and care.

As an adult, I travelled in Polo's directions towards the Far East, curbing my illusions, but not completely. When I was five, I envisioned jade colours in the atmosphere of the East, with gold and emerald jewels lining the streets, but my stays in Japan nowadays are not so green. Automobiles whizz by as I wait for the bullet train and close my eyes to sense the luminous surroundings that I once imagined. Occasionally I reconnect to the mental travels of my childhood, admiring very real and gorgeous silk kimonos in the Tokyo shops or golden temples in

Kyoto built eons ago. The world is still a wonder to me, and so I continue to travel and also to teach as part of this journey. More importantly, through travel I have learned to pay attention to the world that I experience, especially its thickening diversity of people and places. Cultivation of attention to the world outside has also helped me attend more closely at home, and as part of my spiritual path, travel has made me a better person.

Earth and world are quite different, but we often equate them, maybe because both are wide and ubiquitous. I live in Southwest Utah, where the natural surroundings of vast deserts, deep canyons and rivers hold us on earth. The earth is red here, a root-morphic burnt orange and swirling pink container. When I look out of my window at Pine Valley Mountain on the horizon, I absorb the autumn glories of birch trees cleaning the air. As a traveller, I experience cultural and social worlds of other people and the physical givens of earth as joyfully novel yet near, partly through circumstantial luck, but I have also been a good student. I like to study, to pay attention and to learn new things. I have never lost my taste for travel and philosophy, swimming in the ocean or music and dance. Philosophy keeps me asking questions and thinking beyond assumptions of the everyday. Music gives me rest and ecstasy.

And dance? Ahh, that one! Dance brings me closer to others and myself, where space encompasses time, moving with the worlding of the world[1] in spectrums of experience as earth becomes clay to play with. In matching earth and ocean as I dance with them, I sense their organic textures and how colours move within their histories. I have no guarantee that the earth senses me, but the minute I share its softness, I choose to believe that it does, especially at Mukuntuweap, known as Zion National Park to many.

At Mukuntuweap
I meet the horizon,
Dancing in the rivers and canyons
Below the towering cliffs
Of the Ancestral Puebloans.

I don't know if it's sound or silence
Singing to me here.
But I do know, even more,
How it holds me dear.

Dancing brings me joy and is an ethical practice in this respect. Conversely, when depression creeps in, I become a lump on the couch and have less desire to touch the world outside or make a positive difference. Then, I miss connections with others. Doing nothing is sometimes necessary, but turning inward is not always a good thing. Other people, plants and animals, and the otherness of the landscape keep us tuned to world and earth. More closely for me, the earthy call to otherness is intoned through vision, touch and embodied geology.

This essay explores relationships of self, world and earth in dancing, particularly how direction of attention (intentionality) becomes formative. I like to encourage dance through *matching*, as here close to my home in Utah, I dance with others to match the red earth of the desert and swerve of canyons. Matching is an empathic sign of regard, a contemplative and selfless intention towards otherness. In looking towards and matching difference, I become inclusive and my world-sense expands. Matching is correlating, often with a meditative intent, letting the world be without trying to master it. I speak without embarrassment of an ethical world gaze, promising not to dull my feelings, nor be swayed by criticisms of sentimentality.

Somewhere between untenable extremes of optimism and pessimism, action born of joy and hope draws me towards this possibility. World includes earth and goes out beyond bounds, just as the earth that we walk on holds and cares for us. World and earth exceed the human, and yet they include us. We know them, and we belong to them when we feel we do. The earth spinning in space grounds our metaphysical world-sense of belonging. Gravity holds us on earth. Grace sustains us. If this sounds like too much to grasp at once and for real, dance brings this world-sense to us in embodied motion, with feet stamping and arms carving intervals of the heart. Earth, world and nature entwine in language and perception, but they also have divergent aspects to be theorized. Examinations of ethics in dance and attendant relationships of morality also build from there.

Stargazing

As the branch of philosophy that studies experience, phenomenology teaches that consciousness and intentionality ensue from live state standpoints, and at the same time, create them. The experiential gaze of phenomenology relates to this creative, generative stance, but suspends the natural attitude (what is taken for granted). Originating in sense perception, the gaze interrogates attention itself. This attitude of gazing develops curiosity, not closure. Gazing in its very meaning moves psychologically towards immanence and self-reflection. Gazing is about seeing, and it is also about what seeing means and how it happens. How is attention directed; towards what; and to what end? Matters of attention are matters of consciousness, and they form the basis for standpoints and choices, ethical or otherwise.

In constitutive phenomenology through Edmund Husserl, the orientation of attention is known as *intentionality*: 'to perform attentively an act of seeing [...]

to "live" in the seeing [...] to be directed with an active focus to what is objective, to be directed in a specifically *intentional* way' ([1912, 1952] 1989: 5, original emphasis). As the way we orient attention, intentionality has ethical implications. The intentionality of gazing implies an investigation of consciousness, sometimes motivating a deeper look at one's life and actions. In *What is Life*, scientists Lynn Margulis and Dorion Sagan say: 'Life is evolutionary exuberance; it is what happens when expanding populations of sensing, active, organisms knock up against each other and work things out. Life is animals at play' (1995: 170). Dancer Ashley Meeder develops a playful curiosity and gaze in Figures 1.1 and 1.2 below. See also my music videos of these events, '*Land to Water Yoga* in the Water' (Fraleigh 2016a) and 'Levitation Water Dance' (Fraleigh 2016b).

The gaze as an image and metaphor is not new. Stargazing draws up imagery in art, motivates astronomy and refers to daydreams and night watching. Existential phenomenologist Jean-Paul Sartre spoke at length of 'the gaze of the other', which was threatening to him (1956: 110). Conceptually, the gaze has also been popularized and critiqued as 'the male gaze' through the cinema studies of Laura Mulvey (1975). In terms of phenomenology and ethics – the gaze informs perception and understanding. When I gaze at something as a phenomenon (an appearance suspended in time and not laden with belief), I orient my sight and all of my senses towards it. Gazing can be mindful, evoking integrative qualities of meditation and relative to this, *chiasm*, a symbiotic term from Maurice Merleau-Ponty that indicates a crossing over and return; the seer is seen and the knower becomes known (1968: Chapter 4). Attitudes to the body condition such responsiveness.

FIGURE 1.1: Ashley Meeder. Gazing at a misty-red sea star on Holbox Island in Mexico. Photograph © Rames Xelhuantzi, 2016.

FIGURE 1.2: Ashley Meeder. Dancing to match beached driftwood on Holbox Island in Mexico. Photograph © Rames Xelhuantzi, 2016.

Preceding Merleau-Ponty, Husserl also wrote of reciprocal interactions of body, psyche and the natural world, describing the body as 'a point of conversion' ([1912, 1952] 1989: 297–99). Husserl's ideas concerning the body as part of material nature are foundational in phenomenology: 'If we apprehend the body as a real thing, it is because we find it integrated into the causal nexus of material nature' ([1912, 1952] 1989: 167).

Jane Bennett in her political ecology, *Vibrant Matter*, puts the phenomenological issue of perception and consciousness as follows: 'I believe that encounters with lively matter can chasten my fantasies of human mastery, highlight the common materiality of all that is, expose a wider distribution of agency, and reshape the self and its interests' (2010: 122). Husserl's initiation of phenomenology set the stage for philosophies of ecology in explaining over several works that how we understand the world enters into our behaviour towards it. Later in this tradition, Merleau-Ponty created a phenomenology of the human as an inseparable part of the already expressive world ([1945] 1962: 3–5, 35, 53, 67–68). In our current century, the eco-phenomenology of performance artist David Abram extends these sources, recently in *Becoming Animal* (2010). Philosophers Edward Casey (2003) and John Llewelyn (2003) also develop rich ecological perspectives in phenomenology and critique views of humanity as above and in conquest of nature. Similarly, the eco-friendly Japanese philosophy of Yasuo Yuasa defines the human as an integral part of the ecosystem, 'for the human being is originally a being born out of nature' (1993: 188). Yuasa's philosophy, *The Body, Self-Cultivation & Ki-Energy*

(1993), approaches mind and material not in terms of opposition but through their embodied oneness in being moved by *ki* (universal energy).

As we condition the world in our gaze towards it, we direct perception intentionally and are not passive recipients of material nature as other. This does not necessarily dissolve otherness or the magical difference that it can make. Science, ecology and phenomenology attest a physical, material world, which calls our attention to its evolutions when we are listening. Our gaze towards the stars textures them in constellations and spherical music, and the stars return the gaze. We love what we care for, and this affection crosses over our sensate experiences of the live world, returning to us. We can texture our consciousness with appreciation for the world that we share. Consciousness, in its somatic variety, explores this in many shades. Dancer Roman Morris provides an example, as he navigates an icy winter landscape in Zion, Utah, in his video performance 'Weeping Rock: Exploring Grief and Climate Change' (Morris 2016).

Where I stand now
On the red rough cliff of the deserted canyon,
I expect to consult the breeze
by telling it how much it reminds me
of cluttered paths in the muddle of my mind.

Then breathing quietly big,
the desert slips into me,
where I examine conscience and
release failings, not merely on orders.

It has just rained and the sun is out,
my feet miring gratefully
into the wet rust silt
and sandy squish.

What causes my shoulders to
hunch and dance in rhythms,
like repeat reversals
of oscillatory habitats?

Why, I ask, where I stand now
in my kitchen
with a lemon in my hand, do I inhale
ghosts with blank expressions?

Let me return to the soft stones with my name,
to sign it in mud, and with a flourish of toes.

Below, I turn towards soma in affective states that I also think of as *live states* of being. Live states are flesh and blood vitalities, moving as we move, feeling so much like dancing. As Buddhism holds, 'it is not correct to say that life is moving, but movement is life itself. Life and movement are not two different things' (Rahula 1974: 26). At the same time, movement is the very definition of ephemerality. 'Nothing lasts long enough to move', Tibetan Buddhist scholar Miranda Shaw said in 'Dancing on earth' (2016), a seminar that inspired the present journal. I can hardly wrap my mind around Shaw's statement, and yet, I want to. For now, I relate it to immeasurable present time and its resistance to being captured in the live states of which I speak. Live states are what? They are what, where we stand and how we are at any moment. *Intention* is part of this slippery animation, not separate from our dances and disappearances, but very much alive in present time – as past and future obscure while attention intensifies – leaping, swerving or settling.

When liveliness is imbued with dancing purposes, it is not lazy, nor is it selfish; it is present-centred and life-affirming. In being focused, such direction of attention has the potential to elicit moral attitudes and ethical actions, those we might value as good because they are uplifting and vitalizing, also recognizing cycles of life and death in nature.

At the top of my list of live states that animate ethical intent in dance, I nominate *joyfulness* and its intoxications, not those of drugs or drunkenness, but those that might easily appear in heartening movements, and at the other end of the energy spectrum, meditative states of *vastness*, tending towards *evanescence*.

In the following, I explore examples of my study of butoh through travels in Japan and several other countries. This is the form of dance arising from the ashes of Japan in the aftermath of the Second World War. In morphing the human into all that is not human, butoh is not naively joyful but passes deftly through many transformational states in its illogic and evaporations. I am drawn to the meditative, inclusive processes in butoh's now global spread, its healing embrace of performances in nature and its neutral, almost-Buddhist lack of expectations.

Faces of joy and evanescence

The Chinese Book of Changes, *The I Ching*, anthropomorphizes affects of joyfulness in the image of *the smiling lake* and delineates qualities of true joy: 'True joy rests on firmness and strength within, manifesting itself outwardly as yielding and gentle' (*I Ching*, 1967: 224). In their workshops, my butoh mentors the Ohnos,

Kazuo (father) and Yoshito (son), teach in their gentle ways that *dance should be intoxicating*. Well into old age, Kazuo cast spells in his dance. Intoxications of dance are related to what transpersonal psychologists Abraham Maslow (2014) and Mihaly Csikszentmihalyi (2013) call, among other things, peak experiences, being in the groove, riding a wave and being in flow. The affective residuals of these states include spontaneity, unselfconsciousness in action, absorptive involvement and euphoria. 'Unmixed happiness' recognized in trance and very pure spiritual states of *dhyana* attained in meditation are described in Buddhism, which also speaks of pleasure free from sensations both pleasant and unpleasant (Rahula 1974: 18). All of these impermanent states are known at various times in contexts of dance. In technically challenging forms, they arrive through a mix of skill and abandon and intensify existentially through bravery. In contemplative forms, states of joy dive into the mix as possible movements bubble up in gentle bliss. In dancing, joy has many changing faces, and cannot be forced.

These thoughts continue my post-metaphysical research in a chapter of *Dancing Identity*, 'The morality of joy' (Fraleigh 2004: Chapter 9), but with an eye to the joy of connecting to world and earth through attentive performance, noting that performance is not simply a phenomenon of the stage. When I dance somatically in the careens of coral-coloured canyons or find footing with others in the fathomless spirituality of deserts and forests, I breathe in the oxygen that feeds my desires to be better, to be more awake and able to embody worlds of difference beyond my immediate grasp, matching them empathically. I might even identify this as a call to earthly friendship with others near and far, and to an ethic of compassion and peace.

The laughter and joy that ensue from companionship when I dance with others in the environment are worth more to me than impressions of the stage. Most of the somatically oriented performances that I facilitate in nature are not for an audience. Even so, I love enlightening theatre. The self-forgiving joys that I speak of in attuning to nature through dance have much in common with concert dancing and being an audience for stage performances. Both bring us out of ourselves and into community. To do anything in concert is to do it together. I cannot count the performances that I have attended over 58 years of witnessing dance and theatre. Hundreds, no doubt. Theatre dances and earth dances both engage the mindfulness of a traveller, not simply a tourist, but one who is ready for surprise and the inevitable pain of unpredictable encounters. Tourists are insulated in air-conditioned rooms wherever they go. Travellers live with new environments and people, at least for a while, and often without expectations of familiar comforts. Environmental dances like staged performances are not comfortable; their vagaries can be terrifying, but they expand one's reverence for life. Most of all, stepping out into material nature widens attention towards world-spaciousness and livens time beyond time, living in every dance, rock and leaf. Still further, photography, film

SOMATICS IN DANCE, ECOLOGY, AND ETHICS

FIGURE 1.3: 'Blue Muffins in Snow Canyon', dancing into the soft sandstone. Left to right: Sarah Gallo, Denise Purvis and Meghan Brunsvold. Photograph © Tom Gallo, 2015.

and video generate potentials for sharing dance experiences beyond immediate instances, as shown in Tom Gallo's photograph (Figure 1.3).

Attentiveness manifests in various ways, and its generous forms are potentially powerful. Iris Murdoch writes about the moral virtue of paying attention unselfishly to something without expectation (1993). Similarly, Simone Weil's philosophy attends spiritually and socially to world suffering as a way of overcoming self-centredness (Springsted 1986). In advocating a morality of joy, I take another step in the same direction as Murdoch and Weil. But joy, simply as an emotion, might not be moral at all, or evoke ethical actions. Joy is an embodied somatic state that might in any next moment break towards gloom or suffering. Buddhism speaks to such psychological shifting. It delineates a particular kind of suffering that appears in unrequited desire, the dissatisfaction of not being or having enough, evoking endless desires for more. The Buddha is described as 'ever smiling', happy, serene, contented and compassionate (Rahula 1974: 26–27). Buddhism recognizes suffering, while it does not dwell on it.

Impermanence and evanescence are keys to Buddhist thought, just as these often appear in the morphic intentionality of butoh. Somatic states are always passing, and passing through us. What happens when we multiply selfless attentive states and these settle into individual habitus? Might we cultivate the joy of having enough?

In its wake, joy, however fleeting, promotes well-being, and in joyful states, people tend to treat others in light of the gladness that they feel. I cannot prove this, but I do observe it. When people dance expansively with others, and experience a joyful belonging to the world, they do not waste time on petty grievances. Dancing joyfully and reflectively develops human capacity for empathy and enduring curiosity.

* * *

I facilitated a performance in Snow Canyon near where I live in Southwest Utah. To begin the performance, the four of us sat on the curving soft sandstone, as each of us took a turn focusing silently inward using psychologist Eugene Gendlin's guidelines for 'Focusing'. This is a transpersonal process with a witness where people take time to focus attention on an image that arises spontaneously for them when their eyes are closed. The image might be anything: perhaps a sound, a shape or visual image, a taste, a word or whole phrase. The point is that one gets to pay attention to something latent in consciousness, ready and waiting, and this can be anything or nothing at all. Focusing is a reflective experiment in attention, patience and sharing. Participants usually have something to say about what arises for them, as they recount this to a witness.

We four witnessed each other's images and words on this bright September morning in the canyon, and then danced our images to the group, noting that dance is not part of Gendlin's original plan. Each of us danced in solo while the others watched, and 'seeing' was acknowledged as part of 'being seen'. I remember the melting,

FIGURE 1.4: Sondra Fraleigh. Photograph © Tom Gallo, 2015.

arresting tones of each person's dance, the vast earth holding us and sounds of the morning breeze moving through us. Together, we shimmied through multimodal images, our bodies striking the canyon sandstone and bouncing back. Looking up, I understood how heaven drops through skin and stone without prejudice. My music video portrays parts of our imagistic dance (Fraleigh 2015b). Tom Gallo's photograph (Figure 1.4) shows my settling with earth and laughter at the finish.

Texturing world and nature

If joy comes through lively, liberated and concentrated actions, forbearance and patience often occasion thoughtful restraint. The magic trick of dance is in allowing things to change, as earth and nature are constantly changing, and not to get stuck looking back with regret or forward in expectation. In present-centred dance, I lose self-recriminations and have courage. Casting the world as *lover*, as Buddhist teacher Joanna Macy does (2007), emphasizes an interactive mode of attention and ecological relationship. The true lover is not selfcentred, but is concerned with the welfare of others. Sitting or moving for a while in a natural environment, by a stream, for instance, allows the mind to settle and stop 'hopping around'. One might then start afresh and without obsessive attachment to personal concerns. Worries can drift away, and attention can flow as part of the streaming world. Buddhism would carry attention towards suffering, but move at last towards compassion and joy.

In Buddhism compassion is a key principle, and it is also a practice of texturing the world through mindfulness, noticing suffering and joy without attaching to these in any permanent way – all this while acting to assist others. To this purpose, one cultivates the self through some tangible, artful means. Paying attention to ourselves with care and curiosity in dance processes means that we value our own life. Curiosity is about not knowing; it gives up the answers. When we are curious, we can become aware of ourselves almost as if we were another, thus becoming teachable. Curiosity is basic to happiness because it is a prompt to let go of self-judgement, to become present to others and the world in this moment. We can make peace with the past and take joy in the future in such vital moments of dancing.

> My dance is like my body, a fleeting part of the material of the living
> world, a correlate of the world and all life.
> When I dance, I value my part
> in the evolving meaning of the life of this world
> and of worlds that beckon.

* * *

Moving attention towards the natural world helps to change the mind in its restless motions so that something larger than self-interest might arrive in consciousness. But some might say *there is no such thing as nature*, that nature is a learned, culturally constructed point of view. Indeed, Husserl notices that nature even in its objective appearances is constituted in consciousness. It is thinkable, he says, 'that there is no nature at all'. But he sees that such thinking also places consciousness outside of nature. In this attitude, 'consciousness is not positable as something of nature (as state of an animal); it is absolutely non-spatial' ([1912, 1952] 1989: 187). In the many ways Husserl gives text and language to nature and consciousness, he also textures lived space and time as active states of human consciousness relative to nature.

In *Material Feminisms*, Stacy Alaimo and Susan Hekman sidestep consciousness to put the problem in more mundane terms of language and outlook:

> Whereas the epistemology of modernism is grounded in objective access to a real/ natural world, postmodernists argue that the real/material is entirely constituted by language; what we call the real is a product of language and has its reality only in language. In their zeal to reject the modernist grounding in the material, postmodernists have turned to the discursive pole as the exclusive source of the constitution of nature, society, and reality. Far from deconstructing the dichotomies of language/ reality or culture/nature, they have rejected one side and embraced the other.
>
> (2008: 1–2)

I engage the insight of Alaimo and Hekman with a question about nature and our intentions towards the environment. As concerns performance and action, do we act *on* environments or *in* environments? The first intention separates; the second makes humans an integral part of the environments that they inhabit. Do we conceive ourselves as actors on a passive slate of otherness, as artists who mould and shape the environment, or do we embrace environmental emergence and art as belonging to ecological unfolding? In the latter case, we culture (or evolve) art as part of nature and not as a superior comment or event. When we accustom to the subject-object direction of intention in creative processes, and to walling consciousness off from nature as other, making and doing become acting-on or above, rather than acting-with or acting-as. It matters that we dance our way into our human continuities with nature, that we care for material environments vastly wide and far, just as we care for our intimate human terrains.

In order to clarify further, let me define what I mean by *nature* and differentiate it somewhat from *world* through Husserl. We mean many things when we invoke 'world' as a term. Husserl expanded 'world' in his term 'lifeworld', generating several meanings: the environing world (nature), the world of human production and tradition (culture), the world established relationally through social structures and interactions (community and society) and worldly knowledge obtained through carefully coded objectivity and observation (science). He produced a rich variety of topics concerning the world of practical life, ecology, culture and history ([1932] 1995: xiv, 181–92). It is significant that his broad lifeworld concept sees lived continuities across difference and delineation. Ethically, he describes lifeworld inclusively as a world of 'we', one that grasps human continuities with other life, understanding that all life comes from an *environing core*. Husserl's ontology does not separate human subjectivity from nature, but speaks to nature's influence. Nature changes in the grasp of human subjectivity, but still has unity 'as core in its own ontological form' (Husserl [1932] 1995, 189). Nature is materially real in phenomenology, and as lived and known, nature is also complex.

Husserl elaborated lifeworld concepts over the course of two early books and throughout his philosophy ([1900] 1970; [1912, 1952] 1989: 383–90; [1932] 1995: 164–65). In his 1936 publication, *Crisis*, two years before his death, he continued to evolve lifeworld meanings (Husserl [1936] 1970). He managed to combine the physical word, 'life', with the more amorphous expression, 'world'. These are both widely interpreted terms that take on meanings through use. Husserl textured them by delineating and combining them. How could the world be alive unless it included natural processes of growth and decay, for instance? And how could life mean more than the ability to move and reproduce? Life and world commonly refer us beyond such simple boundaries. World as lived invokes multitudes of decisions and choices. World as Earth is where we walk and dance, and it is also a distant marbled globe photographed from space. Lifeworld is the aliveness of the world in its many dimensions: material, physical, social, psychological, anthropological, imagistic and more. All the ways we can study life and world are implicated, including the illusive world of spiritual life. Husserl viewed human subjectivity as having the capacity to experience time beyond objective boundaries ([1912, 1952] 1989: 187–88). This would be one of the ways in which phenomenology explains spirituality. Husserl's early study of varied subjective and intersubjective experiences is key to lived distinctions between the spiritual and the psychological ([1912, 1952] 1989: 412–13).

In expansive concepts of lifeworld, phenomenology generates an ontology of nature grounded in living, moving, environments. It is significant for ecophenomenology that Husserl kept returning to what he originally identified as 'the environing world'. This would be what we commonly call nature, recognized variously in its temporal glacial sluggishness, vital materiality and terrifying physical forces. Nature is not an abstraction in phenomenology, but it can be represented in abstract terms. Like dance, nature is a word and phenomenon of mind and matter; it lives materially in the real time and embodied space of which human consciousness is a part.

As the moth

We began by extolling travel, dancing in coral canyons close to home and gazing at a true-red starfish. Like this star, my body of dance correlates with objective, affective boundaries, expressive bodies of ice and sand, plants and animals with which it coexists, with bee pollen, fuzzy moths and massive grizzly bears. This field of coexistents is not flat on the page, but rather its differentiations are diverse and invite exploration as their vitalities thicken multidimensional timespace bodies in dance, hopefully not in ways that privilege one form or type. In this field, everything is alive with value to share, including the brightness of sky-blue rocks and the journey from water that spawns all life on earth. This liveliness is what sustains the embodied life of dancing. Like water, dance is flow and sharing in the live present. Lifeworld, the vital field of life out of which dance finds its embodied ways, is what the word 'nature' signals most closely.

Correlations with nature (and with culture) arise in sensate life, and can be oriented in many ways. They might occasion as forethought for dancer action, but their broader appearance is through attunement of attention and intentionality. Direction of intention is part of the act of dancing, even as we might speak of intention in terms of lack and missed opportunity. Here we speak of intentionality as a phenomenon that is part of purpose, attention and care. Phenomenologist Paul Ricoeur says of this: 'It is one thing to indicate an action in a project, another thing to act bodily *in conformity with the project* [...]. This relation can be instantaneous, that is, the project and its execution can be simultaneous' ([1966] 2007: 38, original emphasis).

Intentionality, interactivity and affectivity are perennial subjects of both phenomenology and dance. The intentional actions of dance create meaning and can renew bodily responsiveness, assisting participants both on and offstage to realize potential and surpass perceptual habits. The progenitors of phenomenology did not write about dance, even though movement, ecology, body and world were important to them, especially in contexts of choice, individual freedom and social responsibility. I write in the belief that inquiry in dance can expand phenomenologies of the body. The current work of neurophenomenology through Francisco Varela (1996), vital materialism through Jane Bennett (2010) and somatic perspectives of dance assist ontologies that explain freedom and responsiveness as founded in bodily lived affectivity.

An ethic of care assists the attentive work and play of dancing, and comes to life in various ways. Here we speak of it in attunements of 'dancing on (with/ as) earth'. This ethic expands humanity towards other actants (including fuzzy moths, to which I will return), thus expanding the bodily lived foundation of choice and agency. These foundations are based first in somatic sensibilities and understood as meaningful in experience; by extension, we encounter these in social and political life in the freedoms that we proclaim and scrutinize. In recognizing our tenuous relationships with nature, we grasp how corporate interests and big money in politics pose a threat to the environment and to democracy, as Sheldon Whitehouse outlines in *Capture* (2017).

Consciousness is consciousness of something in Husserlian phenomenology. When we perform an act of expression, or understand an act of expression, it means something to us; we have a consciousness of its sense. Intentionality as orientation communicates meaning through the 'aboutness' of the action or what it is about. Dance processes are sometimes about the dancing itself, but they can also point beyond the dance, signalling out into a broader world. Possible meanings that humans share in dance are many, and they are constructed through sense and interpretation. Meaning-making in dance is a hermeneutic process in live terms, even as technology allows us to access life and dance at an objective remove, as I document in this essay through music/dance videos and photographs.

As a dancer, I understand that *dances move in meanings*. If I pay attention carefully, I can discern meaning in movement: in sense, expression and significance. We have said that dance, like consciousness, is oriented through intention, and that what makes an act intentional is its relationship with something. We embody otherness in the way we relate to others and in the 'how' of our doings (call this the intentional quality of actions). These become intensified in matters of performance: in presentation, relationship, transaction and reciprocity. Dancing with others can generate experiences of meaning and sharing. *Dance intensifies perceptual attention* in 'the flowing live present', Husserl's phrase concerning the constitutive function of lived time ([1932] 1995: xiv).

Consciousness is more than being awake. It is being aware of others, self-aware and aware of being embedded in contexts of world and earth. Self is a dynamic unfolding process. Similarly, world and earth continually unfold in consciousness, creatively and imagistically. Images are surely constructed in thoughts and ideas, perceived in colours and sounds, visualizations, rhythmic movement, formal and expressive movement, tastes, smells and narratives. Embodied images are affectively felt and cognitively processed in dance. Tactile-kinesthetic perceptions are among the most potent somatic images that propel dancer creativity. These might be active as sense impressions, or result in cognitive *feelings of knowing* with distinct patterns and attunements that can be described and shared. Dance is a means of identifying with the feelings and thoughts of others and objective otherness, a way towards sharing sense and understanding through imaginative movement.

Art is one of the primary centres of *axiology*, value theory in philosophy and the collective term for ethics and aesthetics. I know this sounds a bit arcane, but it helps locate how values develop through human understanding and affectivity, manifesting in culture and politics in all the ways we can turn the word 'value' towards experience. In dance we find *the good* in experience, intrinsically valued when it becomes meaningful to us aesthetically (affectively) and ethically valued when we find that it moves us towards principled actions, as we understand these. Ethical and aesthetic values are not guaranteed; they are lived in what is fair, what feels and seems right, what is felt and reasoned to be the loving act, what is inclusive and caring. In classical philosophy, the good and the beautiful are entwined. Beauty also has a long history in aesthetic theory, increasing its variable characteristics from formal to expressively reactive, as I have written before (Fraleigh 1999b). Today aesthetic values continue to emerge in curiosity, creative ferment and revolutions. At best, they will lead in the direction of ethical action.

Here at the finish, we lean towards aesthetics and morphology of moths. In ancient Greek philosophy, *Phusis* (to puff or to blow) relates to *Physis* (the Goddess of Nature), the creative principle of nature through gestation, hatching and growing, and thus, of change. Creative principles are an ongoing morphic process of the becoming-otherwise of things in motion as they enter into congruent and sometimes strange conjunctions with one another. Morphic becoming hums within the dance of nature, the dance that we already do in cycles of the spinning world. Binaries disappear in the performative phenomenology of Gilles Deleuze and Felix Guattari (1986, 1987), which draws from Nietzschean poetic philosophy and from Sartre's phenomenology and contemporary writers in science and literature. Their project calls upon several tasks stretching received concepts of subject and object, matter and mind, human and animal, organic and inorganic, also using performative devices such as 'Plane of Consistency' (PoC). If our being is an open project and not determined as Sartre taught in *Being and Nothingness* (Sartre 1956), we can move past binaries, morph and change, and no form is ultimate. It is not too late to re-envision our relationship with nature, to understand and experience our human continuity (or PoC) with all life. We are not other than nature, even if we are also culturally embedded and to some extent shaped through cultural influences. Both nature and culture sediment in human life and are woven into the nervous systems of human responsiveness.

Performativity in the arts can dissipate dual difference, admitting individuation while attending to consistencies, encouraging affective openness to the material and spiritual metamorphosis of all life. I have been attracted to Japanese butoh and its global manifestations for this very reason. Butoh morphs from one state to another, not denying associations with natural, cultivated and wild environments. Nothing in nature rests untouched by time, and this includes humans. In dancing and teaching dance, I adopt aspects of butoh that pay attention to humans in relation to other phenomena. There is somewhere a plane of consistency (PoC) where all life connects, and we can find this in dancing. As Ohno Kazuo-sensei said in our butoh workshops: 'The entire universe imprints on the moth's wing' (Fraleigh 1999a: 164–65). His workshop words state the continuity between human and other beings and allow us to look into the forgotten corners of our lives, including pain and disease. Butoh does not leave suffering behind. 'Do not push away the messiness of life', Ohno teaches. His workshop urgings also promote a Zen ethos, attending to and caring for all life. Speaking of the moth-like universe, Ohno speaks of gestation in utero to motivate dancers in his improvisatory dance classes: 'the mother makes a soup of the universe to feed to her baby, a soup of the moth's wing' (Fraleigh 1999a).

Like Ohno's dance, ours can turn ecological imagery into ethical world actions. His dances inspired others such as Takenouchi Atsushi and this author to dance for peace and in endangered environments. Among the arts, dance brings unmixed happiness and joy to ethics and attentive world gazes.

The ethical task at hand is to become open to the gifts of nature through the life around and within us, and to flow with it in dancing without prejudice or exploitation – like the nocturnal moth, flying and resting through the night. Usually considered clothes-devouring pests, moths are part of a ubiquitous world-wide species considered to be at least 190 million years old, and there are elegant and useful moths: the spinning Chinese oak silk moth, the Japanese silk moth and the Assam silk moth, reserved for the exclusive use of royal families in Assam for 600 years. Rivalling any beauty, the marbled emperor moth is found in Kenya and

FIGURE 1.5: Kimerer LaMothe's charcoal drawing of a white-lined sphinx moth of Colorado and Utah, also called 'hummingbird'. Photograph © Kimerer LaMothe, 2017.

Tanzania, and the wings of the white-lined sphinx moth of Colorado and Utah are laced with bright pink and deep velvet brown. The 'sphinx' is also called 'hummingbird' because of its extraordinary beauty and size. While I was writing this essay, a sphinx moth entered my house through the back door and rested in the windowsill long enough for my husband and me to admire it. At first, we thought it was a hummingbird. As a team, we eventually coaxed it to safety. Kimerer LaMothe, our editor (although probably not named for this moth), has considerable talent for life drawings. I asked her to draw a sphinx moth to illuminate this essay and she joyfully agreed. Dear readers, I hope you appreciate this special moth and Kimerer's drawing as much as I do (Figure 1.5).

NOTE

1. The term 'worlding' has a long history in phenomenology, and was used by Husserl early in the twentieth century. Heidegger and Merleau-Ponty use it later in the same century. I use it first in 1987 in *Dance and the Lived Body* (p. 165), and again in 2004 in *Dancing Identity* (p. 133) to signify an expansive, moving use of language and world in dance scholarship. I continue to use it here and elsewhere through its origination in phenomenology. Heidegger's famous use of 'worlding' signifies a poetic and ever-expanding fourfold-gathering dance of earth and heaven, mortality and divinity (see Heidegger 1971: 163–86).

REFERENCES

Abram, David (2010), *Becoming Animal: An Earthly Cosmology*, New York: Knopf Doubleday.

Alaimo, Stacy and Hekman, Susan (2008), *Material Feminisms*, Bloomington: Indiana University Press.

Bennett, Jane (2010), *Vibrant Matter: A Political Ecology of Things*, Durham and London: Duke University Press.

Casey, Edward (2003), 'Taking a glance at the environment: Preliminary thoughts', in C. S. Brown and T. Toadvine (eds), *Eco-Phenomenology: Back to the Earth Itself*, Albany: State University of New York Press, pp. 187–210.

Csikszentmihalyi, Mihaly (2013), 'A theoretical model for enjoyment', in A. J. Heble and R. Cains (eds), *The Improvisation Studies Reader: Spontaneous Acts*, London: Routledge, pp.150–62.

'Dancing on earth' (2016), Harvard seminar, sponsored by Kimerer LaMothe, Boston, MA, 1–3 June.

Deleuze, Gilles and Guattari, Felix (1986), *Kafka: Toward a Minor Literature* (trans. D. Polan), Minneapolis: University of Minnesota Press.

Deleuze, Gilles and Guattari, Felix (1987), *A Thousand Plateaus: Capitalism and Schizophrenia* (trans. B. Massumi), Minneapolis: University of Minnesota Press.

Fraleigh, Sondra (1999a), *Dancing into Darkness: Butoh, Zen, and Japan*, Pittsburgh: University of Pittsburgh Press.

Fraleigh, Sondra (1999b), 'Witnessing the frog pond', in S. Fraleigh and P. Hanstein (eds), *Researching Dance: Evolving Modes of Inquiry*, Pittsburgh: University of Pittsburgh Press, pp. 203–10.

Fraleigh, Sondra (2004), *Dancing Identity: Metaphysics in Motion*, Pittsburgh: University of Pittsburgh Press.

Fraleigh, Sondra (2006), *Land to Water Yoga*, New York: i Universe Press.

Fraleigh, Sondra (2015a), 'Languor', music video, YouTube, https://youtu.be/7dJfhZvFI0Q. Accessed 19 November 2017.

Fraleigh, Sondra (2015b), 'Blue Muffins in Snow Canyon', music video, YouTube, https://youtu.be/PREImPoEhqE. Accessed 19 November 2017.

Fraleigh, Sondra (2016a), '*Land to Water Yoga* in the Water', music video, YouTube, https://youtu.be/AMeM38OeTso. Accessed 19 November 2017.

Fraleigh, Sondra (2016b), 'Levitation Water Dance', music video, YouTube, https://youtu.be/yfkTv-L2n78. Accessed 19 November 2017.

Heidegger, Martin (1971), *Poetry, Language, Thought* (trans. A. Hofstadter), New York: Harper and Row.

Husserl, Edmund ([1900] 1970), *Logical Investigations* (trans. J. N. Findlay), London: Routledge and Kegan Paul.

Husserl, Edmund ([1912, 1952] 1989), *Ideas Pertaining to a Pure Phenomenology and to a Phenomenological Philosophy* (trans. R. Rojcewicz and A. Schuwer), Book 2, Boston: Kluwer Academic Publishers.

Husserl, Edmund ([1932] 1995), 'Appendices', in E. Fink and E. Husserl (eds), *Sixth Cartesian Meditation* (trans. R. Bruzina), Bloomington: Indiana University Press, pp. 163–92.

Husserl, Edmund ([1936] 1970), *The Crisis of European Sciences and Transcendental Phenomenology: An Introduction to Phenomenological Philosophy* (trans. D. Carr), Evanston, IL: Northwestern University Press.

Husserl, Edmund (1960), *Cartesian Meditations* (trans. D. Cairns), The Hague: Martinus Nijhoff.

Yung, Carl Gustav (ed.) (1967), *The I Ching or Chinese Book of Changes* (trans. R. Wilhelm and C. Banes), 3rd ed., Princeton: Princeton University Press.

Llewelyn, John (2003), 'Prolegomena to any future phenomenological ecology', in E. Casey (ed.), *Eco-Phenomenology: Back to the Earth Itself*, Albany: State University of New York Press, pp. 51–72.

Macy, Joanna (2007), *World as Lover, World as Self: Courage for Global Justice and Ecological Renewal*, 2nd ed., Berkeley: Parallax Press.

Margulis, Lynn and Sagan, Dorion (1995), *What is Life?*, Berkeley and Los Angeles: University of California Press.

Maslow. Abraham (2014), *Toward a Psychology of Being*, Floyd, VA: Sublime Books.

Merleau-Ponty, Maurice ([1945] 1962), *Phenomenology of Perception* (trans. C. Smith), London: Routledge and Kegan Paul.

Merleau-Ponty, Maurice (1968), *The Visible and the Invisible* (ed. Claude Lefort and trans. A. Lingis), Evanston, IL: Northwestern University Press.

Morris, Roman (2016), 'Weeping Rock: Exploring Grief and Climate Change', 18 January, YouTube, https://youtu.be/ehxPjrt_pJY. Accessed 25 January 2016.

Mulvey, Laura (1975), 'Visual pleasure and narrative cinema', *Screen*, 16:3, pp. 6–18.

Murdoch, Iris (1993), *Metaphysics as a Guide to Morals*, London: Penguin.

Ricoeur, Paul ([1966] 2007), *Freedom and Nature: The Voluntary and the Involuntary* (trans. E. V. Kohak), Chicago: Northwestern University Press.

Sartre, Jean-Paul (1956), *Being and Nothingness* (trans. Hazel Barnes), New York: Philosophical Library.

Springsted, Eric O. (1986), *Simone Weil & The Suffering of Love*, Eugene, Oregon: Wipf and Stock.

Varela, Francisco (1996), 'Neurophenomenology: A methodological remedy for the hard problems', *Journal of Consciousness Studies*, 3:4, pp. 330–49.

Yuasa, Yasuo (1993), *The Body, Self-Cultivation & Ki-Energy*, Albany, NY: State University of New York Press.

2

Body and Nature:
Quest for Somatic Values, East, and West

THIS ESSAY IS informed by autobiography and embodied research. It views somatic values through lenses of philosophy both East and West, particularly eco-phenomenology, virtue ethics and Zen Buddhism. Nature, as embodied, is the theme, a current imperative of phenomenology and a growing ecological concern in somatic studies. The text conceives intrinsic (experiential) values of somatic processes relative to body and nature. As a somatic practice for the reader to do, it scripts a Dance Map on neutral attention, or *suchness* in nature, which positions nature as a subjective ideal or virtue in somatic contexts. Photographs and dance/music videos illustrate the essay.

Part 1. *Quest for somatic values, East and West*

I like to participate in somatic processes as a detective. I want to better understand how I might unpack some of my embodied histories to function better and be better. I want to know what I can change and need to change. As a somatic detective, I want to decipher the basics of practice and ascertain their worth (values). I do not seek to embellish my dance but, rather like a phenomenologist, to find it for today. Then for a time, I might heal. Nothing seems settled or solid in my search.

Inquisitive phenomenology asks one to look beneath first impressions of phenomena (anything) to discover what is hidden in plain sight, unearth one's own experience in the finding and be ready for surprise. Phenomenology, first established by Edmund Husserl, studies consciousness and its embodied processes (Husserl [1900] 1970). Its teachings hold that features of experience appear and transform in consciousness. In dance, for instance, the potential for balance is everywhere, depending on the dancer's consciousness. It might be found in falling or standing still, just as phenomenology and Buddhism seek to reveal things as they are in themselves.

What phenomenology calls 'things in themselves', Buddhism conceives as a quest for *suchness*. 'We are not solid beings' (Fraleigh 2020) elucidates this East–West comparison somatically. Suchness is perceptual oneness, experiential knowledge of phenomena (features of experience) arising through neutral attention. In his cross-cultural phenomenology, Shigenori Nagatomo writes of this non-dual awareness through Dōgen Zen as 'casting off (the everyday sense of) the body and the mind' (1992: 153). Figure 2.1 shows Amber Watkins letting go of everyday attachments in contemplative walking, merging body and nature at the Desert Rose Labyrinth in Kayenta, Utah.

To consider something for itself or purely in its presence (its nature at the moment) is suchness; to ask whether it is worthwhile is to seek a value. Values are theoretical until they manifest in some action or state, until they are lived bodily. Lived materiality develops organically and wordlessly and can manifest in felt life through conscious acts of movement.

Experiential values are intrinsic values, and they are only valued when they are realized as the good in experience, including the good we experience in touch with environmental nature (Taylor 1961, 1986). In somatic modes of learning, values and virtues are first and foremost matters of experience. If it is not experiential, it is not somatic. The field of somatics could well be defined as experiential studies of embodiment. Somatic values have a range of experiential, subjective

FIGURE 2.1: Amber Watkins walking the Desert Rose Labyrinth in Kayenta, Utah. Photograph © Kay Nelson, 2015, used with permission.

FIGURE 2.2: In 'Sounding Earth', Robert Bingham explores voice with dance in Snow Canyon, Utah. Still from music video 'Sounding Earth', YouTube: https://youtu.be/Es2xZIR7aFQ. Photograph by Sondra Fraleigh, 2018.

expressions and are open to interpretation. They are often slow, but not always. For instance, Figure 2.2 registers the intensity of Robert Bingham's exploration of voice and movement in Snow Canyon, Utah.

This study recognizes that embodiment is not simply a matter of nature; it is also produced through cultural values and traditions both East and West (Fraleigh 1987: 153–58). My personal values have been derived interculturally, as is true for many people in our globally connected world. I often find myself between two worlds. From my experience of Asian cultures through Buddhism, I understand *compassion* to be a root virtue leading to ethical actions. Still, I sometimes wonder whether the somatic equanimity it implies is too tame and quiescent since I also resonate with the passion of the western mind (Tarnas 1991). Dancing into the difference allows me to explore their overlaps and complements.

In the quiet of meditation and mindful somatics, I seek the peaceful embodiment that Buddhism encourages when I repeat the mantra and universal wish: 'May all beings be happy, may all beings be free'. Turning towards the basics of western culture, I appreciate virtue ethics of *arete* (excellence as a virtue), *phronesis* (practical wisdom) and *eudaimonia* (flourishing). At their best, somatic dance and movement practices embody these enduring virtues.

Virtues enter this discussion of embodiment because they help refine and personify 'the good' in experience and the good aims of somatic practices.

Technically speaking, a virtue is somewhat like a value, but a value identifies something of worth. In contrast, a virtue can be more subjective, singling out those traits we admire and hope to embody in our own character. Revivals of virtue ethics in Rosalind Hursthouse (1997) and Alasdair MacIntyre (1981, 2006) explain this further. These ethicists discuss the nature and definition of virtues, how they are acquired and applied in various life contexts and whether they are rooted in a universal human nature or in a plurality of cultures. In terms of embodiment, I opt for the latter.

The body of somatic studies cannot be universalized; it is individual, psycho-somatically particular, always the personal body of someone and distinct in its gendered and racial backgrounds. The body is not an object. My body and yours is a living subject, unique in its singularity and often puzzling. Jean-Paul Sartre's phenomenology, *Being and Nothingness*, holds that subjectivity is *lived* and *not known* ([1943] 1965: 300, 327). Yet, through the *soma* of self-perception, somatic processes seek to uncover this same unknowable subject. The soma of somatics is uniquely valued and distinguished from the objectified body of muscle and bone charted on a wall. The body experienced in somatic practice is subjective, always in process and, if Sartre is right, ultimately unknowable in any objective sense.

Somatic projects reveal matters of subjective consciousness in various ways, especially manifest in the arts. *Florentis*, a film by Ruth Way shown in Figure 2.3, examines the subjective impact of loneliness on ageing. As concerns our theme, it also reveals caregiving as a value relative to body and nature. The film

FIGURE 2.3: *Florentis*, a film on ageing and loneliness by Ruth Way, a performance and somatics professor in the United Kingdom and a graduate of Eastwest Somatics. Video showing of *Florentis*, *Vimeo*: https://vimeo.com/676093841. Video still of *Florentis* by Ruth Way, 2018.

demonstrates the potential for somatic practice to retain mindfulness and an ongoing engagement with nature to support well-being.

Somatic values are known and cultivated through practice. In practising care for others, we embody and live values of care. Care and compassion are simply concepts until they are experienced. We ought to engage in somatic practices of self-other awareness, keeping in mind that we are not moving and dancing to outdo others but to join them. Somatic practices can be joint or selfish ventures. Letting go of the self in dance and movement somatics, we can uncover warmth and concern for others and connect with them wordlessly in nature, whether cultivated or wild.

The calling of inborn connection influences how dancers absorb (embody) movement. Dance performance on stage can be stressful and competitive. Countering this, somatic processes seek relief and connection. In somatic contexts, *everyone can dance*: this is the practical suchness and virtue of somatic ways. We are embodied in being born, but what do we do with this? We probably forget about it most of the time, but we can also take time to cultivate embodiment, which is a primary occupation of somatic endeavours. The body is never just the body; it is your unique body and mine.

The hidden soma of somatics arrives in uncertain ways, never just as we expect it. The body can hold hidden traumas, for instance. Somatic methods of addressing traumatic events move alongside them until, in their own time, they show themselves – in movement, dance, hands-on restorative therapies and uses of imagery and dialogue. Somatic cultivation in this sense does not imply wilfulness, or mind over matter (mind over body), which invites clichés of body/mind dualist language so pervasive in western thought. Phenomenology and neuroscience both teach that mind and body are not separate or separable. As *soma*, they bend together. The mind is embodied; feeling is embodied; emotion is embodied; spirit is manifested. In the mere bending of a wrist, embodied attributes bend as one. Problems of dualism in somatic contexts are examined more extensively in *Moving Consciously* (Fraleigh 2015: 10–14). According to neuroscience, we have not yet been able to grasp the full significance of soma and embodiment: 'Often the notion that *soma* conjures up is narrower than it should be' (Damasio 1999: 149).

Ideally, somatic practices peak integrative faculties of embodied consciousness. Studies of cognition reveal that consciousness is integrative, and the mind as the knowing part of experience is never separate from embodied consciousness. Mind is always in the process of being shaped and assimilated in consciousness. This process is a significant concern of somatic practices and the valuing of nature. Knowledge is actively shaped in bodily ways and, likewise, shaped in contact with environments. Extending this theme, Louise Barrett (2011) shows how the body and environment shape animal and human minds.

Virtues returning

Understandings of body and nature underlie all somatic work and, for the most part, go unstated. Quests of value and worth quietly sustain such knowledge. These rise to the surface in practice and are sometimes articulated, one of the present tasks of this study. This essay supports a relational unity perspective that body and environmental nature are intrinsically one, and body and mind are one, as in Zen mindfulness. Anticipating more focused discussions of body and nature, this author questions that embodiment is completely formed through cultural constructions, gender, race or wilful control. In valuing nature, we welcome the source of embodiment itself.

Somatic virtues derive from self-perpetuating, embodied experiences of nature and culture, both materially and in consciousness. Speaking more concretely, what are these virtues? Can we identify and cultivate them? Why would one involve specific processes of movement and embodiment in matters of value and virtue? In considering some answers, we look towards the current work of Shannon Vallor, who identifies virtues informed by a diverse group of traditions, including Aristotelian, Confucian and Buddhist. We might look towards other sources, but Vallor considers emerging technologies in social media, robotics, digital surveillance, biomedical enhancement and artificial intelligence. At best, somatic practices help people live better and even heal and flourish in our technological age.

Speaking to the current internet world in her book, *Technology and the Virtues* (2016), Vallor proposes 'technomoral' virtues that people need to cultivate. To my mind, they seem essential; we might encounter these in many life narratives and somatic processes. She includes honesty (respecting truth), self-control (becoming the author of our desires), humility (knowing what we do not know), justice (upholding rightness), courage (intelligent fear and hope), empathy (compassionate concern for others), care (loving service to others), civility (making common cause), flexibility (skilful adaptation to change), perspective (holding on to the moral whole) and magnanimity (ethical leadership and spirit). To her list, I would add respect for nature (listening to its planetary lessons) and fairness in education (encouraging marginalized voices). These virtues remind us how our human existence is entwined with each other in ecological wellness and the fate of our planet.

In educational contexts, a critique of somatic pedagogies can encourage teachers to explore current life challenges, examining potential cultural biases in the values they present for emulation. Paulo Freire offers a way forward from his early *pedagogies of oppression* (1970) to later *pedagogies of hope* (1994). He holds that there is no such thing as a neutral education. Dominant cultural values infuse what is taught, how it is taught and how students are treated, especially those on the margins of the social order. As somatic educators, we can bring about unconscious conformity. Alternatively, we can practise *freedom* as Freire (1994) values it – how people treat each other with dignity and participate in transforming their world together.

De-escalation is a sound somatic strategy for listening to self and others. We can slow down while giving attention to the body's somatosensory wisdom, appreciating nature, practising positivity and fairness. It can be helpful to simplify in discovering what path to take. Embodied learning can be cultivated daily in activities that produce flexibility, courage, care for others, appreciation of nature and common cause in community. In moving consciously, students of somatic dance practices can dynamically engage these virtues. The simple act of moving outdoors, reaching for trees and breathing in fresh air and oxygen can remind us of what matters and what we share.

Part 2. Nature as somatic quest

Ecological phenomenology harks back to Husserl's *lifeworld* concepts early in the last century. *Enworlding (verweltlichung)* is Husserl's ([1932] 1995: ii) description of the lifeworld's ongoing incompletion in consciousness. His theory of 'the natural attitude' holds that we humans naturalize common understandings through bias in everyday prejudicial perception. He questions how we move past ourselves to get out of the way of our ingrained biases, that we might enter the present moment of curiosity and wonder that he calls 'the flowing live present' ([1932] 1995: xiv).

'Eco-consciousness' was not a word for Husserl, but he would have embraced it. His phenomenology is meditative in this regard. It seeks to remove the veil that habitual thinking places over nature so that humans might see their true nature. This is a fundamental quest of both phenomenology and Zen meditation. Waiting is vital in such pursuits, not accepting the first impression that arrives – while noticing that same first impression – in itself. Sitting with patience is a peaceful embodiment technique, and this is not easy; the virtues of silence take time. We can also dance with trees and canyons to arrive beyond ourselves, that our vision might clarify, and more of our intrinsic nature appear.

Husserl's original somatic vision holds that human life is part of the lifeworld. His work envisions the complex phenomena of the psychophysical body interacting with the environing world of nature. He wrote of the human body converging with nature. In this, he founded what eventually propelled ecosomatic phenomenology and aesthetic activism. The monograph *Performing Ecologies in a World in Crisis* (Bingham and Fraleigh 2018) presents several ecosomatic contributions of artist/dancer activists.

I hold with eco-phenomenology that we are not passive recipients of an already constituted world. Humans do not live in the world; we *live* the world. Husserl explains that we *experience* and come to *know* the world by fashioning a world through activity. Human subjects bear every sense of what is meant by *world*; the world of nature itself is alive and has an ontological being (Husserl 1995: 167–89). We create our planet and its ecology in everyday performances: the acts and deeds that surface in theatre and the taken-for-granted rituals of daily life. In phenomenology, the world *worlds*, if you will. *Worlding* is a generative concept in eco-phenomenology, indicating places and occurrences as individuals become increasingly aware of them. The worlding value of *difference* points somatics towards all people's flourishing and to a celebration of diversities. Nature displays values of difference and variety in an endless array.

Nature as quest appears to many in dancing and yoga, to others in painting, music, photography, film or anything else expressive by nature. Nature shines in dancing where emotion is tidal, as moods and movements connect, change and transform. Nature, whether wild or interacting with built constructions, also poses difficulties.

Freedom and nature

Like grace, freedom needs to breathe, and it recedes when pursued directly. In his work *Freedom and Nature* ([1966] 2007), phenomenologist Paul Ricoeur shows that even though we move through intention and volition, we do not control everything. The involuntary nervous system operating below consciousness plays a crucial role, mitigating bodily lived consciousness and voluntary interventions. This lived dialectic of freedom and nature, the voluntary and the involuntary, makes somatics a fascinating field. In somatic movement processes, we cultivate values of conscious awareness, even as we acknowledge the power of acquired habits and the involuntary unconscious. We can move more consciously to live more consciously, including our relationship to a world in ecological turmoil. It is increasingly important in the various somatic fields to question lazy freedoms and speak to ecological ideas and ideals. Philosopher Paul Taylor writes further of ecological ideals and values in *Respect for Nature* (1986). Freedom can only come to those who seek world-friendly liberties of others and cultivate respect for nature, or we could all fail together.

One cannot have a concept of somatics without a vision of nature. I hold with eco-phenomenology and life science that human life is part of all life. As organisms, humans can grow, move and die as plants do, and we also participate in larger ecological structures. We are, however, more than the organic systems that ecology studies. Ontologically, we are complex beings. As both Husserl and Ricoeur studied it, nature is in us, as are potentials for experiential freedom. We are blessed and constrained by nature, not above it.

If we turn East towards Japan and Yuasa Yasuo's work, we find similar perspectives. The ecological philosophy of Yuasa explains the human as issuing from nature. He envisions the human as integral to ecosystems, 'for the human being is originally a being born out of nature' (1993: 188). Yuasa's book, *The Body, Self-Cultivation & Ki-Energy* (1993), does not separate mind, body and nature but presents them through their embodied oneness as moved by *ki* (universal energy). *Ki* permeates and connects us to everything, just as the Buddha Mind is everywhere.

Now, our planet suffers more than ever; thus, we must contribute to its health and understand our human bodies as part of the world's body. Understanding is not all that is needed, but it is the first step. When I walk outdoors in the early morning, the somatic detective in me relaxes and becomes more spongelike. For the moment, I breathe better, and I see the glory of the red cliffs above my desert home in Utah. Suddenly, I am less sure of who I am and more aware of being a part of something wildly beyond me. I give thanks, and the mere act of gratitude assists my search for nature in somatic fundamentals. I am not sure, however, that going retrograde in my search is any better than piling on embellishments, but I believe so.

If I have an embodied nature, it points towards my talents. I believe that I have a heritage of natural propensities and a foundation in experience for using and growing these. My previous interests in bridging East and West through studies in Japan and India assist my growth in relational embodiment and multicultural somatic ethics. Afro-Caribbean and Afro-American students entering my somatic work still bring more richness. The archetype of *the wanderer* informs my life and thus travel as a component of my teaching and writing. An unfinished book about my travels in India and meditations at Sri Aurobindo's first ashram in Baroda has been hiding in my computer for many years. At least it has a title, 'Wandering into the yes: Discovering ethics improvisationally'.

Not going far: Dance Map

You don't have to go far to find nature:

Sit: As your breath slows and stretches into an easy inhale and exhale, your nature will begin to manifest. As you continue to breathe, your thinking mind can also slow down to still its ramblings. Sit and breathe, stilling any busyness of thought. If thoughts remain, as they will, just look at them. Thoughts are just thoughts. Direct your mind to any bodily sensations; pay attention to these as you adjust your sitting to find more comfort.

How are you sitting? If you are sitting on the floor, fold your legs in the most comfortable position you can find. This will serve you somatically as you seek more ease. If you sit on a chair, sit forward with your heels aligned under your knees, slightly apart. Find more comfort as you go, not leaning your back against anything but asking your back to ascend and your head to balance easily upward, like a feather floating.

Meditate: Breathe easily and consciously. Let your face expand towards your ears. The breath will slow down on its own accord, and your nature will become apparent to you as you allow it space and breath.

If you are troubled by any thoughts of unfinished work in a relationship or a project, let that trouble in and sit with it. Array it in light along with your sitting. Then, when you are ready, set it free. The freedom and ethics will be in letting go.

Let go and make energetic progress in the good that is always in front of you.

* * *

Last night I dreamed I was searching for a body. My friend had disappeared, and I was not sure where to find him. We had been together with other friends near an ocean unknown to me. The water and weather were hazy and warm, somewhat aqua-neutral. I had to descend the dangerous drop from the shoreline's precipice to get into the water where I feared my friend had drowned. Suddenly I was waist-high in the water and speaking to a small group of people. They had not seen him.

Near waking, I braided strands of hair together and talked about truth and tyranny to the people in the water. Then the fin of a large ocean mammal appeared on the horizon. I was not frightened, just curious. What suchness I thought as I woke, the comfort of warm water, the vast horizon, the quest unwinding and attachment to results waning.

REFERENCES

Barrett, Louise (2011), *Beyond the Brain: How Body and Environment Shape Animal and Human Minds*, Princeton: Princeton University Press.

Damasio, Antonio (1999), *The Feeling of What Happens: Body and Emotion in the Making of Consciousness*, New York: Harcourt Brace.

Fraleigh, Sondra ([1987] 1996), *Dance and the Lived Body: A Descriptive Aesthetics*, Pittsburgh: University of Pittsburgh Press.

Fraleigh, Sondra (ed.) (2015), *Moving Consciously: Somatic Transformations through Dance, Yoga, and Touch*, Urbana: University of Illinois Press.

Fraleigh, Sondra (2020), 'We are not solid beings: Presence in butoh, Buddhism, and phenomenology', *Asian Theater Journal*, 37:2, pp. 464–89.

Fraleigh, Sondra and Bingham, Robert (eds) (2018), *Choreographic Practices*, Special Issue: 'Performing Ecologies in a World in Crisis', 9:1.

Freire, Paulo (1970), *Pedagogy of the Oppressed*, New York: Continuum International Publishing.

Freire, Paulo (1994), *Pedagogy of Hope: Reliving Pedagogy of the Oppressed*, New York: Continuum.

Hursthouse, Rosalind (1997), *On Virtue Ethics*, Oxford: Oxford University Press.

Husserl, Edmund ([1900] 1970), *Logical Investigations* (trans. J. N. Findlay), London: Routledge and Kegan Paul.

Husserl, Edmund and Fink, Eugen ([1932] 1995), *Sixth Cartesian Meditation: The Idea of a Transcendental Theory of Method* (trans. and intro. R. Bruzina; textual notations and appendix E. Husserl), Bloomington: Indiana University Press.

MacIntyre, Alasdair (1981), *After Virtue*, Notre Dame: University of Notre Dame Press.

MacIntyre, Alasdair (2006), *The Tasks of Philosophy: Selected Essays*, vol. 1, Cambridge: Cambridge University Press.

Nagatomo, Shigenori (1992), *Attunement through the Body*, Albany: State University of New York Press.

Ricoeur, Paul ([1966] 2007), *Freedom and Nature: The Voluntary and the Involuntary* (trans. E. V. Kohak), Chicago: Northwestern University Press.

Sartre, Jean-Paul ([1945] 1965), *Being and Nothingness*, 3rd ed. (trans. H. Barnes), New York: Citadel.

Tarnas, Richard (1991), *The Passion of the Western Mind: Understanding the Ideas That Have Shaped Our World View*, New York: Ballantine.

Taylor, Paul (1961), *Normative Discourse*, Englewood Cliffs: Prentice Hall.

Taylor, Paul (1986), *Respect for Nature: A Theory of Environmental Ethics*, Princeton: Princeton University Press.

Vallor, Shannon (2016), *Technology and the Virtues: A Philosophical Guide to a Future Worth Wanting*, New York: Oxford University Press.

Yuasa, Yasuo (1993), *The Body, Self-Cultivation & Ki-Energy*, Albany: State University of New York Press.

3

Mind Matters:
Mind as Portal and Precarity
in Somatic Experience

'MIND MATTERS' REJECTS the notion that body and mind are bridged or somehow connected in movement. Rather they embody synergistically, constantly emerging in co-creation. It is typically supposed that minds think while bodies feel, but this work holds that minds don't just think; they feel while they think and what they think. *Images* arise subjectively in the process, and they speak to the body, thus to soul and spirit. To write about image as a matter of consciousness is to push the boundaries of mind towards individual character, spirit, or *personae*. Images made of words, sounds, shapes, and senses have the opportunity to linger and grow in conscious modes of movement; consequently, the somatic cultivation of mind in movement and the arrival of ethics.

Introduction: Mind as portal

As a precursor to 'Mind Matters', the essay in your hands, I wrote 'Consciousness Matters' (2000) for the millennial issue of *Dance Research Journal*. Twenty-plus years have passed, and I'm still writing and teaching about consciousness as a birthright, now through the portal of mind.

> My Body is Mind in Movement
> This is how I know myself when I dance,
> not through bones and nerves.
> Moving through dusk encircling a yawn in the open window,
> I breathe with love in mind—on most days.
> Curious colors of latency squeeze-in
> when I falter and trip.

Bodies want to believe in themselves
in minds of stability and certainty,
'but how', the saboteurs whisper,
'when troubles just stick'?
(Be still and don't ask, there's more.)
Gasps of wild imagination hesitate,
halt, and break—
bodying through the awful bungling.
Bodies waver and weaken, fade in a stutter—
Fumble and sway—bumbling through.
Dance precarity, they say, dance lack and not knowing.
Isn't your life-spark worth it?

Mind as a topic may seem strange for readers more familiar with the body as a favoured theme of somatics. Entangled aspects of mind and body, spirit and soul implicate each other in the unity perspective of this essay. These matters connect somatic movement arts to intellectual history through philosophy and neuroscience. The curious potency of these links appears soon, mainly as applied to somatic methods of movement and performance. These links are a matter of mind and an ethical matter for somatic movement arts, as we move and dance with mindful awareness to become more conscious of self in relation to others and alive to the social and environmental world we seek to transform. It is increasingly clear that the embodied mind is bound up in our ethical engagements, as we will explore.

This study of 'Mind Matters' builds a generative picture of mind, moving back historically to the unity philosophy of Baruch Spinoza (1632–77) while inviting the future in the current neuroscience and philosophy of Antonio Damasio (born 1944). The unity perspective of philosophy can be traced in a direct line of thought from the early-modern philosophy of Spinoza in the seventeenth century to the current neuroscience and philosophy of Damasio. Unity philosophy holds that unity in the identity of differences is a lived reality. *Mind and feeling belong to each other*, and as embodied through movement, cannot be separated. However, this doesn't mean that disruptions of consciousness are not real or that corporeality is not precarious.

Unity is also a matter of consciousness. It represents oneness in Zen mindfulness and meditation. In western contexts, unity philosophy is more active, and it conveys nondualism through intra-active complementarities, stabilities, and interruptions. A single cell can divide and multiply into a plurality of possibilities. This study focuses on Damasio's perspective because of his practice-based neuroscience, study of philosophy and psychology, and concerted development of Spinoza's foundational contributions to mind–body unity theories. Damasio's investigation of Spinoza's work unfolds in *Looking for Spinoza: Joy, Sorrow, and the Feeling Brain* (Damasio 2003). Conceptions of emotion and feeling as qualities of mind are unlikely in much western thought, but not for these researchers. Their significant findings are crucial to somatic studies.

I encounter issues of mind and body in dualist juxtaposition, often in the language of my students and colleagues. A unity perspective holds that body and mind are lived as inseparable attributes of experience. We are not integrating the body and the mind in somatic processes because they are entwined aspects of a single substance, sometimes experienced in stability and often in precarity. We commonly identify the body as physical and mind as mental, but the physical and mental are mutually involved features of embodiment and not juxtaposed. The controlling mind/body trope of 'mind over matter', often used about willpower, results from dualism. This essay envisions the mind as evolving in somatics, not opposite the body, outside, transcendent, or in control. It rejects assumptions of mastery and developmental growth in movement as an onward march towards power and empowerment. Somatic learning is complex, and life itself moves towards weakness and death. Where is the weak body in somatic studies?[1]

Feelings in mind

Alongside Spinoza and Damasio's work, this essay recognizes the unity perspective in Edmund Husserl's phenomenology of consciousness and imagery early in the twentieth century (1925–2005). Husserl's lifeworld philosophy envisions a lived convergence of body and nature. In *Back to the Dance Itself*, several authors expand lifeworld values and somatic perspectives (Fraleigh 2018: 12–26). Lived body concepts of Husserl also spur Maurice Merleau-Ponty's oft-cited books on perception (1962) and perceptual entwinement (1968). *Chiasm* (*entwinement*) points to the space of perception in the later work of Merleau-Ponty, where the seer is seen, and the knower becomes known, or 'doubled' (1968: 264). The symbiotic play of *chiasm* animates presence, differentiation, and oneness (1968: 214–15). More recently, phenomenology benefits from the example of Maxine Sheets-Johnstone's influential work, particularly her article on mind in movement: 'Thinking in Movement' (1981).

Through the extensive work of phenomenology and neuroscience, we learn that minds don't just think; they feel while they think as they think in movement. Somatic educators work and play with the connective momentum of mindful embodiment. If this impetus sounds smooth and fluid, it seldom is. As this essay explains, minds develop and potentially flourish in movement and dance, but challenges can reorient any experience, no matter how well-intended. Thinking and feeling are entangled precariously.

How can minds feel anything? As a matter of consciousness and sense, feelings activate movement and awareness and have various thresholds of affectivity and emotional tones, as we explore later with Damasio. Anxious feelings might be the basis for emotions such as fear or shame. Feelings also spur aesthetic expressions and can be opaque and not easy to describe. In somatic education, where individual perception is vital, feeling and emotion exist on sliding scales and ruptures in participants' experiences. Those who have been in a classroom (most of us) might remember the varied and vulnerable atmospheres. What is felt and understood and what it means to individuals is part of the art and fascination of somatic learning.

Most recently, we understand the value of somatic learning for social justice, racial and gender equality, and issues of abuse.[2] Somatic pedagogies can be powerful equalizers as reminders of what humans share, while cultural forces and divisions are also matters of mind and feeling. Struggles for being seen, heard, and belonging fuel minds. Feelings, both positive and negative, guide human awareness and behaviour as fundamental to mind and experiences of consciousness.

Indeed, an ethic arises concerning this. Somatic pedagogies ought to advocate for inclusiveness while featuring a variety of cultural perspectives and teachers. Somatic movement and dance practices can be designed and taught for everyone, not just a privileged few. Pedagogies that work across differences of race and cultures suggest practices that cultivate basic human movement, not highly stylized dance forms; still more, they require a shift of consciousness towards the good of everyone, which is an inherent ethos of unity philosophy. Unity through equality doesn't imply sameness, however. The somatics field faces the challenge of diversifying its topics while providing opportunities for individual development and group work in tandem.

Movement evokes every human emotion. Thus, learning how to attune constructively is important. Corporeal listening can be taught and practiced with patience. Voice and dance improvisations, movement meditations, painting, poetry, and dreamwork are somatic vehicles for a range of emotional expressions. These can engage a wide range of abilities and backgrounds. Group movement in environmental nature is also healing and builds community.

I write for the journal in your hands because I am a long-time teacher, practitioner, and researcher of somatic movement methods and philosophy. In this essay, I seek to connect with somatics-identified readers in delineating mind as embodied and felt in movement. I hope to say more about the implications of this. We don't often define mind in terms of feeling and emotion, but Spinoza and Damasio do, and I do. I appeal to phenomenology for similar reasons. Soon, we take a closer look at these choices.[3]

Spinoza might seem a remote choice, but his work fastens my thesis to a three-hundred-year-old history in the West and recalls even deeper classical roots.

Looking back in Greek philosophy, Plato might be a candidate for consideration because of his classical exposition of the tripartite unification of mind, spirit, and soul. Likewise, Aristotle saw *psyche* (soul) as part of the aliveness in everything.[4] Spinoza stands out for his work's somatic ethos, bond with nature, and in-depth elucidation of mind–body unity.

Part 1. Unity philosophy and somatics

Baruch Spinoza is a philosopher of unity in breaking with his days' theology and Descartes's dualism. Spinoza's lifetime (1632–77) overlapped that of René Descartes (1596–1650). Spinoza spent most of his short life as an outcast Jew living in The Hague in the Netherlands, while Descartes was one of the most notable intellectual figures of the Dutch Golden Age.

After Spinoza

Following Spinoza's lead, Damasio also refutes Descartes's dualism but updates this through science, explaining through neuroscience and in granular fashion how nervous systems create minds and bodies in tandem. Minds are not invisible entities, and bodies not just material substance (Damasio 2003: 183–217). Damasio's search for crucial elements of consciousness, mind, and feeling led him to Spinoza and the implications of his philosophy for science and psychology in *Looking for Spinoza* (Damasio 2003). Spinoza's earlier discoveries of body–mind unity foreground Damasio's neuroscience and inform his study of psychology and affectivity.

Bodily minded generation of emotions and feelings is the somatic scaffolding for these innovators. They both explain mind and body as *parallel attributes* of the same substance, constantly interacting through movement. Our organism contains a body, a nervous system, and a mind that derives from both (2018: 103). The very plastic brain extends into the nervous system and exists throughout bodily substance as vital to conscious movement and the life of the mind. Or, we could assert with Damasio: *No body, never mind*.

In opposition to Descartes's substance dualism, Spinoza saw movement as a quality of nature and all things human, including the mind. His philosophy posited mind as part of an embodied expression and is consistent with today's discoveries in neuroscience and somatics. Somatic practices have a deep interest in tangible manifestations of mind since mind is qualitatively expressed in movement and dance, through dance in nature, and not least in somatic educational styles.

If you want to see my mind, see how I dance; if you want to read my mind, consider what I write and how I teach. The mind of somatics appears in teaching methods that diminish competition, encourage wellbeing, and support choice and diversity. Rather than teaching movement through command, I often ask students, 'what is available to you now'? Verbs of permission such as wait, play, allow, and breathe foster ease of mind and emotion in movement and are crucial to somatic pedagogy. Hold back, fall, and stumble provide more texture and opportunities to disrupt habits, and promote unexpected stability (balance) through precarity.

Varieties of emotion permeate the philosophy of Spinoza – one of the first to challenge the mind/body hierarchy and body/soul dualism of Descartes. Spinoza has influenced the history of biblical criticism, literature, and such different twentieth-century thinkers as Freud, Einstein, and Damasio. Contemporary physicists have viewed his monism as a harbinger of the twentieth-century field metaphysics. The *Cambridge Dictionary of Philosophy* calls him a leading intellectual forebear of the twentieth-century mind–body identity theory (Audi 1995: 759–63).

As concerns somatic studies, Spinoza identifies mind and body as continuous, and the emotions as part of this unity. Could he live in our time, he would encounter the post-metaphysics of Giles Deleuze and others who write of a necessary corporeal precarity inherent to an understanding of human nature(s). Spinoza's contribution seized upon the importance of intrinsic connection, how the whole supersedes its parts. Deleuze's rhizome philosophy viewed such connectivity through PoC, *planes of continuity/consistency* that spread out, not only with upward momentum but more like vines (1987). The propositions of Part III of Spinoza's *Ethics* contain 48 definitions of feelings and emotions: pleasure, pain, desire, love, benevolence, hatred, fear, joy, sorrow, hope, disappointment, humility, anger, pride, shame, cruelty, and further on into the psychological terrain that propels his work.

Spinoza's emphasis on emotion represents a departure from much of philosophy in the West, arising almost exclusively through white male texts, which have had difficulty admitting body, feeling, and emotion as serious subjects. Such texts focus on the primacy of mind through the intellect – setting mind and reasoning apart from body and feeling while degrading the latter. We are not supposed to have bodies and feelings; they are bad actors, animals, untrustworthy, nonrational, and too emotional, as are women and non-whites. Issues of equality are entwined with the diminishment of body and emotion.

The *yin/yang* bifurcations of Asian philosophy also represent the *body* as *yin*, female, earthly, fleshy, and dark, while the mind is light and *yang*, masculine, and intellectual. Issues of gender and race relative to body and nature are prejudicial and consequential in myths across cultures, as I study in works revaluing darkness (1999, 2004, and 2010). In a similar vein, Williamson and Sellers-Young rescue woman's positive relationship to nature through dance in *Spiritual Herstories* (2020).

Spinoza's unity views run counter to metaphysical and mythological dichotomies. Human feeling is part of the flowing seamlessness of life for Spinoza. And to be a body – to have life – is to be a part of God. Spinoza saw God, nature, and humans inclusively (*Spinoza: Selections*, 1958: 384–85), which alienated him from both the synagogue and the church. To view the sacred as immanent and inmost rather than most other in Spinoza's day was heresy. In his articulation of the emotional core of life, we might say Spinoza has a great deal to teach about *soma* – our human and historical body – including his concern for affective life – why feeling minds and consciousness matter

Towards Damasio and extended consciousness

Damasio extends Spinoza's accounts of emotion towards narratives of consciousness and self, delineating autobiographical levels of self in *The Feeling of What Happens: Body and Emotion in the Making of Consciousness* (Damasio 1999). Unlike the primordial account of soma, or the simple representation of organic states involved in self-perception, the autobiographical self can narrate complex structures. This is the fully conscious self we usually address in somatic practices, developmentally and therapeutically. The autobiographical self elaborates implicit memory and changes continuously with new life experiences and complexities of feeling.

Consciousness is not a small book in the head. It is the birthright of living things. Consciousness exists throughout the body in movement and related feelings, especially keen in purposefully directed movement. Motor functions, speech, and consciousness relate to movement and its felt basis in tactility. Bones are immersed in feelings of movement, always, and thus have both an organic and cultural history; how our ancestors lived modelled our bones and the neural structures of our present brains. We learn through somatic education that movement is mapped in consciousness and is developmental; how we feel when we dance matters; ways of practicing all of the arts matter. Practices influence aesthetic (affective and felt) consciousness. Indeed, we expand consciousness through use, and we activate awareness when we move consciously. Consciousness can signal wakefulness and marks deliberateness, intentionality, mindfulness, feeling, learning, and emotion.

How we feel when we move is developmentally potent, potentially positive or negative, or somewhere in between. Damasio explains that we build perceptual complexity in layers of feeling, self-knowing, and subject–object relations that arise somatically from a 'proto-self' towards a core self and finally develop into extended consciousness and memory. He creates a ladder, but not one of surety. One can fall off. Self-knowing and subject–object relations implicate soma: 'Often the notion that *soma* conjures up is narrower than it should be' (1999: 149).

Damasio teaches about soma through the 'proto-self'. This somatic biologic layer of life is not available to consciousness or capable of control. It is, however, the basis for feeling and thus of consciousness (1999: 172). Damasio explains that consciousness is not localized in the brain; it is global and organismic. *We are conscious throughout the body, not in one part.* Phenomenology, like Damasio, teaches that consciousness has content. We can be aware of pain and notice it; we feel joy and relief and name them. We make choices and can improvise in risky terrain to notice difficulty and give it form. Learning often happens in nonlinear paths. We split and seam experiences in memory and imagination.

Damasio further argues in a recent work (2018) that feelings are nature's evolutionary processes for preserving life and making human cultures. Feelings tell us what we care about and motivate human creativity in all walks of life. Conscious awareness of feeling connects us to the objective, tangible world. This is the world of touch that also touches us. Change in subject–object relations activates *somatosensory* felt life (2018: 80, 169). *This is through movement and touch.* Movement and touch are necessarily part and party to consciousness; however, we can be more or less conscious of our movements and generally take touch for granted. We practice somatic modes of movement and touch to become more aware of self and alive to the social and environmental world we hope to transform together. Moving/dancing consciously and developing tactile, kinaesthetic awareness are vital purposes of somatic movement education (Fraleigh 2015).

Consciousness is a great synthesizer, and the psychophysical mind energizes it. Motor adjustments and felt emotional responses to these 'are all coregistered in memory' (1999: 148–49). The *'felt* core self' renews and learns through outside influences and the brain's memory stores. The result of this learning, Damasio writes, is the development of autobiographical memory, an accumulative memory of who we are and can be (1999: 172–73). *Extended consciousness* (1999, 2010, 2018) is at the apex of Damasio's account. This highly discriminating level develops close interaction among feelings and outside happenings.

In the somatosensory feelings of work, art, therapy, and play, extended consciousness responds to practice, particularly in somatic movement arts. Repatterning classes bring awareness to movement structures; experiential anatomy focuses on organic function; somatic yoga and somatically conceived dance improvisations encourage curiosity and precarity as they flow and stutter in consciousness. Ecological site-specific performances draw upon oxygen and nature's healing properties. Tactile-kinaesthetic awareness through fine-tuned touch techniques extends corporeality towards others and the world, admitting feelings of pain and trauma. Values of care sustain such extensions of attention. These practices develop the embodied mind and extended affective consciousness.

Part 2. Mind space

Philosophies of mind fill library shelves, but they seldom speak of mind as embodied (existing throughout an intra-active whole). One of my students asked me to define mind in my way, and I believed it worth a try, having spent my career defining body and in love with mind, first in *Dance and the Lived Body* (1987) and later in more personal work, *Dancing Identity* (2004). Writing quickly into mind space, I connected to my studies of nondualism (unity) in philosophy, neuroscience, and phenomenology. My first thought was to link mind and consciousness. My second was to seek an escape from the snares of mind through what Giles Deleuze calls 'lines of fight'.[5]

Mind takes flight from consciousness. At the same time, it lingers and grows, or else it fades and sometimes falters. Mind is mental, physical, and psychical by way of feeling, change, and imagination. Consciousness is a synthesizer, and the mind is its music. Minds couldn't exist without consciousness and feelings. I feel good, glad, sad, gloomy, or grumpy because I can interpret my feelings and say what possible meanings they hold for me. I can do this through the integrative faculty of wakeful embodied consciousness and the boundless realizations and interpretations of the mind. To my mind, the mind is big – bigger than the head – even as it changes shapes and timings, morphing through felt qualities and emotions in tandem with the ever-malleable conscious body.

Movement shifts the mind and, therefore, the 'self'. Would this be the separate self we assume is ours alone? I notice that the self is an obsession in somatics and not a good one. As I noted earlier, Somatics inherited its self-focus from Hanna, and I want to decentre this outmoded definition of soma. A phenomenologist would say there is no such thing as the self, since we are always incorporating others from birth on, and we are part of the world around us. Any way of speaking about our relationship to the environment would have to account for our being a part of it. The tendency to put ourselves at the centre is a problem I have been aware of since my study of butoh. As a form of dance theatre and therapy beginning in Japan after the Second World War, butoh decentres the self. The morphing nature of butoh makes it difficult to locate a solid bodyself. Instead butoh dancers dissolve the self and enter into a state of *ma* or 'the space between' in Japanese. In the West, we call this space 'liminality'.

Psychophysical felt states move the mind, but minds carry on past the moment of movement – both in general and specifically. The human mind connects to the past and carries the present into a precarious future. Minds have memories quelled or fuelled through bodily states – uplifting states sometimes, or states of fear and loss. Minds also carry intuitive faculties; they can see past what is in front of them, partly through broad experiential associations and informed guesses. Hopefully, they motivate their owners to care for others. Feeling minds can do this. Feelings imbue minds with a conscience. When hurt, guilt and anxiety cross our minds, would we not spare others the same?

Matching

Because minds can feel hurt, they know other minds can also hurt. In many ways, minds match each other. Minds agree somatically through feelings, both empathetic and aesthetic. *Somatic matching* provides perceptual opportunities for attuning with others in nature: walking and dancing together, witnessing, observing, and feeling with others – breathing with trees, matching their minds, and perhaps even changing our own minds.

As one of its primary methods, phenomenology asks into the content and workings of consciousness. Minds couldn't exist without consciousness and feelings, nor could bodies, nor could the minded body exist in isolation from the world. Minds and bodies interact with the world's curiosities; minds and bodies match and tango as one – sometimes in staccato, seldom with stability, and often trembling. I feel glad or sad, gloomy or troubled because I can interpret my feelings and say what meanings they hold for me, and I can do this through the faculty of wakeful embodied consciousness and the boundless realizations of mind.

Minds match selves *to others and environments* unconsciously and naturally. Minds can associate and notice subtle nonverbal attunements through conscious practice. Through the associative faculty of mind, consciousness also roams – as Carl Jung showed in his work with Active Imagination. Damasio helps me understand how matching happens. I learn through his work that *consciousness is global, organismic, and connective*, existing throughout the body and connecting us to the world writ large. Consciousness is a birthright we all possess, a global capacity for awareness, association, and assimilation in reciprocity with the mind.[6] When I attempt to match the mind of others, I listen through movement, gesture, and words; assimilate them, and expand my consciousness through empathy and association.

Images

What is being assimilated and associated in consciousness? What is the content? In Damasio's schema, *images* are the subject matter of consciousness. Like a graphic artist or somatic witness, Damasio understands that images narrate conscious content, the things we perceive and assemble in thought and expression. Consciousness first arises through perception, as phenomenology teaches and thus is alive with imagistic sensate content. Perceptual processes seed vivid impressions, or images of sense experience and knowledge. Such images accrue further corporeal content through somatic approaches and have a lot to say and activate. In assimilation of felt sense and image, minds can roam and ruminate like horses grazing in meadows. Minds flow through dreams, defining their owners to themselves and perhaps influencing others – the narrations of the mind flow in mutuality with bodily lived consciousness.

Embodied minds outlive their constantly discarded skins, but they carry visible fleshiness and the weight of bone and time as manifested. Imaginative minds have hands and feet to take them onto the stage and fingers to touch virtual powers of computer interfaces. Minds listen to many images constituted through sense perception and sentient powers of embodiment. Thus, minds hear and see in parts and wholes. They can also extend outward through consciously performed movement, art, and smart technologies, primal and electronic. People are sometimes characterized through mind as dull or sharp, laid back, fun or practical, angry, cruel, calm, compassionate, spiritual, soulful, and much more. And minds learn. Minds learn to identify: listen, match, and absorb. In desperation, they might even dissociate. Would mindful association as a form of matching be helpful then?

When I dance in ensemble or concert with others, I sense their presence in qualities of movement and character. How we dance together is the goal as we listen through movement. This involves matching the moment of movement in continuity with place, whether in a studio, on stage, or in windy desert sands. These conditions of environment and place all produce impressions or images of their own that remain in mind after the dance is gone. When activations wane, memory replaces the present with more images in association.

Seemingly beautiful bodies

That said, what is a body? For one thing, a body is a visible entity, and bodies can also see outside themselves because they have eyes and senses. Minds are also visual in myriad expressions, including dance and games; they have eyes and are capable of intuition through the proverbial mind's *eye* and in visions. Minds have a presence – expressed in the tenor and tone of the body. Minds are in the likeness of bodies, even as beautiful minds don't require typically beautiful, able bodies, whatever the style or standard. Somewhere there is a beautiful mending likeness. Bodies and minds need each other; one cannot exist without the other. The body is not merely a visible container. It thinks in gestures and feelings and is alive with mind.

Body and mind are co-present, thinking and feeling together in movement and sense. In the flow of dance, they move as one, even when faltering. Movement becomes intelligent when polished with attention in everyday activities or aesthetic events. Witnesses might notice that dance moves from intelligence to stumbling in the blink of an eye, as does everyday movement. I like to watch people walk, not to judge, but to appreciate the many ways of walking. There is mind at play in walking – motor intelligence, the beauty and pathos of emergent steps, and perchance dogged determination, or shyness glancing off.

* * *

Body and mind are two different words in our language, so we ought to be able to differentiate. On the surface and most commonly, we do; but I identify them somatically as entwined and study how through sway and involvement, they create each other. We often attribute qualities separately, however, and cite them knowing they are mere words. Minds, we say, can think; they have cognitive abilities, as they accrue knowledge. But they can't do any of this without embodied nervous systems, brains, and the gifts and cultivations of lively consciousness.

The body has a brain and head, and there is no barrier or seam between the body and the head, the body and the mind. Typical dual views hold that the body is physical material and the mind is psychological, invisible, and transcendent. I hear that minds are in space and bodies are physically present material objects; that we have bodies, and we have minds, and they need to be bridged, connected, or integrated. But do thoughts and thinking not have a bodily-lived physical basis, and the material and mental not reveal each other? Yes, they do. Experientially, however, we speak of ruptures, being distracted or even distant – of not being 'in' our bodies. This would be a phenomenological or *lived dualism* and not a metaphysical split. For instance, this morning I was easily transported by a pot of crimson pansies fluttering face up on my back porch. I didn't leave my body, my mind, or the porch, though I did speed my gaze towards the flowers and the feeling of dew on my eyelids.

Losing my body

I can never lose my body, even when I lose my way, nor can I leave my body. How can I not be 'in my body'? To be 'out of body' is a handy expression for personal loss. Something seems missing – maybe concentration and meaningful connection to others or one's environment. Perhaps this seeming loss of body indicates pain and numbness. Somatic memes speak about disembodied people. No one alive is disembodied. No one can lose their body or be out of their body, except metaphorically. In any case, aliveness is not about *having* a body. With phenomenology, I say, 'I am my body'. I can have a loss of feeling, but this is not disembodiment. It is a loss of sensation or meaningful relationship and can be understood and addressed as such. Therapists and teachers might address someone's 'out of body' experience, or understand out-of-body as an altered state. The approach of phenomenology would be hermeneutic in detecting meanings of experience and describing them. Somatic teachers and therapists might ask into the sense of leaving or losing the body as expressions of existential loss or traumatic numbness.

Do *thoughts get beyond the body?*

Or how do thoughts get beyond the skin? Perhaps in being expressed, thoughts of individuals move out towards others and the outside world. My thoughts or yours might linger on in the lives of others: in written work, in learning together, in music and dance, or anything communicative by nature. Such thought forms are the express extension of the mind. The ability to think animates communication and creativity. This doesn't imply that minds exist in space and need to be integrated with bodies. In action, the physical and mental are co-present. Dance and writing, math, sculpture, cooking, and other material things exercise the human mind. The creative, communicative capacities of the mind represent its effulgent powers and embodied source. The mind does not live in an invisible space outside the body, and body is more than mute physical substance. If the mind transcends, it doesn't escape the convergence of body and world; it moves with the inmost body and catches up with the world. World and earth are already far beyond us, but not outside our felt existence. The human body thinks as the mind does, atonally sometimes and upside down at others, worlding precariously.

Losing *my mind*

Can I split into pieces? Does my mind exist outside of my body, rendering me physical substance and minded distance? A phenomenologist would turn these questions towards experience, since human beings have experiential disconnects and dualisms of all kinds. Sometimes people say, 'I feel split', which is an expression of experience not a split of material substance.

Moreover, separating is essential to science, where objective contrasts in consciousness can be a good thing. Dualisms are not all the same. To see oneself as two or more selves is not so uncommon. I know I have selves that show up differently according to circumstance, and I'm not speaking about being dishonest or the pathology of multiple personalities. I know whatever self appears will change and morph and that underneath circumstantial appearance, I am a continuous self. I can divide in consciousness, image, and experience because I am one and a plurality.

Do I have a soul?

Soul is a word that moves me. I understand it as a variable, poetic, and remarkable quality of being that we all have if we claim it. For today, intensity of feeling is soul for me, and dancing is soul-singing. Soul is generative; it reveals character and expressivity. I experience this especially in longing for something larger than my 'self'. Might this longing be what I most want to develop in my nature? An intrinsic unnamable quality? A snare? A habit?

Special places and people connect me to soul as homecoming and belonging. For today, my soul is here where I am. Here where you are. Aretha Franklin was crowned the 'queen of soul'. Her voice was her soul-home and crowning glory. Might we consider the soul an inborn talent or even a sense of morality and gift? I have a soul and soulful doings and longings that I sometimes claim. These are mine and cannot be permanently lost. My soul can never be lost, except I cease to care for myself, and in this case, it is simply in hiding, not split off from my body.

Soul never leaves me, but I can be more or less aware of soulful emotions and influences in my life. *My soul* is mine and is as constant as my mind. Soul is a quality of my nature and character. As belonging to my nature, my soul is individual, just as yours is. Yet, it connects me far beyond what I call 'self'. It connects me to those I love, to special places, and cannot be separated or stolen from me. I think it can be touched, however, especially in dancing: dancing is soul work.

Nature and soul are qualifiers, words in the English language that have attained meaning in many contexts. They are full of meaning for me. I further know that my little dog has a soul. With her and others I love, my soul calms down. We communicate through our eyes and the feeling tones of our compatible natures.

Do I have a spirit?

Spirit never leaves me, and when I dance, it rises. If I don't always call spirituality to attention, it is nevertheless present, reminding me of more significant matters than meet the eye. As my mentor, Ohno Kazuo-sensei, taught, 'you are not the be-all and end-all of life'. Thus, I see myself as simply a dancer participant living with hope. Like Kazuo-sensei, I keep dancing into old age to summon spirit as moral strength. Responsibility for others doesn't diminish with old age. Duties seem to pile up, and the strength I need to meet the challenge is not simply physical – it is spiritual. There are religious traditions that teach spirit as a precious essence, but my experience of spirit is more actively personal. I don't sense or understand spirit as a spectral essence, something separate hovering around my body or inside that can be tarnished by guilt and shame.

Imagination is powerful in experience. I imagine spirit as a shining quality of experience and see that all kinds of beings shine – including more-than-human beings – shining even in their dimming, dying, and regeneration.

Does a body listen?

Doing somatic phenomenology is about listening wordlessly to the body through the body. This almost impossible feat entails listening to experience in all its precarity of mind, feeling, and image. Phenomenology further asks experience to speak underneath habit and bias. Perhaps experience speaks through felt images of sense perception, as Damasio teaches. Damasio's work shows that images narrate directly to the human organism, while an all-inclusive body consciousness maps and reads imagistic events relative to mind and feeling (Damasio 2018: Chapter 5). Phenomenology through Merleau-Ponty and others teaches that we *entwine* self and world through embodied listening and understanding. Eventually, we might find words for such understanding. Glen Mazis writes about this from various perspectives in *Merleau-Ponty and the Face of the World* (2016).

Listening to embodied images is an attractive idea for somatic work. Mapping/reading images is essential for dance/art relational processes in somatic work. We who work with somatic paradigms know that the body thinks, speaks, and listens to experience. Sheets-Johnstone writes brilliantly about how the body thinks in movement (1981), not in words but nonverbally. Language is just one medium of thought. In my attempts to bring movement to language, I find they don't always match.

How touch listens

Images can narrate in nonverbal ways, *directly through dance, movement, and tactile-kinaesthetic contact*. For instance, through touch, tactile-kinaesthetic images in somatic hands-on education narrate directly to the organism (the nervous system and whole-body consciousness). When I use contact through finely-tuned touch techniques in restorative somatic work, I invite and listen to the other's body. This mindful process opens a space between myself and another as movement and sense images build a story or impression. Sometimes the outcome is literal and verbal, and sometimes it remains unstated. I trust that paths of listening and activation will arise between us.

My hands have learned how to listen to body narratives, and these don't come in the form of words, even if they are telling. I listen to what images say in their narrations of experience and feeling. Good and hurtful feelings both find their way out. Somatic touch (restorative touch through movement) is a mindful conversation without words. Listening is paramount as a nonjudgmental part of tactile conversations. Accordingly, I practice not advising in verbal summaries of hands-on sessions with clients. Instead, as a somatic teacher and guide, I find it better to discuss options. Students and clients can find their own solutions when they are heard.

Homeostasis

Homeostasis is originally a term from physical sciences, but lately, it takes on affective psycho-somatic significance in neuroscience and somatic movement modalities. When I teach yoga somatically, I orient homeward. This means that I assist others in experiencing the power of moving consciously and without stress to find the ease of relaxed at-homeness, and we model this for each other in our easy yoga. Lowering tensions of overwork and achievement, evaluating and transforming feelings of hate and anger, developing feelings of ease in relationships, and expressing strength and power with love: all engender homeostasis (hom-e-o-stasis).

In a fit of inspiration, I composed a piece of music dedicated to Damasio through his somatic view of homeostasis. I call the work 'Tonic Flow for Damasio' because homeostasis suggests the tensional arrival of music back to its tonic key. This would be C in the key of C, or D (for Damasio) in D, a home base of resolution and comfort. These are lived qualities of embodied sound and movement, and we can match them in consciousness.

Qualia of friendliness, trust, and generosity tend towards homing, grounding directions. Optimally, homeostasis expresses itself in wellbeing and joy. Damasio's work describes homeostasis as a state of 'health'. Also, it presents the negative:

> The stress associated with sadness is caused by calling into action the hypothalamus and the pituitary gland and releasing molecules whose consequence is reducing homeostasis and actually damaging countless body parts such as blood vessels muscular structures.
>
> (2018: 198)

Are we to avoid sadness then? That would certainly be a tall order. Sad moments and times are inevitable in life, and paradoxically they also implicate homeostasis. Would we deny the right to be sad or to grieve? Or dismiss human potentials for transformative change? In hopes of flourishing, somatic processes are trustful; they breathe easily and can flutter and wait.

The arrival of ethics

In the introduction, we said that somatic experience emerges through the interaction of the cultural mind with ethical/ecological potentials. The embodied mind is already bound up in our affective feelings and ethical engagements. By definition, somatic movement arts develop an ethos of care at their moral centre. Such care begins with the body and extends towards community. In global terms, *soma* writ large intersects with science, including the science of climate change and its planetary implications. Looking towards governing policies, ecological ethics, and our part in these, we observe that autocratic regimes care more about power than protecting human lives and environmental nature. Our somatic part is to witness, warn, and work towards the good of all.

Somatic processes curry affective dialogue and hold implicit ecosomatic politics. We can pay attention (listen) to these and advocate for ethical–political actions that affect social and environmental change. Audrey Ellis puts this well: 'Dancing does not bracket the body from social, cultural, and ideological forces, but rather registers these forces as corporeal and experiments with the tensions and pressures they create' (2021: 112). As elicited in dance, feelings are powerful motivators; we have only begun to learn how to harness such innate sources towards social transformation. An intrinsic (felt) somatic ethic appeals to fairness in regard to race, age, and ability.[7] We know suffering because we feel it somatically in our bones and minds. Our responsibility to each other and the earth appeals to collective matters of mind.

Ethics are mind matters of life and breath: possibilities of healing arriving through homeostasis amid precarity. These are somatic issues of experience already charged with meaning. As concerns our present actions, the future is already here. The flourishing of all people and planetary health is a somatic issue. Merleau-Ponty says this is what it means to be in a field: a 'belonging' defines the field for us (1962: 4). The somatic field is defined in our human belong to the earth, each other, and all life. Its ethos is not built in major or minor modes but in music that spreads laterally out and spirals beyond the limits of self.

Mind is here
matching the body's example,
not an insignificant stitch
in the social fabric.
Thru hands for touch

eyes for distance
and lungs for breath,
say yes to your exceptional body,
perchance in consent with paradox ...
yes to the flourishing of earth
in the earth of everysoma.
Yes, through and through.

Storyboard

The following storyboard is not exhaustive. It includes process ideas that arose in the writing. Readers might add their insights since this essay aims to stimulate further work and not to suggest closure.

About Consciousness and Images
Consciousness has content.
Consciousness is integrative.
Images energize consciousness.
Images narrate, push, and seize.
Images are both nonverbal and verbal.
Images move and change.
Images arise through sense and perception.
Images are sometimes visual, but not always.
Consciousness integrates and maps images.
Consciousness matters and expands through use.

About Unity
Movement and feeling are inseparable.
Somatic arts work creatively with images.
Somatic arts work with images through restorative touch.
Feelings have positive and negative valences.
Good feelings tend towards states of wellbeing.
Good feelings can elicit states of flourishing. Feelings are tidal.
Bad and good feelings are subject to change.
Movement and body are inseparable.
Body and mind are inseparable.
Soma and psyche are inseparable.
Movement is a quality of nature. Feelings motivate movement.
Qualities of mind are felt and moved in dance.

About Intention and Awareness
Intention makes a difference in life and learning.
Presence with awareness can be cultivated.
Mindful consciousness is more potent than wilfulness.
Thoughts are just thoughts until we examine them.
Movement is just movement until we become conscious of it.

About Healing
Healing is possible. Healing is ubiquitous.
Intention aids healing.
Healing is rich with imagery.
We can heal through intrinsically motivated dance.

About Homeostasis
The body self-regulates towards homeostasis.
In health, the embodied mind wants the best for itself.
Feeling states aid or hinder homeostasis in healing.
Happiness and sadness are valences of movement.
Happiness and sadness are bodily-lived states of being.
Somatic states of being affect wellbeing.

About Movement and Embodiment
Movement can be a source of knowledge and healing.
Moving from deep states of awareness can excavate painful memories.
In admitting pain, the body can listen and allow pain a way out.
We can detoxify painful memories through dance and movement.
We can transform painful memories through somatic bodywork.
We can chart metamorphic paths of change through movement.
Somatic movement practices can link self to others and the world.

About Nature
Humans are part of nature and change.
Attitudes to the body impact nature and culture, or call this natureculture.
Bonding with nature through dance and movement can be healing.

About the Brain and Nervous System
The nervous system influences the whole body.
The human nervous system is marvellously complex.
The brain is adaptive and part of the body.
The brain relates mental and physical capacities.

Non-human animals also have marvellous nervous systems.

About Hands-on Therapies
Somatic bodywork is a conversation without words
Imagistic content of touch has somatic valence.
Good and hurtful feelings both converse.

About Choice, Change, and Culture
We can exercise our powers of choice in movement.
We can exercise powers of choice in somatic practices.
Emotions are not bad actors but guides to the future.
Feeling and emotion motivate cultural creativity.
Somatic processes can reframe cultural conditions for wellbeing.
The flourishing of all people is a somatic issue.

After Spinoza
through Damasio
to mind space
where no movement is never feeling
somatic processes can flutter and wait ...
while images narrate to the organism
through the mind as portal ... the body listens.

NOTES

1. The founder of butoh, Hijikata Tatsumi, danced what he called 'the weak body'. Butoh arose in Japan in the aftermath of the Second World War as a protest form of dance with empathic antiwar undercurrents.

2. Social justice was a major theme of ISMETA's International Conference of 2021: 'Engaging Embodiment: Somatic Applications for Health, Education and Social Justice'.

3. I concentrate much of this essay on the unity philosophy and neuroscience of Damasio. I might have chosen other leading experts on neuroscience. For instance, Mary Helen Immordino-Yang (2015) writes about the implication of affective neuroscience for education, also a somatic theme I engage, and Howard Gardner studies educational virtues for the twenty-first century (2011). *The Embodied Mind* (Varela et al. 1993) presents work closely related to my topic of *consciousness*, but I follow Damasio for his pragmatic synthesis of science, psychology, and philosophy. His work also develops a philosophy consistent with somatic studies and phenomenology. Neurophenomenology arises in his concentration on experience and feeling and his refutation of body–mind dualism.

4. See Gilbert, Catherine E. and Kuhn, Helmut (1972), *A History of Aesthetics*, pp. 62–64.

5. 'Lines of flight' is developed as a major post-structural theme of Deleuze and Guattari (1987) in *A Thousand Plateaus*.
6. Damasio argues that we are conscious throughout the body, not in one part, and he speaks of this unity metaphorically as the 'hidden orchestra'. See *The Strange Order of Things* (2018), pp. 79–80, 174–89.
7. I write extensively about ethics of fairness in a recent article, 'What are feelings for? Towards a somatic ethos of fairness', in *Somatics Magazine/Journal of the Mind Body Arts and Sciences,* in press.

REFERENCES

Audi, Robert (ed.) (1995), *The Cambridge Dictionary of Philosophy*, New York: Cambridge University Press.

Damasio, Antonio (1999), *The Feeling of What Happens: Body and Emotion in the Making of Consciousness*, New York: Harcourt Brace & Company.

Damasio, Antonio (2003), *Looking for Spinoza: Joy, Sorrow, and the Feeling Brain*, Orlando: Harcourt, Inc.

Damasio, Antonio (2010), *Self Comes to Mind: Constructing the Conscious Brain*, New York: Vintage Books, Random House Inc.

Damasio, Antonio (2018), *The Strange Order of Things: Life, Feeling, and the Making of Cultures*, New York: Pantheon Books.

Deleuze, Giles and Guattari, Felix (1987), *A Thousand Plateaus: Capitalism and Schizophrenia* (trans. B. Massumi), Minneapolis: University of Minnesota Press.

Ellis, Audre L. (2021), 'From animation to activation: Improvisational dance as invitation and as interruption', Doctoral dissertation, New York: Department of Philosophy, Stony Brook University.

Fraleigh, Sondra (1987–96), *Dance and the Lived Body: A Descriptive Aesthetics*, Pittsburgh: University of Pittsburgh Press.

Fraleigh, Sondra (1999), *Dancing into Darkness: Butoh, Zen, and Japan*, Pittsburgh: University of Pittsburgh Press.

Fraleigh, Sondra (2000), 'Consciousness matters', *Dance Research Journal,* 32:1, Summer, pp. 54–62.

Fraleigh, Sondra (2004), *Dancing Identity: Metaphysics in Motion*, Pittsburgh: University of Pittsburgh Press.

Fraleigh, Sondra (2010), *BUTOH: Metamorphic Dance and Global Alchemy,* Urbana: University of Illinois Press.

Fraleigh, Sondra (ed.) (2015), *Moving Consciously: Somatic Transformations through Dance, Yoga, and Touch*, Urbana: University of Illinois Press.

Fraleigh, Sondra (ed.) (2018), *Back to the dance Itself: Phenomenologies of the Body in Performance*, Urbana: University of Illinois Press.

Fraleigh, Sondra and Bingham, Robert (eds) (2018), *Performing Ecologies in a World in Crisis*, special edition of *Choreographic Practices*, vol. 9, 1st ed, Bristol: Intellect Press.

Gardner, Howard (2011), *Truth, Beauty, and Goodness Reframed: Educating for the Virtues in the Twenty-First Century*, New York: Basic Books.

Gilbert, Catherine E. and Kuhn, Helmut (1972), *A History of Aesthetics*, Westport: Greenwood.

Husserl, Edmund ([1925] 2005), *Phantasy, Image, Consciousness and Memory 1898–1925* (trans. J. B. Brough), Heidelberg: Springer Verlag.

Husserl, Edmund and Fink, Eugen ([1932] 1995), *Sixth Cartesian Meditation: The Idea of a Transcendental Theory of Method* (trans. and intro. R. Bruzina; textual notations and appendix E. Husserl), Bloomington: Indiana University.

Immordino-Yang, Mary Helen (2015), *Emotions, Learning, and the Brain: Exploring the Educational Implications of Affective Neuroscience*, New York: W. W. Norton.

Mazis, Glen A. (2016), *Merleau-Ponty and the Face of the World: Silence, Ethics, Imagination, and Poetic Ontology*, Albany: SUNY Press.

Merleau-Ponty, Maurice (1962), *Phenomenology of Perception* (trans. C. Smith), London: Routledge and Kegan Paul.

Merleau-Ponty, Maurice (1968), *The Visible and the Invisible* (trans. A. Lingis), Evanston: Northwestern University Press.

Spinoza, Baruch (1958), *Spinoza: Selections* (ed. J. Wild), New York: Charles Scribner's Sons.

Sheets-Johnstone, Maxine (1981), 'Thinking in movement', *Journal of Aesthetics and Art Criticism,* 39:4, pp. 399–407.

Varela, Francisco J., Thompson, Evan and Rosch, Eleanor (1993), *The Embodied Mind*, Cambridge: The MIT Press.

Williamson, Amanda (2018), 'Falling in love with language', in S. Fraleigh (ed.), *Back to the dance Itself: Phenomenologies of the Body in Performance*, pp. 78–98, Urbana: University of Illinois Press.

Williamson, Amanda and Sellers-Young, Barbara (eds) (2020), *Spiritual Herstories: Call of the Soul in Dance Research*, Bristol: Intellect Press.

4

A Future Worth Having:
Somatic Ethics of Flow and Curiosity

ECOLOGICAL WELL-BEING with understanding of the body as part of a nature-culture continuum motivate the examples of this essay. Place Dance site-specific improvisations show that learning through curiosity is vital to somatic encounters and ethics. Virtue ethics and value theory position this work, where values arise first as possibilities or promises, actualized in our lives and dances but not guaranteed. Here we recognize an abundance of somatic values as guides to consider in a future worth having.

Promises of soma and ethics

This investigation views crucial concerns of somatics and ethics as relational and ongoing. The inquiry considers somatic learning relative to values, virtues, gender fluidity, lived experience, ecological awareness, pedagogical hope and communal well-being. Values arise first as potentials and possibilities – promises not guaranteed – actualized in our lives and all of our dilemmas and dances. *Values motivate the ethics of somatic movement arts*, even when they go unmarked. This essay recognizes somatic values as guides to consider in a future worth having.

I use phenomenology as a method to study embodied relationships – here, through the lens of ethics as a branch of philosophy. This approach underlines the experiential, relational scope of somatic endeavours. In giving examples, I explore kinaesthetic and lived values of *flow states* and values of *listening* and *emotional intelligence* in somatic contexts. The last section provides a short sample code of ethics for touch in somatic bodywork and a sample code of ethics for attending to emotional processing in learning environments. The *Springboard* and *Storyboard* at the end summarize experiential and relational values of somatics.

Part 1. Somatics and ethics as relational

Is somatics something?

In movement and dance education, it is. Developmentally, somatic education is concerned with transformative potentials of embodied life rife with affective and cognitive possibilities. Through its diverse methods, somatics can also cross between movement and dance as mindful means to improve movement skills and performance. The thing (the phenomenon) of somatics appears when we move with awareness. The very thought of somatics might draw an inward or outward accent in perception. We are not passive recipients of an already constituted world. The thing we call 'somatic' moves inward towards consciousness and out towards others and the world we actively embody. It manifests ethically when we develop individuality and empathy in tandem. Lived materiality grows organically and wordlessly – brought to light through the embodied subjects of dance.

Figure 4.1 shows a dance in process that shifts consciousness away from self and towards place, as the dancer and photographer ask permission of the canyon to perform there. I believe that the canyon hears such requests in ways I barely fathom. As stewards of Mukuntuweap, the Paiute were predated by the

FIGURE 4.1: Cave improvisation in *Mukuntuweap* (Zion Canyon, Utah). The canyon was named *Mukuntuweap* by the Paiute, the most recent Native Americans to inhabit the canyon as a sacred place. Place Dance of Nathalie Guillaume. Photograph © Sarah Jeffreys, 2019.

now-extinct ancestral Puebloans who venerated the canyon and believed future people would come there for spiritual enlightenment.[1] Today, environmental activists work to keep the extensive landmass and its environs free from fracking. Over four million people visited the canyon last year; canyon officials are considering limiting the flow of tourism, even though the canyon is miles long and extensive.

I wonder how human ontologies might strike a healthy balance with the wild beauty of *Mukuntuweap*? From the time I was young, I revelled in the canyon's grandeur, its vast soaring heights, the sweetness of its pools and weeping rocks. I carry these experiences with gratitude. *Mukuntuweap* is a majestic gorge that gives meaning to the word 'gorgeous' – its canyon ontology shakes me to my core. When I lie down at the foot of its giant trees and greet its wandering wild turkeys, I believe the canyon holds me.

Yes, somatics is something

In ways of witnessing, being and belonging, somatics includes both first-person and relational phenomena. It names a wide field of practices that studies lived experience and is not purely about self or self-perception, as is often supposed. *Interactively, somatics develops movement modes that encourage participants to receive and interpret sensory information as they interact with others and environments.* A phenomenologist would say that there is no such thing as self-perception in a pure sense. 'Human life is we-life' in a cultural and environing world constantly in motion (Husserl [1932] 1995: 192).

In its almost global acceptance of Thomas Hanna's original definition of *soma and self-perception* as the basis of somatics, somatic movement education developed a self-referential ethos as its sustaining principle. Consequently, it omitted the defining matter of self: there is no self without others. I know myself to be 'a self' because there are others, other people and the perceptual complexity of emplacement. In reciprocity, we carry otherness in our bones. Loss and desire move from soma to self to other and world – emerging in love and sorrow, sometimes illness and grief. The world of history and nature is not simply a container for human emotions; it is a part of them. The world is in us as we are in the world, and history never goes away, even when its stories are reimagined.

Hanna is primarily credited with founding (or naming) the field of somatics as a first-person view of self and perception. He defines soma and self dualistically and mechanically, describing the *mind's control of body and movement* in his book, *Somatics: Reawakening the Mind's Control of Movement Flexibility and Health* (1988). A philosopher and early student of Moshe Feldenkrais, Hanna writes that:

> Humans are self-sensing and self-moving subjects while, at the same time, they are observable and manipulable objects. To yourself, you are a soma. To others, you

are a body. Only you can perceive yourself as a soma – no one else can do so [...].
Humans can learn to perceive their internal functions and improve the control of
their somatic functions.

(Hanna 1988: 20–21)

In his pathbreaking work, *The Feeling of What Happens: Body and Emotion in
the Making of Consciousness* (1999), Antonio Damasio, famed neuroscientist and
psychologist, teaches that the somatic biologic stratum of life, what he terms the
'proto-self', is the core foundation for feeling and consciousness (172). Consciousness is global and organismic, not a local brain property. He further argues that
feelings are nature's evolutionary solution for sustaining life. Conscious awareness of feeling holds connective potency. Changes in body state, cognition and
subject-object relations activate *somatosensory* felt life (80, 169). 'You simply
cannot escape the affectation of your organism, motor and emotional most of all'
(148). Movement and emotion are inseparable in his neuroscience.

Damasio says that the 'somatic' or 'somatosensory' system is not one system but
a combination of several subsystems that signal the organism's state to the brain. He
groups the signaling into visceral, vestibular, musculoskeletal and fine-touch divisions.
Motor adjustments and emotional responses to these 'are all coregistered in memory'
(1999: 148–49). How then do we draw upon somatic potentials? Or as Damasio
would ask, 'what are feelings for'? (1999: 284). The story of somatic endeavours in
education and therapy is composed of such questions. Damasio's science explains that
we build perceptual complexity in layers of self-knowing and subject-object reference,
as the proto-self rises towards a core self and finally extended consciousness and historical memory: 'Often the notion that *soma* conjures up is narrower than it should be'
(1999: 149). Damasio paints a complete and consequential picture:

> You rise above the sea level of knowing, transiently but incessantly, as a *felt* core
> self, renewed again and again, thanks to anything that comes from outside the brain
> into its sensory machinery or anything that comes from the brain's memory stores
> toward sensory, motor, or autonomic recall [...]. The consequence of this learning
> is the development of autobiographical memory, an aggregate memory of who we
> are and can become.
>
> (1999: 172–73)

Damasio further elaborates on extended consciousness, which permits close interaction among feelings of self and external happenings (2010, 2017). This would
include our relationship to earth and world. We extend consciousness through
somatosensory use in the natural curiosities of work, play and art – and we further
expand these by design in somatic movement arts: movement repatterning classes,

experiential anatomy, somatic yoga, somatically conceived dance improvisation, fine-touch techniques and ecological site-specific performances in places of both beauty and peril. In such ways, we expand our reach towards others and the world and activate ethical concerns. *Moving Consciously* researches modes of somatic movement arts with several authors (Fraleigh 2015). This essay urges somatic methods of movement towards the promise and responsibility of ethics.

Why somatics?

I often ask, not 'what is somatics', but 'why somatics'? And 'how much can we expect from it'? As Hanna held in his initial insight, somatic learning through movement rightly places value on the mover's experience. But is this enough? While personal experience is important, somatic education should also promote experiences of sharing through movement and environmental awareness, including the soul and lessons of particular places. My mentor in butoh, Ohno Kazuo-sensei, said he couldn't dance for healing at Auschwitz until he saw 'the pain in the stones', quite a somatic turn of mind for a Japanese veteran of the Second World War. Pain in stone is an illogical and potent somatic image. As lived in bodily experience, images can materialize in mind, movement and dance. Indeed, the mind's intuitive eye holds healing potential in all the arts.

Sharing space

Somatic methods focus on aesthetic (affective) learning and happenings. Somatic methods and movement patterning that animate the Feldenkrais work and the Alexander Technique typically focus introspectively on individual learning and improvement through movement, while somatic methods as applied to improvisational dance are both solo and relational. Sharing space with others while moving with trust and risk of unknowns is a relational ethic of somatic learning, eliciting respect for boundaries.

Sharing space teaches us that we are not alone; we coexist in a world of otherness: of people, animals, insects and specific locations. These might be your places or mine: natural, wild, historical or newly built. I appreciate my home as a place of somatic recovery and connection. Likewise, I breathe easily in meadows, mountains and valleys. Canyon-desert atmospheres uplift and soothe me at once. I sense I am a part of them, somatically, and I grieve their past and current endangerment where I live in Southwest Utah. I wrote *Dancing Identity* (2004) partly as an attempt to witness the disasters of nuclear testing that began in 1952, continuing for seventeen years at Frenchman's Flat in Nevada near my ancestral home in Utah. The detonations started when I was 12 years old and didn't end until I was almost

30 and living more at a distance. I wanted my writing to witness this national disgrace and to warn of the harm we do to nature and human natures in the name of country and security (2004: 4, 170–73). We were the human disposables of this environmental tragedy and convoluted ethics. The nuclear fallout and radiation travelled widely across America and Canada, also infecting the food supply.

We share spaces and places widely and with all life. We don't own space; we live it, just as we coexist the space and the spirit of specific sites along with their history. Awareness of place and nature-culture now propel a large part of my ethics, as somatics morphs to ecosomatics in my teaching and writing. Metaphysically, I step into nature to experience more of my nature; my character or *suchness* in Buddhist perspectives, like the catness of cats and the coming and going of everything. In the Zen image of 'holding up the flower', we respect nature and care for all life.

I continue to learn that somatics encompasses a wide field of studies, practices and empathies, especially as it takes various forms internationally. Attempts to fasten definitions of somatic movement methods to present examples will eventually fail. Thus, I envision the future with confidence. Somatic education develops a field of movement practices and processes with a fluid, evolving identity. Its programs, big and small, are made up of people, and people have values and make choices whether stated or not. In refining definitions of somatics and revaluing somatic movement education, this essay looks into these.

What are values, virtues and ethics?

When people see the word 'ethics', they often take a step back, assuming they will get a lecture. Ethics is not primarily about what not to do and impending punishment. Ethics is hopeful; it details virtues: those aspects we admire in others and seek to emulate. Related to this, it identifies values as the good we seek in our lives and activities. Don'ts based on prohibitions represent just one aspect of ethics.

In ancient philosophy, the *beautiful* (aesthetics) and the *good* (ethics) were not separate. Today aesthetics is more broadly indicative of the affective, including a wide range of felt influences and emotions. Ethics takes expanded forms, including increasingly important voices, since feminist ethics first called for the inclusion of marginalized voices: Simone de Beauvoir in *Ethics of Ambiguity* ([1948] 1992) and Carol Gilligan in *In a Different Voice* (1982). When Beauvoir and Gilligan were writing, technology had not developed profusely as it has today, and social media and artificial intelligence were just on the horizon. Ideas and opinions circulate more widely and dangerously in technology today, accompanied with the rise of hate speech. On the other hand, people of all races and genders agitate for the status once granted to white men only. The creation of a multiethnic society is increasingly valued in higher education, raising concerns in somatics.[2]

What Shannon Vallor identifies as 'technoethics' now informs the broad landscape of values and virtues (Vallor 2016). Topics of ethics also cross into education with specific concerns for educational values and opportunities. Regarding oppression, pedagogies of hope observe how dominant voices drive some values and render others invisible. Paulo Freire identifies this as an evolving concern of social justice (Freire, *Pedagogy of Hope: Reliving Pedagogy of the Oppressed*, 2015). Kelly Ferris Lester focuses her inquiry on somatic pedagogy in dance and relational environments for somatic learning (2015).

Fluidity and relational values: Curiosity in ethical reasoning

Gilligan's social science research into gender bias caused a revolution in ethical thinking across all intellectual disciplines. *In a Different Voice* (Gilligan 1982) studies how women come to ethical decisions, seeking their way through complex issues with curiosity by asking what effects their actions might have on others. Previous research had used men only as subjects, showing how ethical choices arrive from objective positions (1982). Gilligan found that women value relational thinking and seek to make the most loving decisions. Women participate in dialogical and subjective reasoning, establishing the importance of making decisions through curiosity and compassion. Thus, feminism has impacted inclusivity in social change and gender identity issues.

Women have also become more prominent in somatic fields. Experientially, however, somatics belongs to everyone who calls it home. Men and women have both been formative in the development of movement somatics, as Don Hanlon Johnson's work demonstrates (Johnson 1995). My memorable mentors in Feldenkrais studies were Larry Goldfarb and Frank Wildman: Goldfarb for his humour and kindness and Wildman for his lean, morphic movement workshops. The significant power of *naming* in somatics redounds to men: Thomas Hanna in naming the field of somatics (1988); Edmund Husserl in early philosophical identification of somatic phenomena ([1932] 1995); F. M. Alexander, Moshe Feldenkrais and Thomas Hanna in naming their somatic practices after themselves.

Awakening curiosity through the body

Ideally, somatic education offers a doorway to awaken curiosity (indeterminate awareness) through the body: *anybody*. But the body is never just the body. Bodies are always *somebody* through individual nature and social habitus. Embodied ethics underlie all somatic work and go unstated for the most part. This essay states a relational perspective; it doesn't accept that embodiment is completely formed through race, cultural constructions, gender or wilful control. All of these are influential, however. Everyone moves, but movement is complex, being individual, natural and cultural at once. Naturalcultural complexity is apparent in the acts of arts of dancing.[3] How one directs attention (awareness and curiosity) in movement is formative.

Discipline in dance knits together the cultural, natural and artfully artificial – too often problematically, without reflection on the dancer's experience as a person. What then is the hope of discipline? If one prefers present-time flow over the taming and mastery of the naturalcultural human body, *excellence* is a better hope than *mastery*.[4] If control is our only story, we should be sorry for not asking for more freedom and choice. Contemporary somatic education should cultivate fluid ways of moving, thinking and doing to show that life is sustained through an interplay of many kinds of beings, ages and ethnicities; this, amid concerns for gender fluidity as hard and fast distinctions between sexes are increasingly challenged. If somatic movement practices value relational aesthetics of care, they will reject exploitations of nature and competitive climbing over others.

Through inclusive aesthetics, somatic dance and movement practices value dialogue and creative curiosity, increasingly speaking between the personal and pluralistic while bridging self with diverse others in community and awareness of place – whether crowded city streets, disappearing forests or backyards. The activist workshops of Sydney L. Mosley in Harlem, New York is an excellent example of how dance-making in community includes somatic awareness of place. Her pedagogy engages students in multiracial community building through dance as art-making. Workshop participants consider the potency of their creativity regarding such issues as safety for women in the streets, expressive choice and social justice. I participated with Mosley recently on Zoom. My age was not a limitation, since we moved improvisationally with questions in mind, always aware of the community as a whole and our part in it (17 September 2021).

Detecting ethics

To detect is to sense and perceive: I participate in somatic practices as a detective. I want to investigate what I can change and need to change in my relationships, both near and far. We all have complex somatic histories; the good news is that we are not captives of the past by necessity. We humans have choices to make in building a sustainable future. Turning towards the basics of Western culture, we identify qualities of virtue in ethics of *arete* (excellence as a virtue), *phronesis* (practical wisdom) and *eudaimonia* (flourishing). I have pursued excellence as a virtue in dancing and scholarship for much of my life. By now, I'm equally interested in right thinking and right actions for building pluralistic communities and planetary health. With others, I act to build community through the conferences we sponsor, most recently featuring somatic practices in nature (Elmira NY and on Zoom, October 2021). Fortunately, the technology of Zoom permits us an international reach.

Perhaps my push towards excellence redefines for me what is important in performance as I look past self-perception towards the world I inhabit with others. Together, we consider our part as artists and somatic movement detectives in creating healthy environments. It all starts, as everything does, with each person's responsiveness to the whole. Dancing, writing, teaching and activism comprise an ethics tool kit. Detecting ethics is not so difficult when each person contributes their time and talent to causes that call to them. Somatic studies can broaden its base, turning self-focus towards a more just and friendly world. Robert Bingham and I brought multiple voices to the fore in our co-edited issue of *Choreographic Practices: Performing Ecologies in a World in Crisis* (2018).

More technically, this essay benefits from revivals of virtue ethics in Rosalind Hursthouse's (1997) work and Alasdair MacIntyre's (1981, 2006). These ethicists discuss the nature and definition of virtues, how they are acquired and applied in various life contexts and whether they are rooted in a universal human nature or a plurality of cultures. MacIntyre argues that any account of virtues should be generated out of the community in which those virtues are practiced. The very word *ethics* implies 'ethos', or the guiding values of communities as grounded in particular times and places. I opt for this. It doesn't matter how old I become, I know my time is now, and my work in the somatics field is cut out for me. As a detective, I need only pay attention and learn along the way. Creative, proactive detectives discover how to contribute and continue to examine assumptions.

If we accept that communities for somatic studies vary, then what values hold steady in ascertaining what counts as somatic? Or where does somatic value originate? Answers to this would vary, but my answer lands on *experience*. In somatic learning modes, values and virtues emerge in light of *experience*. If it isn't *experiential*, it isn't somatic. Somatics is corporeal experiential work, primarily. *Somatics as a field could well be defined as the experiential study of embodiment.* Somatic values in dance are derived from *human movement* and, more specifically, developed through individual and community consciousness of movers in myriad contexts. I nominate *experiences of well-being and flourishing* as basic motivational values of somatic movement modes and hope to elucidate further that *somatic values are relational* and not simply personal. They relate humans to each other and the environing world, unfolding a somatic and inconclusive ethics of flow.

Part 2. Experiential ethics of flow and creativity

Few experiences are so enjoyable as complete absorption in movement and dancing. Through their extensive research, Mihaly and Isabella Csikszentmihalyi discovered that people find genuine satisfaction during a state of consciousness they call *flow* (1990, 1996, 2006). In flow states, people are completely absorbed in an activity, especially those that engage creativity.

When one is wholly absorbed in movement and dance processes, one can lose self and self-consciousness. One loses oneself in the flow of doing in other words. I experience absorption and pleasure in movement and dance when my self-limitations dissolve in action. The opportunity to move within my abilities and push the boundaries of these is part of what I enjoy in somatic movement and intuitive dance processes. This requires that I freely chose the movement and don't feel forced to accomplish more than I can. I start where I am in ability to move, learn from there and progress as I do. Engagement of *creativity* in learning depends on this level of engagement. I can't learn if I over exert or become stressed. If I seek to learn through force and stress, that is what I embody. I don't want to get worse; I want to get better; *I seek flow*. This resonates throughout my perspective and teaching of somatics through movement, dance and yoga, especially as these engage community.

What might be the reverse of such flowing engagement? How about compression and tension as somatic qualities? If one is paying attention and not simply forcing solutions, resistance can be productive in movement patterning. Push patterns can invite certain kinds of resistance while also embracing directional flow. Encounter and resistance relate to both self and environment. They can reference ecological somatics where flow qualities connect to physical properties of strong winds, for instance, or evoke the difficult politics of climate change. *Tensegrity* describes a somatic value of balance between tensional integrity, floating compressions and extensions. I appreciate emergent qualities of tensegrity when I feel light after a somatic movement process or mindful quest in nature.

Flow signals a state of consciousness and attention. To be in a state of flow is to be in between the doable and the challenging. We have said that people take pleasure in activities they can accomplish within their skill level when the activity offers new and novel challenges. Flow is basic to Csikszentmihalyi's psychology of optimal living (1990) and his psychology of discovery and invention (1996). His inherent ethics of curiosity and creativity are important to well-doing and thus to well-being. Ideally, flow reaches towards optimal states of happiness and joy. When we aspire to such states in somatic contexts, we call them 'somatic values'. Hope is generated from the somatic flow of 'I-Can' do this movement; 'I-Like' this way of dancing. Yes! Can-do is not the same for everyone; there is always something a person can do.

Hope does not overreach; hope indwells and swells. Hope flows like water and doesn't have ethnic, ability or age boundaries. It seeks a path towards free-flow and the well-being of everyone. Such flow states are ongoing and unfinished. In somatic endeavours, they elude bodily mastery, favouring modes that listen for 'yes' in ways of connecting and opening. 'No' stops. 'Yes', flows.

I aim for *flow* in my teaching. I value the concept of flow because it aids my thinking about how to teach a diverse group of participants who are not all at the same level of experience and comfort with somatic movement processes and may not be adept movers. Teaching with flow requires having a clear understanding of flow as a process. Flow processes need to have forms and concepts that are easy enough for most people in a class to accomplish, and in addition, the teacher needs to find ways to keep the learning fresh and alive for everyone, including advanced movers.

Let me explain with an example. If I begin a session of somatic yoga with the easy 'mountain' posture, anyone can do this, even from a wheelchair. But I might texture the traditional yoga mountain with somatic nuances and movements that often surprise students. After all, yoga means 'yoke', which means to connect and surprise. I sometimes take the mountain into a walking pattern that I call 'mountain stride'. It uses the foot in its rolling possibilities, from heel to toe and from toe to heel. If you are running in dance, you might use both of these possibilities and more. The easy upright mountain posture can move in many directions, even in reverse. Symbolically, the mountain stands for stillness; thus, we carry stillness into movement, which stimulates the imagination and can bring creativity into a mindful focus. Mountain Stride has many permutations and offers teachers and students a creative springboard, in addition to which it is fanciful and fun. Not least, its simple movements can be simulated from a wheelchair. How does one walk in a wheelchair? By matching walking motions or imagining them in mental rehearsal. As we just noted: there is always something a person can do.

This is a short example of a somatic movement process with many possible permutations and several built-in functions: reaching, ascending, walking, turning and stilling. The teacher can also encourage ease of breath in the movement or stop it somewhere to add a breath pattern into the mix. All of this is easily doable, and in practice, it gains complexity along the way as elements are added. Mountain Stride can also be carried into a dance exploration. In somatic studies, both teachers and students learn how to build from basic forms or patterns into more complex challenges, and teachers can observe how the particular class at hand is doing.

My overall goal in teaching somatics is to create an environment of learning that stimulates curiosity and imagination, improves movement and mood and builds skill. I assume that this leads to more optimal living through creativity, but I have no proof of this unless someone tells me that their lives have improved through our work. Sometimes they do tell me. Valued states of flow and well-being are fluid in somatic work, often lingering between the possible and the actual. We can identify them provisionally. They present us with the possible and lean towards the actual. They aim to engender trust, to increase confidence in creative endeavours and performance in the everyday.

Embodied fluency

Somatic values of well-being and well-doing are part of moving well, improved performance, aesthetic enlivenment, creativity through permission and encouragement, and inclusion of diverse populations. These are all values demonstrated in somatic practices, and increasingly so. *They constitute ethical dimensions of practice, even if they are not always realized.*

Values related to well-being and well-doing are not abstract for me. Sometimes I stop to ask myself about a particular pattern or process: 'what is this worth', or 'why do it'? And so, I stop the class to ask students these same questions. I want to know what they are getting out of the processes we undertake. These are value questions. I can observe whether students are 'getting it', but I don't always know what they find valuable. When we stop to discuss this, sometimes I get blank stares, but more often, students are eager to share their somatic experiences, and they express somatic values of these in affective ways. After hands-on contact and yoga repatterning, some common responses are: 'I feel lighter'; 'I feel heavier'; 'my pain has gone away; I float'. Sometimes someone will volunteer a temporal and psychological sense of self: 'I can move on now'. People sometimes cry or laugh. I have responded with feelings of wanting to run in my own processing. What a relief, I can still run! I don't feel stuck. Suddenly my life flows, and my words have fluency. I feel connected and at ease in my body.

Such realizations are about giving attention to *feeling*, as somatic work does. The key to somatic attending (attunement) lies in aspects of permission. We provide a lot of permission to *think* in our educational environments but little or no permission to *feel* anything. Feelings and emotions are what we are not supposed to have; bodies are what we are not supposed to have; and minds, which we value, are not embodied. Such is the unquestioned state of most education. Most educational systems are oriented towards objective knowledge, and somatics has a subjective, intersubjective and interactive emphasis. Subjectivity is the subject of somatics – to put it in a happy circular nutshell. Somatic movement education encourages and studies subjective processes of embodiment ranging from self-focus to alterity. Such methods can also be motivated by concerns that have a basis in objectivity and form. Overall, however, somatics in action circles back to subjective values in feelings of well-being. If we teachers of somatic movement arts don't pay attention to sensate embodiment in movement to value the good in experience, who will?

Do we take embodiment for granted or cultivate it? Phenomenology and neuroscience both teach that mind and body are not separate or even separable: the mind is embodied; emotion is embodied. We are embodied. OK, then what? Do we not incorporate the possible and make it actual in moving and dancing?

In dance, as in life, sensations and feelings flow and stutter. *Emotion is also tidal* as moods and circumstances change. We should be glad for this. It means we don't need to be stuck; we can move and change and feel better. In validating feelings, we can also connect with others. *Somatic connectivity* and *empathy* are possible values of somatic quests.

Convergence: Embodied choices

Somatic values are ubiquitous. Yet, they don't come ready-made and are not unmovable, even if they are already present in personal habits and in societies and families. Values develop personally and culturally over time and are malleable. In dance and somatic movement processes, they are lived and interpreted. I am interested in how values form in the first place. In the case of movement, we find that emergent powers of the will animate all movement, whether skilful or clumsy. The work of phenomenology explains how will and value are connected through intentionality and the corporal involuntary. Husserl's student Paul Ricoeur writes of this extensively (2007: 122–34). Going unnoticed, our choices are embodied organically through repetition – and in consent or refusal (Ricoeur, 'motives and values on the organic level', 104–22). Somatic movement processes encourage students to consider how choice converges with movement and becomes embodied in life on a more conscious level.

Somatic values are derived from affective/aesthetic life. They are not all pleasant or soft, even as the field of somatics has gained a reputation for softer qualities. Human movement itself contains a range of somatic values from gritty, messy feelings to uplifting ones. Somatics would indeed be lopsided if it only admitted gentle, slow values. We need only observe how dance improvisation provides access to a wide range of movement expression and associated values. Identifying movement components (such as shape, durational and emotional tone) allows us to say what we discern or interpret and even value in movement experiences.

Take the significant value of freedom, for instance. In his study of freedom relative to the will, Ricoeur writes that the body takes the form of the will (1966, 249, 328). Freedom is a democratic ideal, as we know, but what we seldom consider is that freedom roots in movement experience. Dancing is a study in freedom and agency. So is movement *per se*. Moshe Feldenkrais famously taught that if you don't have at least three ways of doing something, you don't have a choice. Will and freedom are faculties of moving well, making choices and dancing better, sometimes beautifully. In making choices and encountering precarity, we sharpen and mitigate freedom in movement. In somatic movement education, we have a chance to practice the lived values of *freedom* in learning how to move, improve and adapt. We might even learn that complete control isn't possible or even desirable.

Part 3. Somatic attunement: A future worth having

Life did not take over the globe by combat, but by networking.
(Lynn Margulis and Dorion Sagan)

If somatic values are embodied through movement, they also exist in relation to others and to pressing matters of ecology in creating and sustaining a future. Competition for resources and power dissolve in *a new ethical imperative of cooperation, interaction, listening and mutual interdependence*. These values are essential to the ethics of survival. The popular notion of survival of the fittest is a misinterpretation of Charles Darwin's work, cited by many scientists. The updated view of Lynn Margulis and Dorion Sagan in *Microcosmos: Four Billion Years of Microbial Evolution* conceives of evolution in interactive terms. 'Life did not take over the globe by combat, but by networking' (1986: 14–15).

Somatic ecology and bodily convergence with nature

A critical and under-theorized aspect of somatic movement education is its engagement with nature and what might be called natural, which is fraught if it is not defined. Husserl developed his philosophies through relational lenses of 'environing nature', 'the lived body', 'motility' and 'the life world'. These express his comprehensive somatic visions of embodiment and nature ([1932] 1995). From the time, Husserl first wrote that the human body is a point of convergence with nature and the environing world, phenomenology has investigated our relationship to nature and the environment.

Husserl's student Paul Ricoeur in his phenomenology, *Freedom and Nature* ([1966] 2007), shows that we don't control everything even though we move through intention and volition. The involuntary somatic nervous system operating below consciousness plays a crucial role, mediating bodily lived conscious interventions. This dialectic makes somatics an intriguing field. In somatic movement processes, we hope to cultivate values of listening and conscious awareness, even as we acknowledge the power of habits and the involuntary unconscious. We can move more consciously to live more consciously, including our relationship to a world in ecological turmoil. It is increasingly important in the various fields of somatic endeavour to question lazy freedoms and to speak to ecological ideas and ideals.

One can't have a concept of somatics without a concept of nature. I hold with phenomenology and life science that human life is part of all life, and I hold with neuroscience that all mammals are conscious (Damasio 2017). As organisms, we are as capable of growing, moving and dying as plants are and we also participate in larger ecological structures. Ontologically, we are complex beings, and the ontology of nature is also complicated. Nature is wild and can also be cultivated. It exists in multifarious faces of the human and more-than-human. Nature is potential as much as we are, and we need to care for nature's potentials and better understand them as part of our own. As our planet suffers, now more than ever, we must contribute to its health and understand our bodies as a part of and through the world's body. Understanding isn't all that is needed but it is the first step towards a future worth having.

A pragmatic turn: Emotional intelligence as a virtue in somatics

Once more, what is a virtue? We can't ask this question enough. Hursthouse holds that a virtue is a positive character trait, or more broadly, the good in human beings. Thus, she distinguishes virtues as belonging to a person's whole character

FIGURE 4.2: Tree Reflection in Water. Oak Creek in *Mukuntuweap* (Zion Canyon, Utah). Photograph © Sarah Jeffreys, 2019.

and not to single actions or feelings (1997). Shannon Vallor, in her book *Technology and the Virtues* (2016), proposes 'technomoral' virtues that people need to cultivate to flourish in the current socio-technological internet world. She includes *honesty, agency, justice* and *humility*. Her work further involves *courage*, as intelligent fear and hope; *empathy* in compassionate concern for others; *care* shown in service to others; *civility* in creating community; *magnanimity* in moral leadership; and *flexibility* in skillful adaptation to change.

Her summary of virtues is reflected in many somatic practices, especially in processes that focus on adaptation, perspective, community, care, respect and agency (choice in action). Glancing back to key concepts of the present essay, I would add curiosity, creativity and flow as motivating values of somatics. Vallor applies virtue ethics to the global challenges of an interconnected technological world and argues for a twenty-first-century framework for a future increasingly clouded by uncertainty. Her work is informed by a diverse group of traditions, while taking account of emerging technologies in social media, robotics, digital surveillance, biomedical enhancement and artificial intelligence. Her task is impossibly large in addressing challenges that demand extraordinary cultivation of collective moral wisdom on a global scale. But then, she is speaking to a future worth having.

I relate Vallor's account of virtues to emotional intelligence in the teaching and learning of somatics practices. IQ isn't everything. Emotional intelligence, EQ, is more important than intellectual intelligence for functioning in today's complex world and in somatic contexts. One can know a lot and still not be able to apply it or navigate the complexities of relationships and society. Most simply, emotional intelligence is a marker of how well we get along with others (Goleman 2006). Ultimately, this is a matter of verbal and nonverbal communications that promote peaceful interactions in personal relationships and communities. Topics of emotion and somatic attunement (or corporeal listening) surface in such considerations and in somatic work.

Springing from emotional terrain

We have said that we give permission to attend to feelings in somatic processes and that subjectivity is important. It is here that we enter the terrain of emotion. I understand emotion as fluid in somatics and celebrate the opportunity to engage it through embodied and aesthetic means. But I am careful to say that I am guided by creative processes of somatic movement arts, not by raw emotional expression. I choose to address emotion in somatic education through explorations of emotional intelligence and corporeal listening – in the hope of promoting harmony and fairness in group work while not neglecting transformative potentials for individuals.

In teaching groups, I attend to emotional intelligence through communication principles, emphasizing active listening, not fixing others, nonjudgment in respecting the emergent story of others without substituting one's own and practicing attentive healthy boundaries. We call this 'holding presence' for others and 'somatic attunement'. Facilitating a community of individuals who respect differences and each other sometimes means stepping back from immediate emotional reactions while at the same time recognizing that emotions are not bad actors. Emotions are what people are supposed to have, and they can flow with ease, stutter, withhold or take a turn towards violence. Ideally, educators of all stripes develop approaches for responding to emotional reactions in present time and have resources for referral in case of emergencies.

Scope of practice and corporeal listening

Much somatic learning is accomplished in classes and workshops, and these should clarify limits that respect open-minded curiosity and emotional intelligence. People can learn how to validate and respect vibrant life responsively without aggression, especially towards others. *The ability to respond well in the moment is a mark of emotional intelligence.* Nevertheless, I know that somatic programs vary in their approaches to topics of emotion. For example, the Feldenkrais work is objective, while Rosen Breathwork and Holotropic Breathwork can be outrageously emotional. In a Holotropic Breathwork session, I spoke in tongues, slobbered profusely and cried to see God. My body remembers the exposed feelings overcoming me. Around me, I heard people sob, bark like dogs, scream, threaten and swear profusely.

Losing my ordinary sense of time and place did me a lot of good but this reminds me of educational aims of somatics and my role as a teacher. The founder of Holotropic Breathwork, Alexander Grof, is a psychiatrist, and I am not. I teach therapeutically and educationally through movement and dance, not the raw expression of emotion and complete loss of boundaries. Some somatic methods in psychology and psychiatry encourage extreme expressions, including rage. This requires facilitators who are experienced in ritualizing and managing emotions towards creative and therapeutic ends, as in Holotropic Breathwork and Reichian Breathwork.

Subtleties of listening are keys to success in somatic learning. Corporeal listening (somatic attunement) can be taught and practiced in dance improvisations, painting, sounding, voicing, movement meditations, poetry, dreamwork and somatic bodywork. These are safe somatic methods for emotional expressions and can be applied across cultural and age differences in many situations. Group improvisations through somatic practices in nature also heal as they build community and planetary awareness. Somatic facilitators can provide time for students to attune to felt life and emotion through witnessing and communicating with each other, painting and journaling.

Emotion is part of movement, and thus emotional processing is constant in small or large measures through somatic movement practices. Teachers/facilitators can be prepared for disturbing or weepy responses, readying places where students might be alone for a while, or be with someone they choose to talk with. Having a blanket handy for immediate comfort is also important and can afford feelings of privacy and protection. This is usually enough. It is important to remember that teachers and fellow students are not responsible for solving the problems of others. Still, they can listen in safety when personal and group boundaries are respected.

Listening is an essential ingredient of communication in somatic practices on all levels, whether in workshops, classes or individual therapeutic settings. Effective listening starts with nonjudgment, an easy concept in principle but not in practice. *Nonjudgment* is a learned communication principle in somatics and also an indicator of emotional intelligence: in learning how to listen responsively and not reactively, thanking people for their thoughts, not substituting one's own story as a preferred narrative and not advising or asking probing personal questions. I studied this somatic approach in Selwa Said's workshops on effective communication (2003), which is based in the humanistic psychology of Carl Rogers. Later I published a somatic vision of my study with Said, 'The ways we communicate: Somatic dance and meditation as a bridge' (2012: 14–17). One can somatically attune through effective communication principles.

Ethics in somatic laboratories: Movement and touch

Somatic workshops and classes provide laboratories for the practice of ethics. The student/teacher relationship in education is dialogical and a study in ideas and ethics of learning. When movement is the medium for learning, we prioritize it and attend to ethics via movement. In somatic movement arts, movement is the educational medium and avenue for somatic experience, not just any kind of movement, but embodied movement, which is always the movement of *someone*. Thus, ethics in somatic work is both personal and interpersonal.

Somatic touch techniques develop a special kind of interpersonal communication and corporeal listening. *Listening is a virtue in somatic touch.* Listening through touch is about respect for the client's embodied experience, and thus it involves emotional intelligence as a study in patience. In this, a nonverbal ethic passes between the practitioner/guide and the receiver or student/client. This perspective on listening through touch is not unique. I have studied several hands-on practices of movement education that proceeds mainly nonverbally with patience and openness towards unknown outcomes. The practitioner has the potential to become an artist in this work. It takes time and patience in classwork and goodwill as people listen, speak and learn together through relational somatic attunement.

In practice, we know that emotions will be present in all of our work as part of embodied life, and we also know our limits. We touch with permission and care, hold presence for another and listen. We are not doing anything heroic to anyone; instead, the guide is a catalyst for the other's potential or bodily nature. The curiosity and creativity of somatic hands-on practices intrigue me, not the hope of being a healer. Somatic hands-on practices heal in the variable sense that the body of the other holds healing potentials. The guide is a skilled listener who attunes to the other, not a doer.

Agreement circles: Ethics agreements for group learning

I like the idea of establishing ethics for group learning through agreements, and I do this with the involvement of all students, or in smaller groups who report back to the whole, somewhere near the beginning of a workshop or series of classes. For instance, do we agree not to talk over each other? Do we agree to respect everyone in the class? Do we agree to listen and wait for discussion to offer thoughts and questions? Do we agree that it is alright to disagree with the teacher and others and express a point of view with curiosity and without aggression or blame? What other agreements do we want to make? Do we need agreements about emotional and physical safety in our group?

Agreements can arise in community and establish the tone and intention of an entire workshop. The teacher's syllabus and the declared orientation of a class are foundational in agreement settings. What will this class be about? What do students need to succeed in the work? What are student agreements with themselves? Do they want to record these in their journals?

On the other hand, ethical codes are more than agreements; they state right and wrong – as in the following two examples.

Sample code of ethics regarding touch in somatic learning environments

Touch only with permission and with care. Practice nonjudgement. Practice patience. Be objective and neutral by not imposing yourself or your story. At the same time, be fully present to your practice partner (or client). Touch to serve others, not your own needs. Use touch with somatic movement and purpose. Sexual contact and solicitous touch are not permitted.

Sample code of interpersonal ethics in somatic learning environments

Strive to foster ethical interactions in learning and educational environments. Give priority to the physical and emotional safety of individuals and groups as a whole. In context of group awareness in somatic processes, people sometimes cry and express a range of emotions. This is natural; excavation of emotion is part of authentic movement and depth movement dance, but overall, somatic movement methods have creative, restorative and educational goals. Emotional venting in uncontrollable screaming, temper tantrums or aggression toward others, whether fellow students or teachers is not permitted in somatic classrooms and workshops. Become acquainted with available resources for psychological emergencies. In group work, draw attention to learning and sharing through movement and dance. Include everyone fairly.

Introducing the Springboard and Storyboard

The Springboard begins with scattered thoughts on ethics in somatics as they have arisen in the writing of this essay and often discarded in revisions. I use these initial wanderings as a springboard for key organizational principles as they appear later on the Storyboard. In his first reading of this work, Feldenkrais teacher Ray Swartz equated the Springboard to 'early somatic explorations where one is immersed in sensation and often does not know how to organize the experience, and then how over time those experiences begin to take place in the map of self that is forming and clarifying' (Conversation of 2018).

I invite readers to enter this process by adding to the story, first in scatters, then finally stating their organizational principles on a Storyboard.

The Storyboard summarizes significant values in somatic movement education, which also represent ideals, aspirations and promises that can be understood as virtues when personified. Values and virtues indicate worth and provide ethical directions. Somatic values of movement education prioritize *experiential change*: effective, enjoyable, useful, transformative change. Somatic movement values are inconclusive and not guaranteed, but they can serve as guides. Finally, I emphasize that my value groupings are by no means the only way to state or organize topics of ethics in somatic movement education.

Springboard: Ethics in somatic bits, values and scatters

Encouraging positive change
Experiential learning
Emotional Intelligence
Creative agency
Networking
Honesty
Embodying ease
Happiness
Kinesthetic connectivity

Empathy
　　　　Civility and service to others
　　Creative engagement
　　　　　　　Embodying peace
　　　I-Can
　　We-Can
Adaptability
　　　　Interaction
　　　　　Sharing Space
　　　　　　　Emotion
　　　　　　　　　I-Care
　　　　　Well-being
Movement Integration
　　　　　Mindful Relaxation
Expressive range
　　　　　Responsive agency
　　　Enjoying movement
　　　　Exploring limitation
Exploring liminal movement experiences
　　　Gender fluidity
　　　　　　Wonder
Pedagogical fairness and hope
　　Extending intuition and imagination
　　　　　　Discovery modes of learning
　　　　　Strength with flexibility
　　Alertness
　　　　Coordination
　　Patience
　　　　　　　Practicing risk
　　Mindfulness
Flow States
　　　　Optimal living
　　　　　Moving better
　　　Performing better
Well-doing
　　　　　　Adaptability
　　Tactile-Kinesthetic empathy
　　　Balance
Ecological connectivity
　　　　　Personal development

Professional development
Building self-confidence
Matching not mastery
Beginning where you are
Improving body image
Joy in the body
Movement as curiosity
Art/dance experiences in/with/as nature
Bridging restraint and freedom
Revaluing darkness   Revaluing the earth
Revaluing culture
Revaluing power
Resistance as a value

Storyboard of ethics in somatics

Values and aspirations of somatic movement practices

o   Well-doing
o   Well-being
o   Flourishing
o   Improved Performance
o   Interactive Embodiment
o   Effective Communication
o   Patience
o   Mindful Presence
o   Fairness
o   Empathy
o   Adaptability
o   Somatic Attunement

Values of movement integration
o   Harmonious Flow
o   Ease with Facility
o   Balance with Readiness
o   Balance with Resistance
o   Grounded without Effort
o   Centered through Choice
o   Adaptable through Choice
o   Reversible at Will

- o Expressive with Range
- o Agency with Awareness
- o Strength with Flexibility
- o Alertness with Coordination

Affective values of somatic movement
- o Emotional Ease
- o Optimal Engagement
- o Easy Concentration
- o Immersion
- o Fascination
- o Hopefulness
- o Somatic Empathy
- o Emotional Awareness
- o Emotional Intelligence
- o Mindfulness in Motion

Educational values of somatic processes
- o Learning through Curiosity
- o Not Knowing
- o Respecting Liminality
- o Moving without Fear
- o Moving past Command
- o Moving toward Discovery
- o Encouragement for Learning
- o Taking Time to Learn
- o Matching, Not Mastering
- o Gaining Hands-on Movement Skills
- o Extending Creativity through Movement
- o Relating Movement and Art
- o Inclusive Attitude to Others
- o Sharing Space
- o Respecting Gender Differences
- o Respecting Gender Fluidity
- o Embodying Adaptability
- o Practical Wisdom

Conceptual values
- o Addressing Oppression
- o Revaluing Aesthetics

- o Revaluing Nature
- o Revaluing Human Ontology
- o Revaluing Ontology of Nature
- o Cultivating Hope
- o Remaining Curious

Activist values
- o Acting on Ecological Regeneration
- o Engaging Cross-cultural Community Building
- o Practicing Civility
- o Awareness of Unequal Power Dynamics
- o Permission in Performance

Ethical conduct in somatic studies and practices
- o Do no Harm
- o Touch only with Consent
- o Touch with Care
- o Listen to Others
- o Credit Sources
- o Speak your Truth
- o Respect Others
- o Practice Fairness
- o Learn with Joy
- o Be Patient
- o Teach with Care

NOTES

1. I learned this in a drum circle at *Mukuntuweap* as part of a larger gathering, 12 December 2010.
2. Social Justice was a major theme of ISMETA's International Conference of 2021: 'Engaging embodiment: Somatic applications for health, education and social justice'. ISMETA is the International Somatic Movement and Education and Therapy Association.
3. 'Natureculture' is a term that comes from cultural anthropology, primatology and feminist science studies. It refers to a 'synthesis of nature and culture that recognizes their inseparability in ecological relationships that are both biophysically and socially formed'. See: Ovenden et al. (2017: 1–2).
4. The taming and mastery of nature to the detriment of culture and all life on earth is the topic of Anna Lowenhauput Tsing's work, *The Mushroom at the End of the World: On the Possibility of Life in Capitalist Ruins* (2015).

REFERENCES

Beauvoir, Simone ([1948] 1992), *The Ethics of Ambiguity* (trans. B. Frechtman), New York: Philosophical Library.

Csikszentmihalyi, Mihaly (1990), *Flow: The Psychology of Optimal Experience*, New York: Harper and Row.

Csikszentmihalyi, Mihaly (1996), *Creativity: Flow and the Psychology of Discovery and Invention*, New York: Harper Perennial.

Csikszentmihalyi, Mihaly and Csikszentmihalyi, Isabella Selega (eds) (2006), *A Life Worth Living: Contributions to Positive Psychology (Series in Positive Psychology)*, New York: Oxford University Press.

Damasio, Antonio (1999), *The Feeling of What Happens: Body and Emotion in the Making of Consciousness*, New York: Harcourt Brace & Company.

Damasio, Antonio (2010), *Self Comes to Mind: Constructing the Conscious Brain*, New York: Vintage Books, Random House Inc..

Damasio, Antonio (2017), *The Strange Order of Things: Life, Feeling and the Making of Cultures*, New York: Pantheon Books.

Ferris Lester, Kelly (2015), 'Environments for self-learning', in S. Fraleigh (ed.), *Moving Consciously: Somatic Transformations through Dance, Yoga, and Touch*, Urbana: University of Illinois Press.

Fraleigh, Sondra (2004), *Dancing Identity: Metaphysics in Motion*, Urbana: University of Illinois Press.

Fraleigh, Sondra (2012), 'The ways we communicate: Somatic dance and meditation as a bridge', *Somatics Magazine Journal of the Body-Mind Arts and Sciences,* 16:4, pp. 14–17.

Fraleigh, Sondra (ed.) (2015), *Moving Consciously: Somatic Transformations through Dance, Yoga, and Touch*, Urbana: University of Illinois Press.

Fraleigh, Sondra and Bingham, Robert (eds) (2018), *Performing Ecologies in a World in Crisis*, special edition of *Choreographic Practices*, 9:1.

Freire, Paulo (1994), *Pedagogy of Hope: Reliving Pedagogy of the Oppressed*, New York: Continuum.

Freire, Paulo (2015), *Pedagogy of the Oppressed*, New York: Continuum International Publishing Group.

Gilligan, Carol (1982), *In a Different Voice: Psychological Theory and Women's Development*, Cambridge: Harvard University.

Gilligan, Carol, Taylor, Jill Mclean and Sullivan, Amy (1995), *Between Voice and Silence: Women and Girls, Race and Relationships*, Cambridge: Harvard University Press.

Goleman, Daniel (2006), *Emotional Intelligence. 10th Anniversary Edition*, New York: Bantam Dell, A Division of Random House, Inc.

Hanna, Thomas (1988), *Somatics: Reawakening the Mind's Control of Movement, Flexibility, and Health*, Reading: Addison-Wesley.

Husserl, Edmund and Fink, Eugen ([1932] 1995), *Sixth Cartesian Meditation: The Idea of a Transcendental Theory of Method* (trans. and intro. R. Bruzina; textual notations and appendix E. Husserl), Bloomington: Indiana University Press.

Hursthouse, Rosalind (1997), *On Virtue Ethics*, Oxford: *Oxford University Press*.

Johnson, Don Hanlon (ed.) (1995), *Bone, Breath and Gesture*, Berkley: North Atlantic Books.

MacIntyre, Alasdair (1981), *After Virtue*, Notre Dame: University of Notre Dame Press.

MacIntyre, Alasdair (2006), *The Tasks of Philosophy: Selected Essays*, vol. 1, Cambridge: Cambridge University Press.

Margulis, Lynn and Sagan, Dorion (1986), *Microcosmos: Four Billion Years of Microbial Evolution*, New York: Summit Books.

Ovenden, Kathryn and Malone, Nicholas (2017), 'Natureculture', in *The International Encyclopedia of Primatology*, New York: John Wiley & Sons, pp. 1–2.

Ricoeur, Paul ([1966] 2007), *Freedom and Nature: The Voluntary and the Involuntary* (trans. E. V. Kohak, foreword D. Ihde), Chicago: Northwestern University Press.

Tsing, Anna Lowenhaupt (2015), *The Mushroom at the End of the World: On the Possibility of Life in Capitalist Ruins*, Princeton: Princeton University Press.

Vallor, Shannon (2016), *Technology and the Virtues: A Philosophical Guide to a Future Worth Wanting*, New York: Oxford University Press.

5

Walking Well:
A Play of Touch and
Restoration in Three Acts

A SOMATIC MOVEMENT detective accepts that there is more than meets the eye in movement, even in walking. Walking is fundamental to humans. We all do it, but for the most part, we don't give much attention to it, unless we consider what walking holds in its power to reveal individuality and personality, or that postural balance in walking can deteriorate quickly when any part of the foot loses feeling or function, especially the big toe. The play we enter here includes my detective work in movement and touch with a client I call 'Amy'. Parts of the play might be read as a case study in a somatic process focusing on the whole person through the feet and big toes. My case study with Amy is embedded in matters of body image, approaches to touch, instances of attunement and matching, and the consciousness of the teacher/practitioner.

I love to walk
when the sun is high and hot, and there is just enough breeze to ruffle my coiled sarong,
just enough to stir the chartreuse leaves in metallic music against the sky.
Walking arouses gratitude in me for the kid practicing his saxophone as I pass by,
for those whose brilliance I have never doubted.
I will walk till stillness overcomes me, and I am awake,

Act I. Balance in walking and faith in the unknown

When I walk and pay attention to acts of walking, I am aware of moments when my back foot releases and lifts from the ground and that for a time, my front foot is balancing and holding the weight of my whole body. My big toe is the last part of the back foot to leave the ground. It is, therefore, mightily crucial for propulsion and balance. Then I am aware of an expanse of time when my body is balanced on the front foot in faith with the Earth, and the back foot and leg experience an abyss as they empty towards unknown outcomes. I hope my back foot will find a forward footing and become the new balancing point for my walk. This happens most of the time but I could stumble or get my foot caught in some trap I didn't see coming.

This happened to me this morning. I caught my back foot in a loose strap holding my movement mat. My brisk walk forward was suddenly halted, and I took a forward dive. Fortunately, I was close enough to a wall that I fell into it and didn't get hurt. Puppy ran to my side and tried to help. So, I recovered quickly, but I still remember the air moment when I was suspended in space with both feet off the ground. Suddenly all my taken-for-granted faith in walking erased, and I panicked. On recovering, I remembered having had this same suspended feeling before, once when carrying a big bag of groceries out into the parking lot of the market and stumbling over a rock. My body went flying as I experienced a mysteriously empty and sweet expanse of time before the crash landing. I was in my mid 70s at the time, and it was scary to land hard on the cement. I got badly bruised and scratched but had no broken bones. I managed a wild crumple on landing, intuitively and somatically. After all, I am a somatic artist and detective.

In my early sixties, I had another opportunity to call upon my somatic skills when I fell down a flight of stairs and broke my left big toe. In working with my compromised toe over the space of many years, I learned a great deal about the importance of toes, the flourish of walking, and the overall postural organization for any kind of movement. Big toes are no joke!

Act I – Scene I. Somatic artist and detective

Can one really be a somatic artist? And what would a somatic detective be? Somatics encompasses a field of theories and practices concerning movement and dance education, with accompanying hands-on therapies. Certainly, one can become an artist at something in this mix, but it takes time, dedication and practice like any art. There are skills to be developed and matters of excellence. My part in somatic movement arts is that of teacher and practitioner.

My background studies for somatic work accrue in dance practices and through the Feldenkrais work, primarily. Dancing expands elements of walking, or it makes them apparent. Walking is a simple transfer of weight from one foot to the other. Acts of dancing are usually more complicated, but basic rudiments can be distilled. The Feldenkrais Method works with small incremental movement patterns like walking when dissected according to the small and large patterns that make up the whole.

As an artist, I understand the individuality of walking and pay attention to personal styles, which are endlessly fascinating. As a teacher, I work with students to expand their repertory of movement understanding. Through my study of the Alexander Technique, I always include walking as basic and telling in terms of posture and intention. I adapt such somatic techniques for walking at Eastwest Somatics Institute and include instances of attunement and matching, as I will get to later.

A somatic detective accepts that there is more than meets the eye, even in walking. Walking is fundamental to humans. We all do it; at least most humans walk at some time or another. But for the most part, we don't give much attention to walking. Unless we consider what walking holds in its power to reveal individuality and personality or that walking and postural balance can deteriorate quickly when any part of the foot loses feeling or function, especially the big toe. The play we enter now includes my detective work in movement and touch with a client I call 'Amy' and identify anonymously. Parts of the play might be read as a case study in a somatic process involving the big toes and body image. My case study with Amy is embedded in matters of body image, approaches to touch and the consciousness of the teacher/practitioner; thus, we ask into these in several introductory scenes.

Act I – Scene II. Body image in walking

First, in any somatic process, I appeal to what I know, and, at the same time, I hold faith in what lies beyond me. I'm not speaking of anything supernatural, but of trust in nature itself, the nature of the body, that is, which is always teaching me something new. Somatic detectives know what they don't know and have faith that they will be able to discern unexpected matters of body and movement in working with others over time. In my practice of movement and touch, I seek to access more of the body's healing nature, my client's healing, of course, and my own. I am not a neutral bystander. Somatic detectives experience the values of their findings. Both partners in the somatic exchange stand to benefit and in a variety of ways. This play concerns the distinct values of walking as human and variable.

People walk in restricted ways and sloppy ways, in dainty ways and in bold swaths. Some walks travel far in space but go quickly. That would be me. Some are slow and meandering. That would also be me, sometimes. The pace and intention of my walk change often to meet the exigencies of the day. Some walks spraddle widely, and some walks squeeze the feet together. As a detective and dancer, I look at these matters of expression and style, but what interests me as a reflective phenomenologist is how movers themselves feel about their walking, and thus about themselves. What kind of self-beliefs and self-images arise when people give attention to their movement, especially when they have a chance to play and work with the timing and size of their walks.

SOMATICS IN DANCE, ECOLOGY, AND ETHICS

What do people say when they walk beside and *match* someone else's walking in somatic group work? Do they enjoy the matching process or become frustrated? How is their kinaesthetic sense of time and timing affected in walking with others? These are open questions, with meaningful answers from movers themselves as they test their feelings in moving with others, interpreting their feelings and experiences. My outside eye as the teacher intersects with the learning of movers. Most likely, I pose a question or two that might peak the mover's awareness. Questions like, 'was this exploration of matching in walking fun for you, or did you find moments of difficulty or frustration'? If someone is apparently lost in the exploration, I let it go and just listen to any impressions they share.

Act I – Scene III. Walking in nature

My job as a somatic detective in an educational setting is care and observation, not analysis and assessment; instead, I try to provide engaging processes that engage students in their own images of self and self in relation to others. The setting for exploration is often in a studio, and we also travel to some green or rocky knoll outside. Walking outside is the best, since it aids people in building positive body images. I know this through experience and the testimonials of students who appreciate the opportunity to feel the support and wisdom of nature, which is not about doing anything, but in letting go and letting be. I also remember that oxygen heals.

Philip Barr, a veteran of the Iraq war and one of my long-time students, told me he used his somatic studies consciously when he walked the entire Appalachian Trail. The use of somatics with hiking was one of his ways of healing from the trauma of war. Attending to his walk's somatic subtleties sustained him, he told me, and made his 20,193-mile hike enjoyable and doable (well, more manageable). This trail is the longest foot-path only trail in the world, ranging from Maine to Georgia, and Philip walked it for daily recuperation in appreciation of each foot-fall. He practiced the somatic value of allowing things to be as they are without wishing them to be otherwise. Values of letting-be can come forward in practicing movement in nature, with nature, as nature, and allowing our bodies to belong to nature.

> Sondra, I was just thinking about you! I am currently hiking the Appalachian Trail from Georgia to Maine, and the experiences I have had with you and your work are bearing amazing fruit! I have basically been (over 1300 miles, so far) re-learning to walk. My spine stacked, my muscles relaxed, and – as I remember you showing me before – walking as if I was simply falling and catching myself over and over! I would not be having such a pleasant (though VERY strenuous) hike without the kinesthetic awareness I developed through the now life-long practice of somatic awareness. So thank you!
>
> Philip Barr

FIGURE 5.1: Philip Barr in Somatics Class with Sondra Fraleigh and Kelly Ferris Lester at the State University of New York, Brockport in the early 2000s.

Act II. Patterning and faith in the known

Sometimes I pause to count the many years I have spent learning movement patterns as the basis for self-regulation and hands-on therapies. I also have conversations with myself about the uses of these in hands-on therapeutic touch. 'You mean there is more than one kind of Hands-on Therapy?'

Yes, there are many uses of touch in somatic contexts, not mistaken for massage, which is the most common hands-on method that most people understand. Massage uses manipulation, moving the muscles against the bones or stretching through tissues and adjacent structures, sometimes with deep pressure. On the contrary, somatic hands-on work distances from manipulation, forceful pressure or controlling contact. Somatic methods relinquish control, employing languages of exploration and discovery in modes of quiet listening and waiting. Somatic approaches are made of the cloth of listening, adaptation, acceptance and discovery. Somatic detectives are ready to accept differing unknown outcomes. When I inquire into the core of my development of Shin Somatics hands-on methods, I see how they ride close to meditation.

Act II – Scene I. Aims and purposes of movement patterns

That said, 'are somatic therapies completely empty of form and distinctiveness'? No, they are very distinctive and have specific aims and purposes. My students practice movement patterns, many of them, in simple objective repetitive forms. They do this for self-regulation and embody the forms kinaesthetically and visually to later use formal knowledge of patterning as a basis for hands-on work with clients. For example, a simple movement pattern emerges in lifting an arm up in a relaxed way with the wrist leading, then lowering it softly. We have a name for this pattern. We call it 'cat's paw'. It feels wonderful to dangle the whole hand from the wrist and makes us laugh as we lift it high and let it float down.

Likewise, we practice specific ways of walking to get used to the feeling of taking the weight through the outside of the foot, or on the inside, of lifting the big toe to unbalance the walk, then putting it down to feel the balance. These become *known patterns*. Sometimes we dance in loose, improvisational patterns, letting an arm guide or letting the tail bone or shoulder lead. Then we test how the elbow might guide while paying attention to what happens to the shoulder. Lifting and lowering the shoulder is a straightforward and helpful pattern. In this case, we might pay attention to the psychology of body image that arrives when the shoulders are lifted and held tensely: fear for some or hiding for others. It is telling to see how people see themselves when they release the shoulders, loosen the neck and let the shoulders relax downward. I would rather hear students' own interpretations than offer mine. In this way (and others), *movement patterns* constitute knowledge to be referenced and used in hands-on restorative work.

Act II – Scene II. Case study with Amy: Conversations without words

When we play with walking patterns, we get to know them intimately and notice patterns in others' walking. Recently, I worked with a new client I will call Amy, whose walking was at issue. She was aware of the disfunction herself, which is rare. People generally don't pay attention to their own ways of walking, even when their shoes are wearing out towards the outside, and their ankles and knees become painful. Amy had undergone back surgery and knee surgery. Now she was thinking of having surgery on her big toes. They were 'floppy', she said.

When she walked, I noticed how she flipped her lower legs and feet outward in small circles to avoid using her big toes. They were losing tone and power, and they were also painful. In walking, her back leg veered immediately towards the small toes and lifted from the floor early, taking a forward step before reaching the large toes. In lay terms, she was not 'rocking' through the whole foot from the heel to the toes in transferring her weight directly forward in walking. Thus, her gait overall had a halting punctuation about it and a side-to-side elliptical sway.

So how did my knowledge of movement patterning and experiential work with walking help her? First, I didn't judge her walk and call it 'bad'. All walking to me is just the way people walk.

* * *

I tell her I think we might be able to encourage a functional pattering of her whole body through hands-on work, which might give her strength and confidence in walking and use of the fullness of her foot. I say it will be 'fun' to try and that she might not need surgery on her big toes.

She agrees, so I proceed by asking her to lie down on the bodywork table on her back, which is a simple way to begin that I use with many people. The ability to lie down and the way people do it are always revealing. Technically speaking, this gives access to what somatics teacher Amanda Williamson speaks of as *fulcrums of support* through the resting pressure of the occiput, scapular, spine and sacrum. Sensing the related parts can support my client in resting on the table, and we might accomplish hands-on affirmation of this support. I think immediately of the simplicity of a pattern from back-lying I call *Seahorse Wave* in my yoga teaching, one that uses the breath softly to influence these fulcrums of support.

But there is a problem: Amy tells me she can't lie down on her back because of 'hardware from her back surgery'. So, I ask her if she can lie down on her side. She says that will be OK, so I assist her in this, and we start supine in side-lying. I need to adapt my plan immediately, and I consider that working with the breath from a side-lying position will also be a good way to begin. I know that the qualitative manner of my first touch and hands-on contact will tell her everything she needs to know about how our work together will unfold.

First, I settle my stance by bringing attention to my own feet in standing. I soften my knees and shoulders, so my touch can be deliberate, and I can hold my own weight without placing any of it on Amy. In my mind, I am practicing an aspect of somatic teaching and leadership that encourages independence in hands-on work. Hands-on therapies are sensitive to mutuality and should be objective, not incurring dependence. I don't think I will be doing anything to Amy; instead, we will be moving in touch with each other. In the beginning, her breath guides me, and as my contact becomes acquainted with the subtleties of her breath, I gently guide her breath to non-habitual places of renewal. Curiously, I am matching her breath without miming it.

Somatic touch is about the clarity of contact and emptiness for me, about listening and waiting for my client's body to speak to me. And when it does, it communicates without words. In the silence, I hear Amy's body say: 'I respond well to this kind attention; I can breathe better and relax into this process'. I hear this in her breath as it begins to expand, moving in response to the neutrality of touch and movement facilitation. This part of our work is nonverbal. I experiment with slightly different directions of touch, asking her breath if it wants to move here or there, and I pay attention to the path it takes. Her breath guides my hands in this part of the conversation. And I give up any expectation for outcomes in order to be in touch with the meditation.

Working with the breath is fascinating and endless. I have worked with many different people by now and from a variety of cultural and racial backgrounds. The breath is always just human and familiar; yet, it is also the breath of life, and everyone is vulnerable and alive in this sense. But the breath of each person has distinctness, as distinctive as their ways of walking. This makes the wordless conversation with breath fascinating. People manifest unique and unexpected patterns in the form of breathing. In my experience, the breath is an orchestra that makes wonderful music in its improvisational tones and patterns. I listen for the music, always in process, moving as life does.

Act II – Scene III. Lifting the limbs

I expand my work with Amy in side-lying because I see she is responding well, and I believe that cradling and lifting her leg slightly while holding its weight will

FIGURE 5.2: Eastwest Graduate Alaina Deaver lifting and cradling the leg from side-lying. Photograph by Sondra Fraleigh, 2017.

bring more attention to the relationships of her extremities to her torso, especially through the hip joint. I know it will take normative work (habitual efforts of holding) out of the leg and lend it lightness. I want to be careful in any case because I know that lifting the leg in side-lying will influence her back, and I want to respect the surgery there.

> Eastwest graduate Alaina Deaver accomplishes the lift by reaching from behind her classmate, Denise Purvis, then holding the knee and ankle by *matching* them patiently with her hands. Alaina waits until she feels the leg and hip release weight and any holding patterns.

The lift can be done in several ways, much depends on the two participants, the size and strength of each person play a role, but most crucial is what the practitioner discovers in silent conversation with the movement responses. She wants to be in tune with the leg's potentials, demonstrated movement habits and ease or difficulty in the hip joint. Alaina keeps her attention wide, not simply on the leg. She observes how the back moves in relation to the leg lift.

In my work with Amy, I also give special attention to Amy's arm, to its facility and how it might speak to me at the moment. Below we see Alina's work with Denise's arm in our classwork at Eastwest. I note especially how neutral and fully attentive to the moment Alaina remains throughout the process.

FIGURE 5.3: To begin, Eastwest Graduate Alaina Deaver lifts slowly with attention to movement potentials from under her partner's elbow and wrist. She knows the shoulder, upper back and ribs will be involved in association with the lift. Photograph by Sondra Fraleigh, 2017.

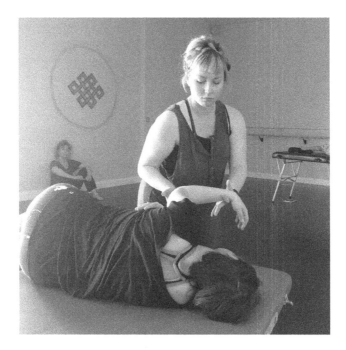

FIGURE 5.4: Eastwest Graduate Alaina Deaver lifts the arm slowly and a little higher, matching two points of touch, the elbow and wrist, while she listens to the willingness of Denise's arm to be in the movement. Photograph by Sondra Fraleigh, 2017.

FIGURE 5.5: Alina waits for Denise's arm to settle into her hands and then begins to place the arm and hand down while listening to the shoulder. Meanwhile, Alaina gives attention to the breath through the ribs and upper back. Photograph by Sondra Fraleigh, 2017.

FIGURE 5.6: After the arm is in a good resting position, Alaina settles the head gently on its horizon. Throughout the process, Alaina is conscious of her own movement and doesn't go beyond her capacity; she takes care of herself. If she remains focused and free of stress, she has a good chance of promoting a calming effect in Denise's nervous system. We think of the nervous system in terms of whole-body responsiveness and listen for clues of well-being. Photograph by Sondra Fraleigh, 2017.

Act II – Scene IV. Leadership and listening

I know I'm the guide or leader in undertaking somatic therapies with clients. So, I'm ready to assume this position and to call upon my studies of movement patterning, dance and finely tuned touch techniques. I'm not just touching people and hoping for some unexpected result. I have faith in what I know and stay ready for the next idea in my conversation with a client. In my leadership role, I risk new ideas and am also prepared to give up wilfulness. I don't know everything or even enough yet about the person I'm working with.

I tell Amy that I think she can roll from her side to her back safely if she plants her feet on the table as we accomplish the turn together, and I caution that we will do this slowly. I will guide her, and if she feels any discomfort, we can give it up immediately. In our nonverbal conversation with touch thus far, she trusts me. She says: OK, we can try. I help Amy move onto her back as we become further acquainted through touch and movement. She says she feels fine on her back and notices the support from having her feet planted on the table.

I begin with a simple play of most/breath & least/breath, noticing where the breath comes up clearly and where it is not moving. My hands contact the most breath and then move to the least. The breath will typically flow with the touch, and if it doesn't, I will try another approach.

I don't doubt myself in such processes. I know that if Amy can plant her feet on the table, her lower back and surgery can feel supported. It will help her back let go of any work. This position is one of ease and is restorative. Amy and I worked our way towards the back without any problem. She is resting on her back for the first time in three years, she says. Her feet are planted with the soles down on the table. This support from planting the feet is protecting the site of her surgery. I can work with several patterns from back-lying and renew the breath. I check to make sure the plant of her feet is steady, and if not, I bring the feet broader or narrow the stance.

Now, what was the goal I set for us? The goal was to help her find balance throughout her whole body to facilitate 'wellness' in walking (dare I say 'elegance'?). Getting into restful positions in side-lying and back-lying helped us both to access the body as a whole. It was never my intention to simply work on her big toe. But I bear it in mind, as a balance point of walking, and I know she is protecting it for a good reason. It hurts! I also know we can get to the toe more effectively *by not touching it directly*. That will simply call more attention to the pain. We will work instead through supportive positions and movements. The goal is to gain trust in balance throughout the body, allowing her body to shift

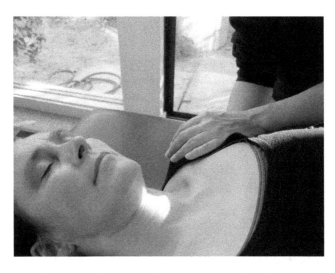

FIGURE 5.7: Eastwest Somatics Graduates practice in class. Darby Sheridan encourages breath in the movement of the shoulder and scapula. Ruth Way receives. Photograph by Sondra Fraleigh, 2015.

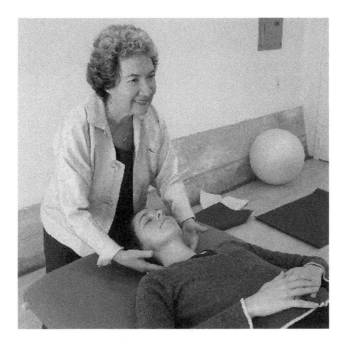

FIGURE 5.8: Through minimal touch, Sondra's hands find breath in the neck. She waits there and listens as she continues to teach a class on restorative touch. Photograph courtesy of Sondra Fraleigh, 2015.

toward better function. I know some of this through personal experience with my own big toe.

Act II – Scene V. Sondra's left big toe

This I know about my big toe
it is often painful because I broke it falling
one fine day.
And this I also know about my big toe
I have had to love it into wellness
with doctors telling me it could be fixed somewhat
but never completely to my satisfaction.
I got my toe into dancing shape without surgery and
with daily somatic care, talking it into leaping flight
with every possible direction of gentle movement,
with special attention to wobbly knees and ankles
and surly hips adapting to the greater
being of my body as a whole.

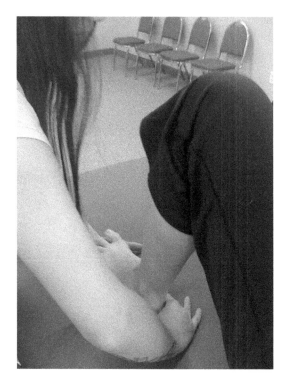

FIGURE 5.9: Eastwest students in classwork with particular attention to the foot and left big toe, affirming the heel's connection to the ground while lifting the front of the foot, and encouraging the toes to settle into the touch. Soon this toe will be ready to go wherever it wants to. And for now, it feels just great! Photograph by Sondra Fraleigh, 2012.

Act III. Big toe surgery, or Land to Water Yoga?

Our work took a serious turn towards practice, as I taught Amy how she could assist herself through movement and creative uses of simple yoga and meditation. She initially thought she would need surgery on her big toe but she hoped to avoid this through our work. We decide it is worth a try.

Act III – Scene I. Teaching movement in hands-on practice

Amy settles into the table on her back with her feet in standing, and I facilitate the *Seahorse Wave* as a breath pattern that involves her whole back in a gentle floating wave from the sacrum to the cranium. This pattern and its benefit are fully described in my small guide book: *Land to Water Yoga* (2006: 73–75). Along the way, I teach Amy how to do this breath pattern by herself at home. The book will help her to remember small details of the seahorse, which is not incidentally associated with the root chakra (energy vortex) of the feet and legs.

I also perform specific gentle work on her foot to help her feel its tripod shape and multi-directionality through the ankle. We explore the foot and ankle connection, not forgetting the foot's relationships with knees and hips. All the joints of the foot and leg influence each other. I mention this to her later, but don't want to overload her with anatomical functionality in our first meeting. Then I assist her in rolling back onto her side, so she can easily come up to sitting, rest a minute and finally come to standing.

After she walks to regain uprightness, I work with her in sitting to facilitate some postural principles without her needing to bear weight on her feet. I help her settle in sitting on a chair upright with ease while teaching her how to express her

FIGURE 5.10: Students assist each other: finding balance in sitting while bringing the chin and eyes to the horizon. A tap to the top of the head opens awareness to the space overhead and the entire length of the torso. Photograph by Eastwest Graduate, Michelle Ikle, 2010.

FIGURE 5.11: Amber Watkins-Olpin practices Mountain Stride in walking the Desert Rose Labyrinth in Kayenta, Utah. She expresses her horizon and her full height. Photograph by Sondra Fraleigh, 2015.

horizon by looking out widely instead of looking down, which most people do by habit. Then, I sit on the floor in front of her and pedal her feet, noting the response in her knees and hips. This is easy to do and pleasant for both of us, as we simply observe her responsiveness to touch and gentle play in the joints.

When Amy stands up, I teach her the yoga mountain pose and emphasize a back-leaning variation before standing. The Mountain is about standing still with balance throughout the whole organization of the body. It is both easy and challenging because it is just about standing tall and steady, but there are many details to pay attention to in expressing one's full height and balance in standing. In the *Land to Water Yoga* book, I explain further and detail both the *Mountain Stance* and *Mountain Stride* as practices (2006: 5–13).

I give Amy the book to take home after teaching her how to stand in *Mountain* and roll her foot fully through the Shin Somatics practice of *Mountain Stride*. This constitutes the hands-on therapy and use of our first session's movement together, but she wants to share something with me about her walk.

Act III – Scene II. Agreements and meditations

She tells me that she regularly asks her husband to look at her walk, and he tells her how to improve. I ask if he is helpful. She says she isn't sure. Then I ask her if she feels better about her body and her toes through our first session of work. She expresses trust and says that she can tell her weight and walk have shifted. She feels she can practice *Seahorse* in lying on her back (feet in standing) at home; she can practice sitting and playing with the relationship of her joints, ankle, knee, hip and finally toes, as we have done in hands-on explorations. She will remember how to do the Mountain, then reaching high and back to lengthen her back. Amy says she wants to practice *Mountain Stride* because she is experiencing more feeling in her big toe and learning she can take her body's weight through the whole foot in walking to include the toe. Magically, it doesn't hurt because of the shift in her entire body balance. We take time to talk about the processes of the day and their results so she might recall them in words and feelings.

We finish the practice by sitting quietly together, matching each other in well-balanced seated positions. I emphasize that in 'real-life', one doesn't always centre so easily. But once having experienced an easy distribution of weight and balance throughout the body, one can find it again. It just takes a little practice. I teach her how to pay attention to her breath and that she can let any concerns or worries travel away on the out-breath. In short, I begin to teach her rudiments of silent meditation. I don't add visualization; instead, I leave her to absorb feelings of trust in our work together and introduce her to the quiet mind of meditation. Silence is a great healer, and oxygen is a great healer. Amy says she wants to walk outdoors incrementally. We agree that she will walk barefoot in the house a lot, so she can pay attention to the feeling in her foot and all the wonders of its many joints.

We agree to meet again and continue working this way. We can recall and repeat anything that seems missing.

Amy came faithfully to twelve sessions, and we made a lot of progress with the result that she decided not to have surgery on her toes. We both celebrated that she was walking towards wellness.

Act III – Scene III. Trust and responsibility

I did not discuss what seemed to me Amy's dependence on her husband's willing assessment of her because I thought it would fade. I hoped so, even as I tried to stay neutral in a Zen way. After all, she came to see me because of her toes. I felt if I dwelt at all on her habit of asking for judgment from her husband in assessing her walk and body that she might give up our work altogether.

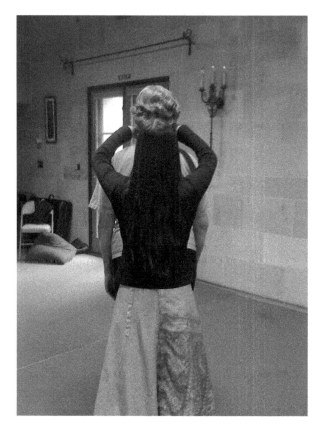

FIGURE 5.12: Michelle Akane Sugimoto assists Ann Guhman in standing tall, balancing the head on top of the spine, and walking well. Photograph by Sondra Fraleigh, 2012.

I don't know enough to introduce the psychology of co-dependence. This is not my work. I trust that my movement work with Amy can help shift her conversations with her husband and help her take responsibility for her own well-being. I know that I will leave her with objective tools for balancing her body throughout and walking well. This includes an ongoing relationship with meditation, sitting quietly alone inside the warmth and comfort of her own breath. Amy and I have trust through standing and walking. The rest is up to her.

Act III – Scene IV. Who am I?

And now to the crux of another matter: my consciousness. It matters how I consider myself in any interaction with a client or student in somatic work. Who I am will resound throughout the communication, whether verbal or through touch. As a teacher and somatic hands-on therapist, I want to gradually disappear, like any good teacher who encourages independence, and this involves what I think of as a conscious use of neutrality.

In entering such psychological terrain, I need to be prepared for unexpected responses, including my own. It matters how I feel in my work with others, but I don't want to attach to my feelings; instead, I practice *nonattachment*, as it is sometimes called in Zen. Both the good and the bad, or what I perceive to be the case, lands in the same place in my consciousness. I let them go, empty my touch and assume meditative neutrality, which is curiously complete and valuable. I let myself 'off the hook' of expectation, so to speak, which doesn't mean I don't care. Such neutrality contains a productive 'not knowing'. It is also a place of vulnerability and a clearing, as in somatic bodywork where uncertainty, risk and emotional metamorphosis reside. I want to be surprised in my work with clients, surpass myself and make discoveries, and at the same time, I seek the best for them. I confess I don't know what that is. The human body is more intelligent than I am. So, I trust in the nature of the body that wants the best for itself, and I listen.

Sometimes I wonder about love in this conditional mix. Students often think that touch involves unconditional love, but I think not. Our work is not about consoling or loving others, even as it requires care. We empty, wait, listen, follow, guide and discover, but we don't fall in love or dependence through touch. This I know: love is not neutral. Ideally, it is freely given but often brokers attachments and disappointments. Love is a condition of mind and heart that is incredibly subjective and risky. Neutrality in somatic bodywork and leadership is ready to give up common attachments to love, to be open to learning and to attend to the good as it presents itself.

What students and clients think of us as somatic practitioners is not up to us. We don't seek approval and have no control over what other people think. The best to hope for is respect and maybe appreciation. Neutrality more than love shines the senses, even as we recognize our passions and attachments. I love my work but I also need to be objective. Somatic hands-on work teaches me how to be in the deliberate manner of touch. For myself, I empty my stores of expectation and let things be. I don't want to fall in love or worry; I want to fall into meditation and listening. I hope to be able to listen deeply to my client's bodily disposition and to my own associations, and I want to do this without doubt or fascination. I am in a curious place of engagement while letting go. I am attentive but not concerned; I can always be kind and caring without display.

I'm speaking about the kind of meditative presence that I have been cultivating for many years in Shin Restore hands-on therapies. I teach students that

FIGURE 5.13: Classwork with Sondra Fraleigh: checking in with each other at the end of a hands-on therapy session. Photograph by Sondra Fraleigh, 2006.

the minute we touch someone in our work, the touch should be clear, present and not solicitous. The latter means releasing worry and the need for outcomes. It would be good if some positive result should arrive, but we don't expect it. Rather, we wait to hear or see whatever result emerges from the changes that occur for the client.

Act III – Scene V. Healing through walking

Such results, however ongoing and never final, are most often surprisingly affirmative. Of course, we care. This is at the root. We have some affinity for outcomes and a lot of experience with client descriptions of their experiences of touch. There are always unexpected outcomes to carry us forward. The simple presence of touch brings unanticipated rewards. I don't believe that I'm transferring any magical substance through my touch. I understand that if I am well-grounded in my relationship to gravity, especially in my own embodied presence, my client or partner can relax into the moment of their own bodily existence.

When we finish a session, I often hear from clients that pain has subsided, that they feel lighter and taller, or the opposite, that they feel heavy. If heaviness is the result, we can go with it and let that speak by encouraging giving into weight. People also describe images that come to them: landscapes never visited or birds flying away from them and escaping the chest. Everything depends on the personality and specific embodied life of the person describing their experience. Some recipients of hands-on therapies don't speak about the experience at all. Many will simply show results in expressions, confidence in walking and often in the release of crying.

In the many interactions I have had with clients and students of hands-on work, I have yet to hear from anyone that the experience was utterly lacking in value. There is always something that changes for the better, or at least towards more understanding. 'My big toe is now part of me. I can feel it now'. This is one of the most recent telling results from my work with Amy. It may seem a small thing but not to her. She has discovered that the way she walks can direct bodyweight directly through from the heel to the front of the foot and into her toes. She can do this safely. Thus, as she walks, she can strengthen her toes instead of stopping short of them and walking flat-footed. This can be learned. Nothing is irrevocably written as habitual. If Amy does this incrementally, it won't hurt and overtime might heal through walking.

One of the great values of somatic touch therapy is that with minimal work and a lot of attention, we can learn how to trust the goodness of our bodies, not getting attention stuck on 'bad' backs and toes. How do we develop a 'good' body image then? Well, I would say, drop by drop, and through having good experiences that teach us how to listen to and trust our bodies. Somatic touch therapy can be enormously helpful in its trust with movement and the body's natural healing capacities. The human body is a marvel and can heal if we send it in healing directions.

I love to walk
when the sun comes up in the morning,
my puppy meanders among purple weeds and flowers,
softly sniffing everything in her path.
Walking arouses gratitude in me for cerulean blue skies
above, and insects moving mid peach-dappled rock.
I will walk till stillness overcomes me, and I am awake, awake.

6

Everyone Needs to Breathe

THIS ESSAY IS written with an eye towards the future and a foot in the past. It is partly autobiographical, and in each of four parts offers reflective somatic practices. The author is sheltering at home, so her thoughts centre on the meaning of home, family and pets. At the same time, she articulates somatic skills to cultivate embodied presence, insightful verbal interactions and healing touch. Her writing invites readers into somatic movement explorations and somatic communication practices through poetry. Life and death, love and war, ground her essay. The section on Simbi involves global shadow work through butoh and the healing essence of water. Golden shadows appear as elemental and ecosomatic in Morphic Curiosity, a butoh invitation to site-specific dance. Video links and photographs further embody the work. The final section, Dance back the world, presents somatic witnessing as an extraordinary process of intimate notice and care. Becoming friends with the whole world is an exhortation of Mahatma Gandhi, and the life work of this author. Her essay was written before the brutal murder of George Floyd and the international protests that began in America as cries for social and racial justice. Now we have a new imperative for Gandhi's call, because everyone has a right to breathe.

Prologue

He who would be friends with God must remain alone, or make the whole world his friend.
(Mahatma Gandhi, *An Autobiography: The Story of My Experiments with Truth*, 1929)

Love in the Time of Cholera (originally *El amor en los tiempos del cólera*, 1985) is by Nobel Prize-winning author Gabriel García Márquez, known affectionately as Gabo throughout Latin America. His novel takes place between 1880 and 1930, just over a hundred years ago. An English translation was published in 1988, and a movie adaptation was released in 2007. Gabo's descriptions suggest the story takes place in Colombia in fictional cities based on Cartagena and Barranquilla, both of which I visited in 1989. I looked for signs of the novel in my travels, surveying for traces of steamy rat-infested streets, mingling in the lives of the characters. Now we have *life in the time of COVID-19*, where death has proliferated everywhere as in Gabo's saga. COVID-19 now was *el cólera* then, the fatal disease that swept through intermittently in terrible epidemics. *Cholera* is also defined somatically as *choler*, or *anger*, which in the extreme becomes war, a related plague on a massive scale that Gabo also brings to the fore in his heart-breaking novel.

Against this dark ground, I write this piece knowing that lives far beyond my reach or intimate knowledge are incredibly precious and precarious. As in Gabo's story, I write about family, war and love, but I write for my time, and with narratives of trust and love rather than tragedy. I stay home as wife and mother, maintaining safety for my extended family, while I also attend to the unfolding politics of the body in the public arena. I am keenly aware that power and greed rather than health and recovery are the driving force of our late and sorry national response to COVID-19 in America. In our slip towards tyranny, we are also fighting a culture war that devalues the body and the truth, but we fight amid the heroics of science and medicine and the eternal unselfishness of good people everywhere. From abroad, the Irish returned an old favour, helping Native Americans battling the virus. In 1847, the Choctaw people sent $170 to help during the potato famine. Irish donors are citing that gesture as they help tribes financially and with great spirit during the pandemic. COVID-19 has afflicted Native America profoundly, particularly the Navajo Nation not far from my home in southwest Utah where water is scarce.

In my reflective and slightly autobiographical essay here, I keep an eye towards change and the future, while using what means I have as a teacher and author to promote health and well-being against the tide, because everyone needs to breathe. The majority of deaths from the virus are among the poor in African American and Native American communities. As I finish this essay in the last week of May 2020, we have extreme unrest and rioting in America, with Minneapolis burning during the time of COVID-19, and many of our large cities in turmoil over the murder of George Floyd, an unarmed African American. As caught on camera, his breath was literally taken away by a police knee to his throat while he was handcuffed.

Somatically stranded between grief and *choler* (anger), our country has an imperative to use the historical lessons of pandemic to change its body politic, fundamentally. In the first week of June, legitimate protests are being infiltrated by looters and violent trouble makers, but peacemakers also abound. I don't want to get lost in despair, and so I have hope, as I pray for systemic change in 400 years of cruelty against Americans of African descent. Becoming friends with the whole world is an exhortation of Mahatma Gandhi and of this essay, I wrote it before the international protests that began in America as cries for social and racial justice. I hope the essay's somatic themes of world-friendly inclusiveness, resilience, breath and healing might resonate in these turbulent times. Change is blowing in the wind, blowing and bending towards a better, more moral future.

Warrior trooper

My husband Warren is resilient. One could even say *he is a trooper*. Warren is 95 years old in 2020, and he has remained a reliable and uncomplaining guy these 53 years I have been married to him. He has also been a warrior who served on a submarine in the Second World War. Warren belongs to 'the greatest generation', and in my eyes, he deserves to. He also lived through the Great Depression and the more recent Great Recession with another one now in process. What is the secret of his resilience? Well, he has been a mover all of his life, and a lover of sports and fair play, which he has written about (Fraleigh 1984). He founded an academic organization for the study of the philosophy of sport, which now awards a world prize in his name. He continues to keep up with his community of activities and friends, even at a distance.

I want to create a somatic practice out of my understanding of Warren's resilience. But where to start? I think I will start with submarines because of Warren's wartime service. He and I watch every submarine movie that comes around – most recently, *Run Silent, Run Deep*, starring Burt Lancaster and Clark Gable. Imagine how old that one is! Movies aside, real warriors have to pass rigorous tests to be on submarines, and have nerves of steel. They might get depth-charged and can't freak out. Warren's submarine was attacked near the end of the war just off the shore of Japan. The sub surfaced at twilight so men could fire the deck gun and disable a radar station near Sendai. Warren remembers diving quickly, then waiting quietly with the motor off, everyone hushed amid chaotic explosions outside, not knowing what the next moment would bring.

Fast forward to today, and some of Warren's best friends and professional associates are Japanese. We see how things change a great deal over time if we are resilient and far-seeing. Every evening over dinner Warren and I mull over our memories, which often entail our travels and studies in other countries, especially Japan. The world becomes friendlier when you listen to differences and learn from them.

Troopers walk, because they are foot soldiers, even on submarines. Troopers continue on, even when they don't feel their best. They brave the unknown and learn how to stay calm. So I want to create a warrior walking process that people

EVERYONE NEEDS TO BREATHE

can do indoors or out, one that has continuity, choice and obstacles, and I dedicate it to Warren. He has a difficult time walking now, and I notice how he chooses to sit down when he is tired. That's smart! But he also challenges himself and tries to find balance between rest and activity. So much of life is a struggle to find balance, especially in times of crisis.

Warrior troopers walking

If you are not already standing, stand up from wherever you are. Wait, hesitate, be patient, some direction will appear to you.

Decide now
Do you want to walk indoors or out?
Go out if you can.
    if you can't, that's fine.
Look up from the ground
and bring your gaze to the horizon
Look out
    way out
    and see where you are going
    when you arrive at the next place
    stop
Breathe for a while
    and just concentrate on this
    as you notice where you feel the breath
    moving in your body
Wait for a while, hesitate ...
    everyone needs to breathe
Decide now ... and begin to walk again
    go far if you choose
    and if you need to use a walker
    that's fine.
    See along the way
        Stop
Sit if you want to
and bring attention
to your breath
Wait and see
as you look toward the horizon
sensing

how everyone needs to breathe
Stop frequently
    check in with your standing or sitting
    let your crown float upward like a balloon
    as in the Alexander Technique
    Feel your feet on the ground
    as in yoga
    while you find balance in your stance
    as a yogic warrior would
Make the stance wider to experience
a broad base of support in your root chakra
surging from the spinning earth
Remember you belong here
that you are not alone
neither large, nor small
doing nothing at all.
At ease
everyone needs to breathe

FIGURE 6.1: Warren Fraleigh in 1944, a veteran of the Second World War and 95 years old in 2020.

If the breathing becomes difficult
don't panic
Adapt. Find a way.
If breathing becomes impossible
Let the way find you
Should time and space loosen their hold
Breathe as you do
Rest.

Readers are invited to move from 'Warrior Endurance' to 'Embryo Floating Meditation' through this link to *Land to Water Yoga* with Sondra Fraleigh: https://youtu.be/esqMBVTN5Xs.

Death wish
When I die
    I want
to negate, reject the sense of loss
the down, down taxes of the deceased
which fasten damp death Velcro to trees.
So please, dear friends
       exile
ballooning black bunting, flags at half mast
muffled cadenced drums
speeches of what was fondly desired
and by all means, curses hurled into the cosmos.
Don't wail, gnash teeth, rent garments
        rather
raise a fluted toast to the richness of grace
for the sight of
    humming birds,
    pink-gold sunsets,
    red roses,
    a loved one.
for the sound of
    children's
    laughter,
    cable car bells,
    a cat's purr.
for the smell of

jasmine,
newly mown grass,
a lover's,
fresh skin.
For the taste of
pea pods,
crisp-tart apples,
Pinot Noir,
roast lamb.
for the touch of
a love kiss,
a cashmere neck scarf,
a rain-clear
cool breeze.
for the feel of
a pured iron,
a gliding waltz,
a springing step,
a rhythmic Lindy.
for the blessings of
dear friends,
shared memories,
family meals,

FIGURE 6.2: Photograph of Sondra in 'Cow Face' from Hatha Yoga. Photograph by Kelly Ferris, 2002.

vibrant debate,
the end of war,
great art, good sport,
the fullness of time,
a joyous spirit,
the quiet Presence.
When I die
    I want
to go gentle into that good night
and praise, praise, the yet glowing light.
(Warren Fraleigh)

In touch

For Today
Blossoms fall like snow—
Butterflies chase the dog's ear
Prayers rise up and up
    Every day, I walk in the park with my puppy
    she is eight years old, but I still call her puppy
    because she is small and looks like a honey bear
    She is in charge of our walks, so we meander
    smell every weed, breathe easily
    with tulips and iris in spring—wave to people or bark
    keep a safe distance, while weaving today's haiku

We who lavish affection on our pets boost our immunity. In turn, they bond with us somaesthetically, especially clear in times of stress or grief. If I sneeze, Annabella runs to my rescue. Last year when I fell atop the ice on a rare day of frost here in the desert, she fit her furry body around my head like a halo until help came. Now that I'm in touch with Warren, our daughter Christina and Annabella through sheltering in place, I realize how much we touch and are touched by each other in sound, word and deed. And I notice what kind of touch we encourage. Not rash, our kind of touch is the familiar kind, practical, protective, listening and laughing. My immediate family is small, but it extends to my siblings and their children, and also to students who have been with me for many years. Some have adopted me as a second mother, and I take my role seriously. So we keep in touch.

Families are in touch when they get together, and barring this, when they call each other on the phone. Well maybe? To be in touch is a qualitative matter. It means we

FIGURE 6.3: Annabella with Warren. Photograph by Sondra Fraleigh, 2020.

FIGURE 6.4: Annabella with Christina. Photograph by Sondra Fraleigh, 2020.

FIGURE 6.5: Annabella on her way to the park. Video link to 'Walk in the Park' with Annabella and Sondra, https://youtu.be/BlVtt63F8ho. Photograph by Sondra Fraleigh, 2020.

know what others are doing and care about them. To be in touch implies affection, understanding, friendliness, support and forgiveness. Touch can evoke the capacity to be quiet together, transporting empathy from an abstract ideal to a prescient reality.

Now that we are sheltering at home in this crisis, family is magnified in importance. I ask what somatic skills I might hone so that my physical presence and verbal interactions are conducive to insight, and my touch heals. The list below comes to me first, and as I look it over quickly, I wonder whether these are virtues rather than skills. …

smile
listen
forgive
forget
love
let go
wait
share
breathe

serve
enjoy

I see them first as virtues and even as events, but wonder if they might be practiced as skills of finely tuned communication. To be touched is 'to be moved', artfully and interactively in any exchange: in dancing, through writing, in therapy and in learning. To be moved is an event of relationship and spiritual empathy.

In touch without words

With those close to us and far away, we have the opportunity to practice empathy in communication. I can think of nothing more helpful in this attempt than the erasure of self through 'no mind' in Zen. To adopt an attitude of no mind is to release ego attachments and expectations, to quiet discursive thought and judgement. In quieting the habits of mind, one can practice the freedom to listen to others and respond without hesitation or fear. I envision this as a somatic practice that improves and expands over time and with use.

In any case, don't forget to breathe. The breath is a great help in practicing peaceful relationships; it is key to restoring family rifts and frayed friendships. It also helps us navigate chaotic unknowns of partnerships and marriage.

The poiesis below is based on quieting the mind and skilful composure in communications aided by the Zen concept of no mind. Attitudes of mindfulness might also apply, but not quite. Through no mind, we seek the somatic ability to move in any direction out of a balanced, empty centre.[1] Mindfulness is applied very loosely nowadays and implies a focus of awareness. What if we could focus emptiness, I wonder? Of course, human consciousness is never completely empty of emotion, cognition and memory, but we might bracket these, setting them aside for a time to become curious, especially in tense moments of a relationship, or as a palliative to the suffering of others.

Quiet mind reset
Artful listeners offer
artful explorations
not solutions.
Empathic listeners
hesitate
and breathe …
empty
of thought,
and full of heart.

The story
is the one
being told,
not
    your
        story.
    People want to be heard,
    not bettered.
    everyone wants to be heard.
    In no-mind
    and not-advising,
    connections ruminate.
    Interrogations
    and rude reminders
    suck.
    Practice not asking
        not telling
            not judging.
        Respond without stealing the story.
        remember, eyes speak volumes,
        and words can soothe.
        What you say
        is not as important
        as how you say it.
            Listen
            with your porous body,
            everyone needs to be heard.
        Forget your mind
        Open your mind
            soak-in feeling tones.
        Suspend assessments
            and corrections
                breathe. …

Global shadow

My butoh path is ecosomatic, as I will explain in view of Japan and expanding world gazes. For now, I introduce butoh as a somatic way to morph into otherness and darkness, or seemingly so. In butoh, dancers can become stone, sky and insects, and they can move as one with water or mud. Butoh is elemental and ecosomatic in that way.

A plethora of butoh visions can also be shared as theatre. I follow in this path as well, but more as a scholar and witness than as an artist (Fraleigh 2010). I am interested in how somatics intersects with butoh in its appreciation of ourselves as part of nature, where darkness is admitted and not feared. Butoh revalues darkness and has implications for how we see a full spectrum of colour in the human family. Human beings come in many colours, and all of the colours are beautiful. Butoh is multidimensional. Not reaching out and skyward only, it admits difficulty and anguish. Darkness is not evil in butoh; it is absorptive and humbling. 'Don't push away the messy refuse of life', the very resilient centenarian grandfather of butoh, Ohno Kazuo, advised. Thus in performance, one might smear the face with paint or mud.

What if I don't push away COVID-19? What if I dance into my shadow relationship to it? Morphing through the global pandemic of it? Then might I surprise myself, shocking my psyche-soma shadow? Would I encounter suffering? How could I emerge in tact? I would want to be resilient like my husband Warren and my butoh mentor Ohno Kazuo, seeking a fluid adaptable state. We are, after all, more water than anything, and this allows us the freedom of flow and evaporation. We don't have to be stuck.

Butoh shadow work

Butoh comes out of post-Second World War Japan, springing from its shadow, especially through embodiment of social crisis and pain. The larger ethos of butoh expresses the wide shadow of war in both Japan and the West. The Second World War was in its own way – a pandemic. As a butohist and also a Japanese veteran of the Second World War, Ohno Kazuo put this way: '[w]hen I dance, I carry all the dead with me', and he didn't mean just the Japanese dead, he meant *all the dead*.

This war engulfed the world and changed it. America dropped two atomic bombs on human beings: Hiroshima (6 August 1945) and Nagasaki (three days later). It also fire-bombed Tokyo, including much of the Japanese countryside, leaving total destruction in its wake. The bomb ended the war on 2 September 1945. I was born in 1939, the year Hitler invaded Poland. By the war's end, I was 6 years old, but even at that young age, I remember the vivid photographs and news reels of Hitler's tyrannical rants and rallies, and the atrocities of war.

When I was 24 years old, I went to Germany to study dance with Mary Wigman, the legendary source of modern dance. Germany is vivid for me in research and aesthetics, as well as personally. I eventually had the privilege of teaching several wonderful students from Germany, and have thought a lot about the war that put us on opposing sides and how we finally found ourselves in touch. Now I witness political hysteria in my own country, not nearly so distressing in terms of COVID-19 viral threats as it is in threats to free speech, loss of civil discourse and erosions of democratic goals, as we see increasingly around the world. COVID-19 will one day lose its grip, but how will we repair if we lose faith in truth and truth telling? What kind of dances must we do?

Before my studies in Germany, I experienced atomic and nuclear fallout from America's testing of bombs at Frenchman Flat in Nevada, about a hundred miles from my home in Utah. The tests, escalating from atomic to nuclear, began when I was a child and continued through my late teen years. By the time I went to college in Cedar City, Utah, closer to the testing, I had unexplained seizures. At first, I found ways of working through my pain with strange dances. Eventually I encountered the strange improvisational dances of butoh as a resource for healing myself and others.

Takenouchi Atsushi, an acolyte of Ohno Kazuo, says butoh is 'the ancient dance already happening in the body'. The basic elemental nature of butoh allows it a global circulation. It springs from circumstances in Japan after the war, but not as a direct response to the war. I believe the founders of butoh – Hijikata Tatsumi, Ohno Kazuo and his son Ohno Yoshito – were finding their post-war footing. Their work came out of root creativity and curiosity. Dance as art and healing can be a way of finding out more about who you are and how your life is being shaped by matters beyond your control. Like the advent of modern and postmodern dance in the West, butoh is inventive and imaginative. Its anti-nuclear ecological stance orients it as antiwar, but unlike most dance, butoh also draws on imagery of disease. Hijikata's full concert work, *Summer Storm* (1973), includes a tender section called *Leprosy*, and is a nativist prayer for peace.[2]

Shadow work in butoh, as also in Jungian depth psychology, requires giving up control and entering into the unknown. Jung developed 'active imagination', a process of working with imagery in dreams and the unconscious; while in butoh, the shadow process is metamorphosis: change itself. Curiously, you are not really yourself in butoh, you might find that yourself as singular dissolves and that you multiply to become bigger than you know. I don't want to scare anyone, just to offer something beyond the ordinary in my butoh poiesis and invitation to dance the unknown.

Morphic curiosity
Go out into the environment
take most of the day for this

SOMATICS IN DANCE, ECOLOGY, AND ETHICS

or a half-day would be good
Let yourself be drawn to a particular place
some place that has natural beauty
or rugged warmth
or challenge
like Rocks
Dead Lava Rock
Smooth Rock
Mud
Fallen Leaves
Or perhaps a Construction Site
Water if you can find it
yes.
Be alone
smear your face with paint
or mud if you choose to
wrap yourself in some found element
Pile leaves over your body
or Sand
or any loose matter
Water works well
    Let soft, gooey,
    or heavy matter cover you
    be the matter you are
    as you matter more
    Hide for a while
    not being available
    to anyone
    Be still for as long as you wish
    remove the matter
    sit or stand up
    Wait …
Everyone needs to breathe
free of obstacles
free of self
Unbidden, your shadow will come to you, perhaps later in dream.
Pay attention. Dreams have something to teach you, a gift to give.

Your golden shadow
    Someone you admire

FIGURE 6.6: Nathalie Guillaume, an Eastwest Somatics graduate, with Joan Englander at the Eastwest Retreat in Santa Barbara in 2012. Nati encourages breath in the heart space, remembering that the heart is the central organ of the body and is multidimensional, out-breathing and inward at once. Video link to 'Seahorse', https://youtu.be/xuFf-EUQQuc, a somatic process with Sondra Fraleigh. Music and video by Sondra. Photograph by Sondra Fraleigh, 2012.

    inelegant before affectionate
    like you in the mirror
        Rugged and daring
    shattered and standing
    close in the mirror
        Undisclosed and bare
    dull and tangibly lucid
    ordinary mirror

Enter your dark and golden self. Try. We learn from shadows, and we can also fall in love. To embrace shadows in discomfort and beauty is to fall in love with the world with all its warts and viruses. In his 1929 autobiography, *The Story of My Experiments with Truth* ([1929] 1940, 1983), Mahatma Gandhi said one should

FIGURE 6.7: SIMBI, Nathalie Guillaume. Photograph courtesy of Nathalie Guillaume, 2020.

avoid exclusive friendships. It is good to have friends if we realize that they can lead us astray, but we are not here to cultivate close personal friendships. We are here to make friends with the whole world. Everyone suffers. Some suffer more because they are poor or helpless or struggling for acceptance. Open your eyes to the injustice around you. Do the good you see in front of you.

Everyone matters.

Everyone needs to breathe.

Simbi

To encourage a healing vision for 2020 through the soothing darkness of water, butoh dancer Nathalie Guillaume created SIMBI, seen in Figure 6.7 and the video link below. (Guillaume also appears in Figure 6.6.) As a native of Haiti, she teaches that Simbi in Haitian Vodou is a diverse family of spirits, neither male nor female, living in the depths of the waters where creativity is infinite. Guillaume demystifies Vodou, exposing wide-spread misunderstandings of the spirituality of Haiti. Its African-based religious life still carries the heavy burden of colonialism through slavery in America, where indigenous beliefs were distorted and vilified in their conflicts with Christianity. In practice, Haitian Vodou teaches love and support within the family, generosity in giving to the community and to the poor, and respect for elders. Guillaume says that Haitian Vodou emphasizes wholeness of human life within the material world, and human symbiosis with the interconnected forces and beauty of nature.

Here are some flowers from Nati's garden, stretching from Haiti to her new home in New York and featuring another butoh dancer, Seattle-based Vanessa Skantze. In the following link, experience SIMBI with dance and music by Nathalie Guillaume: https://youtu.be/23tL7v5wSEY.

Dance back the world

Witnessing can be extraordinary as a somatic process of intimate notice and care. Many of us involved in somatic studies know witnessing as an Authentic Movement Process, and part of the structure of the whole, where one partner witnesses the dance of the other and then reflects the experience back, either verbally or in painting. I include *Dance Back* as a way of witnessing. This is a simple turnabout, as the witness dances to return the dance to the dancer.

What if we danced as witness to the time we are living through together now? Not with any particular plan or fears, but simply to be present to the moment? What if the world is already dancing, and we just don't see it? What if we danced the witness side of depth psychology as a worlding process? Then we could be witness to the motions of the whole world, whatever that might mean in the moment. Most of the world is responding to crisis now, but everyone has their own relationship to pandemic. It would be difficult to say what the whole world thinks or how it responds, but in dance, many things arise in the psyche-soma, larger than the rational mind can grasp.

I invite you to dance back the worlding of the world right now. What if you don't give it too much thought? Begin by assembling some painting materials, paper and crayons will do, or anything you have handy. Now, set these aside and start to move spontaneously without a plan.

> Dance the world back to the world
> > when you feel moved to move
> > > finish when you finish
>
> Have patience
> Wait
> Reflect

FIGURE 6.8: Ashley Meeder, 'Dancing Back the World'. Selfie photograph by Ashley in 2020.

Paint your feelings
   and the happenings
      of your dance
In silence
muster the courage
to rip your painting
into a few pieces
and reassemble the pieces
by chance into a collage

We change places in the act of witnessing, when witnessing means I see you; I am here with you; we belong here in the dance of time beings. Moving past language and judgement, we can be quiet together, as we see with Ashley Meeder in Figure 6.8.[3]

A new painting

This new painting reflects your dance back to the world, your painting of it and the unpredictable collage resulting from ripping and reassembling the painting. You are returning the world to itself, to its worlding motions and trusting ...

We are always returning the world to itself through our bodily-lived perceptions and interpretations. They disappear into the whole. Physics becomes metaphysics in the exchange, spanning the world interval. Dance is the physical and affective connection, relating to a larger ...

World Body Continuum
Moving with breath in vision dances
   the tangible darkness remembers falls
      and mends cuts our limited minds withhold
         forgiving everything

My body is made
    of moonlight when I dance
       My body is made whole

Hang my bones
from a silver tree
and let me dance –

Two Haiku by Sondra

NOTES

1. *Quiet Mind Reset* uses effective communication skills I studied through Selwa Said and her workshops in Monterey California in the late 1990s. Her work derives from the teaching of Carl Rogers. See Fraleigh (2012). My essay and *Quiet Mind Reset* also derives inspiration from the Feldenkrais Method of Functional Integration, which starts from a place of not-knowing and listening hands.
2. *Summer Storm* is described in *Butoh Metamorphic Dance and Global Alchemy* (Fraleigh 2010: 81–90).
3. Ashley Meeder is a graduate of Eastwest Somatics Institute and teaches our work at her own institute in a small city an hour outside of Mexico City. On 9 May 2020, the front page of the *New York Times* reports that the COVID-19 pandemic is overwhelming Mexico City in the amount of cases and unavailability of hospital beds. Ashley is taking care while remaining calm and resilient for her baby, due in July. Find her institute at: www.eastwestsomaticsmexico.com.

REFERENCES

Fraleigh, Warren (1984), *Right Actions in Sport: Ethics for Contestants*, Champaign: Human Kinetics.

Fraleigh, Sondra (2010), *Butoh: Metamorphic Dance and Global Alchemy*, Urbana: University of Illinois Press.

Fraleigh, Sondra (2012), 'The ways we communicate: Somatic dance and meditation as a bridge', *Somatics Magazine Journal of the Body-Mind Arts and Sciences*, XVI:4, pp. 14–17.

Gandhi, Mohandas Karamchand ([1929] 1940, 1983), *An Autobiography: The Story of My Experiments with Truth* (trans. M. Desai), New York: Dover Publications.

7

Talking to Tremors:
Somatics in Dance, Dialogics,
and Silence

As an author in the field of phenomenology, I have wondered how its insights might be applied to individualized hands-on somatics practices. The following is the result. It draws upon work I did a few years ago with Alice in which she learns to talk to her tremors, making friends with them and moving past fears. She gave me permission to write about this, and is identified anonymously. I explain our work together through notes I took at the time, which I also discussed with Alice. In application of phenomenology, I contextualize our somatic process using Mikhail Bakhtin's dialogics as a recurring conceptual ground bass. In light of Bakhtin's work, the present essay explores dialogic, extralinguistic states of silence and utterance as stepping-stones towards healing – also employing the neuroscience of Antonio Damasio and Eugene Gendlin's somatic focusing process – further delineating changes towards feeling better and becoming well. My background as a Feldenkrais and Shin Somatics practitioner aid this study, as also my studies and teaching of dance.

Structure

I see myself through three lenses in this essay: that of dancer–author, phenomenologist and *somatic movement guide* in dialogue with Alice. She in turn is the *primary mover*, author and interpreter of her own therapeutic process and eventually becomes her own teacher. Part 1 builds through Bakhtin's linguistic phenomenology and explains extralinguistic or dialogic aspects of movement through *silence* and *utterance*. Part 2 summarizes and reflects on my work with Alice in light of movement dialogics. The end of the essay includes three somatic movement lessons I developed for Alice that readers can do for themselves. In hopes of building a bridge

SOMATICS IN DANCE, ECOLOGY, AND ETHICS

between theory and practice, I insert thumbnail phenomenologies of *silence in movement and dance*, indented reminders of the central dialogical theme of the study.

> Silence – intelligible sound (a word) – and the pause constitute a special logosphere, a unified and continuous structure, an open (unfinalized) totality.
>
> (Bakhtin 1986: 134)

Part 1. Utterance

Movement is a non-linguistic utterance. It does not speak as words do, and like dance, it cannot be read in the same way that spoken and written language is. Relative to this, dance is special, playful and often urgent utterance, intrinsically before language and characterized by changes inseparable from expressions and emotions. Such affective extralinguistic elements of movement and dance contribute to unique genres of somatic communication. Somatic movement and dance practices are particularly rich in extralinguistic aesthetic and kinaesthetic aspects of utterance, the sphere that falls between linguistic and purely semantic analysis that Mikhail Bakhtin sees has entirely disappeared for science.

'The utterance as a whole', he says, 'is shaped as such by extralinguistic (dialogic) aspects, and it is also related to other utterances. These extralinguistic (dialogic) aspects also pervade the utterance from within'. From his standpoint, 'everything linguistic is only a means to an end' (Bakhtin 1986: 108–09). The primary dialogic aspect I explore in this study is movement as extralinguistic, preverbal *utterance* and, relative to this, the place *silence* plays in healing through somatic methods.

> *Silence is a quality of stillness in the middle of movement, in the middle of music or sounds of the environment, unfinished time in stillness.*

This analysis shows that stillness is bonded to phenomena of movement, silence and timelessness. And in human life, silence and stillness hold a well of emotions from joy to sorrow that can be activated towards healing through dance and movement.

A basic problem in somatics in dance is how to link extralinguistic utterances of movement to linguistic expression, how to bring movement and soma to language in other words, and more specific to somatics perspectives, how to become more receptive to therapeutic potentials of movement utterances themselves.

The ethical concern of somatics in therapeutic modes is how to build a communicative context that will support the mover while respecting a neutral or objective relationship. Bakhtin's work on utterance and expression respects linguistic context and a wide spectrum of possible genres of communication. As he puts it: 'we speak in diverse genres without suspecting they exist' (1986: 78, 98). The somatic genre I describe here has several layers of utterance all imbued with aesthetic/affective imprints and mindful of ethical distance in therapeutic settings.

Dialogics in somatic dance practices

We all move, and movement is fundamental, but as a phenomenon that ranges from silence to utterance through its reach into expression, dance is more than movement.

In my somatics work with individuals, movement as utterance develops first through the individual client, or *primary mover*. Then the somatic therapist/teacher, *the guide* in our case, responds to, receives and sometimes supports or matches the client's movement. The primary mover initiates the movement in form and expression and is eventually an author in reflections of insight and change. The underlying place of silence out of which both participants in the dialogic process move, speak and listen, waits upon the unknown. I underscore this aspect of silent waiting, which creates neutral spaces between the mover and the guide, and releases assumptions towards results.

In distilling utterances of movement, however these arise, the guide speaks in a mode of reflection, stating briefly the essence of what she gathers from the movement explorations and what the mover tells her about her immediate experience. The guide's task is to listen actively without exceeding the emergent meaning of the moved and spoken insights of the primary mover. The guide's general task is to make sense of the mover's process as a witness – to be herself in other words – reflecting back, whether in movement or words, as briefly as she can at crucial points to let the mover know how she is assimilating moved and spoken utterances. For me, the entire process is like a dance with rich choreographic challenges and improvisatory elements.

As a guide in such dialogues, I match in my body the movement images, emotions and feelings that arise in the mover while safely remaining outside of them, so that at some time, I can shift from guidance to support. If and when it seems right, our communication is aided through dance. Using dance, both as metaphor and practice, I improvise and sometimes I choreograph. I am conscious of structuring boundaries for our conversation, delimiting small 'chunks' of conversation or movement that keep us focused. Once set in motion as choreography, the unfolding of restorative potentials begins to guide me improvisationally. Some participants are more comfortable thinking of the process as movement, not dance. From the time we begin, I am guided by the moved and spoken utterances of the other. I start where she or he is.

My healing comes through giving myself to the process as a dance, using my hands-on skills choreographically and dancing intuitively, often minimally, as I have learned through many years of dance experiments. I seek a fullness of presence through paying attention to the emergent process as a whole and matching my own intentions of health and wellness as I work. I breathe smoothly, attending to my use of self and self-moving in form and feeling. Not forcing movement, I follow the lines of least resistance into stillness until the utterance of movement seems complete. I clear places for silence in my body's capaciousness, creating space for greater ease and joy, while attending to any affects that arrive. Moving consciously, like other dancers who think somatically, I become more alive to myself and thus to the other.

Silent insight, righting dances and falling down

Silence can be achieved in the midst of sound, just as stillness can be experienced inside motion. In dancing we encounter a phenomenology of silence – the relationship of stillness to movement, timespace and consciousness.

Encouraging utterance through a silent core, I often relate to individuals through sitting still or in gentle repetitive patterns: rocking back and forth, pushing and pulling, turning and returning movement in waves. Repetition lulls; it fosters forgetting in release of the will while assisting intuition. Stomping and clapping also provide avenues towards insight, probing the resonance of silent rebound and the intrinsic dancer in everyone.

A silent centre is obvious in stasis, but can also be perceived at the top and bottom of rebound and in the mid-line of repetition. Simple movements that return in some way, encourage positive bodily affects in those who give themselves permission to move towards heightened states of silence, either intuitively or through guided movement processes. Such intrinsic uses of dance for pleasure and healing are more fundamental than theatre art. The phenomenon of silence goes to the heart of dance as healing and somatic movement therapy, and the benefits of somatic modalities are available to all through simple guided movement processes, not just those who typically define themselves as dancers.

I understand healing as a process and not an end point. Healing is discernible change or movement of the body towards well-being, a kind of 'righting' dance the body does for us, one we can access, when we pay attention to the insights of silence in consciousness and allow the body to shift towards health, as I discover in this study.

Disturbances might also manifest in silent intervals, interrupting the body's balance, its sense of safety and preservation. Antonio Damasio's neuroscience speaks to the body's propensity towards balance and stability, commonly known as homeostasis. The body has a limited range of possible states, he writes, and for a good reason. It wants to preserve its organism against the assaults of the outside world, which changes dramatically and hourly (Damasio 1999: 142). The body at its most innocent self-sustaining level wants to move away from the imbalance of bad feelings and harmful happenings quite naturally. Of course, there are exceptions to this tendency in cases where people seek self-harm or deliberately sabotage their well-being, but these are exceptions not the rule.

We could even observe that the bodyself is intrinsically 'good' because of its propensity to make things right, and to make them even better when leaning towards joy. Healing is not a one-time occurrence. People commonly heal from illness and accident, and seek emotional healing in the very wish to get better. Damasio's neuroscience takes the natural righting dance of bodily minded states a step further, identifying the propensity of the human organism towards joyful emotions as the stepping-stones of 'virtue' ('The foundations of virtue'; Damasio 2003: 170–75). 'Joyful states', Damasio says, 'signify optimal physiological coordination and smooth running of the operations of life. They are not only conducive to survival, but also to survival with well-being. States of joy are also defined by a greater ease in the capacity to act' (2003: 137). Joyful states heal and are the basis of feeling good and becoming well, which I add to my definition of healing.

Of course there are cases where, as a matter of consciousness, people cannot give themselves permission to feel good. When something goes wrong, the body knows it, feels it and sets about immediately to make things right, unless intention is directed towards being ill, or for some reason impedes self-healing tendencies of the organism. The harbouring of guilt and negative feelings can interrupt the natural capacity of the body to set itself right – just as the righting reflex that wants to bring the body into an easy upright relationship with gravity can also be over-ridden when we lose balance. Giving attention to imbalance is helpful in somatic education and therapy, as in dancing off-balance, probing the edges of falling, actually falling.

When we fall intentionally in dance, we are over-ridding the righting reflex. We prepare for the plunge, and let it happen, moving past the point where we might recover an upright stance. There can be trepidation in the moment of falling, depending on the level of risk, but also thrill and surprise. The entire enterprise of falling – the movement that Heidegger says gives us 'proof of our existential mode of being in the world' ([1928] 1962: Section #176) – is rehearsed for choreographic result or improvisational play in dance. We fall deliberately; directing intentionality along the existential fault, our everyday bodies gloriously awake in release to gravity. Being is a venture in falling that Heidegger borrows from Rilke's poetry, a venture 'flinging beings loose' (1971: 163–86). To practice falling is to venture a bodily becoming, to give up control and to trust. The many ways of falling consciously undertaken in dancing serve a sense of adventure and renewal. There is a great silence at the heart of falling when the world seems to go away for a few precious seconds. After a fall, we get up, brush ourselves off, rebound and return anew.

Affective silence and somatics in movement

The dancer breathes in the silent air and stillness of her dance, whether performing on stage or in a somatically conceived movement design. This allows her to better attune her body to gravity, to find a friendly relationship to it – in her reaching and falling, turning and crawling. Her movement carries the potential of stillness at its core. Otherwise she would simply spill forward in timespace with no memory of backspace, no trace of the place and moment she just passed through. Stillness proffers the expansive sides, diagonal twists, and volume of her dance, grounding her danced sensations of center, balance and falling.

When we move attention deliberately towards sensations in silence, we have the possibility of feeling ever more clearly what lies within body consciousness, be that a place of confusion not yet defined; or a deep well of unexpressed grief.[1] The silent moments of movement bring us most clearly into an affective world, or felt senses of self in the psychosomatic contents of body consciousness. This is not necessarily the bright surface of conscious thought, but often touches the hidden or 'dark' consciousness acknowledged by Carl Jung and in Buddhist philosophy and Japanese phenomenology of the body.[2] Our intuitive connection to this shadow is an extralinguistic source for a potential shift in the dance of healing. It may never come to language, which does not mean it is not real and operative in the somatic life of the body.

It is most fascinating how the aesthetic, affective life of the body can move and change when it is given attention. A morphology of wellness begins in the silent, meditative spaces of dance and movement somatically conceived. The body, when we listen to it in silence, can speak its wordless messages directly in the unmediated play of consciousness.

The well of dance, as not already expressed, is already falling down, rising and attuning to joy and sorrow. Muttering in darkness or light, we hold these possibilities patiently in the morphology of waiting, and in common with the intrinsic dancer in everyone.

Quite often we can excavate these messages and reflect on them in words in the same way we might interpret the meaning of a dance. Meaning in dance is derived first from the body, the whole person in motion and stillness. It ensues from the entire context of the dance, the dancer, the setting and the witness, and is not restricted to a single interpretation. That is what makes dancing and witnessing dances so interesting. We interpret them from our own understanding, much like a Rorschach inkblot; thus, the truth is tested according to what the image evokes in affects, moving along an interactive chain of related dialogics in bodily shifts, as in my following work with Alice.

Part 2. Talking to tremors

Recently in my somatic dance and movement practice, I have been talking to tremors: to fear, confusion, feelings of worthlessness and the dark spots of depression. Such extralinguistic utterances can emerge in dialogical practices that facilitate the use of imagery in somatic situations. As I did with Alice, I often begin a somatic session by asking my client/student if she or he would like to sit in silence and pay attention to whatever image may come to consciousness – a sound or a picture, a colour or smell – a person, taste, feeling or perhaps a movement. In focusing the image, the client/student eventually describes something (anything) that comes to her. This is related to a transpersonal focusing process pioneered by somatic psychologist Eugene Gendlin that has inspired many movement-based somatic practices. For example, Amanda Williamson explores Gendlin's somatic therapeutic process as linguistic and phenomenology in a recent book chapter, 'Falling in love with language' (Williamson, 2018).

Waiting and sensing together

To explain somatic focusing more fully, I shift to examples from class settings where somatics and dance overlap, and the process emulates work with individuals. In my somatic classes and workshops, students work with each other in partners, as I teach them how to focus an image in sitting together, eventually carrying images into dance and hands-on somatic bodywork. In class sharing of somatic experiences, I have heard about beautiful images of birds trapped in the heart that find their way out, and also about hopeless darkness in the same place. Some images point to ethereal sounds coming from far away, rays of sunshine, stars and clouds moving in heavenly hues or sharp objects that can hurt lurking somewhere in the room.

In my experience, this way of working with imagery can to some extent be understood and shared across cultures, because images have kinaesthetic, dialogical elements that come directly from participants themselves, and their discernable feelings and characteristics are described, interpreted and shared by them. Caribbean students in my somatics workshops imaged tactile-kinaesthetic feelings of burning fire and thorns, animals caught in thickets, figures dancing, rainbows and more. In my Japan workshops, students spoke and danced about profuse visual and nature imagery, images of death and life transitions, some stated in floating tones, others visualized in smoke or with chimes in the distance. Akiko Kishida who teaches somatics workshops in Japan, showed me her students' paintings and danced images of tsunami destruction, and shared paintings of their group dances holding hands in community circles to help rebuild confidence in moving forward together. In London and UK workshops, I taught students from wide and varying backgrounds; their images also ranged widely, from snakes and beautiful swans to grating dreams, noises and nightmares. In India, students imaged doorways, burials, trees, underground rivers and much more.

At some time in imaging processes, I ask students or clients if they can locate the particular image somewhere in the body and if they can describe what it feels like – its somatic, kinaesthetic character, in other words. There are times in somatic focusing with individuals when nothing is stated, but nevertheless a felt sense of peace or crisis permeates the silence. As a guide, I do not expect anything, and I do not desire anything. Rather I wait in stillness and silence, empty of self. I welcome this relief from the burden of self, as I wait to serve the emerging image of the person in front of me, respecting his/her body history and ability to transform through movement, image, expression and dance. Sitting in silence, sets the stage. By now, the reader may have noticed that this kind of sitting has remarkable similarities to meditation. Silence is the ground that unlocks speech and life's deepest mysteries. Silence is to speech what stillness is to dance. Silence and stillness are both characterized by emptiness, space and waiting. In stillness, silence may be sensed as a timespace interval when the body is pausing or waiting for new movement to form, even as the new course carries the body's memory of the completed one, slipping into the past. The body becomes quiet, not needing anything in the silent dynamic and peaceful resolution of waiting. Any sound (or lack of sound) becomes inseparable from lived time and its spatial character.

From the beginning, my client/student and I become partners, trusting the somatic (felt) terrain to yield. Invariably, she or he expresses a feeling, shape, colour or sound, or perhaps a concern or fear. Sometimes a beautiful panorama unfolds, or my client (and dancing partner) begins to move. At this point, the guide in me emerges and I respect my partner as the primary mover. Some people want to dance, and some do not. If my partner wants to move, we both stay with it, moving together intuitively in any way that comes about between us, also speaking if words come. Or maybe we sit together in silence with just the breath moving between us. Some movers want to stomp, clap, or simply rock in place, but eventually we go back to silence and stillness. We trust that in a quiet interval the body will excavate its troubles and hopes. We wait without expectations and without stress; until the bodily held silence speaks to us or moves us. As a somatic guide and dancer, I ask the client questions to help focus the image kinaesthetically. 'Does this image have a location somewhere in your body?', 'Can you describe how it feels?'. In other words, I ask them to locate the image in or around the body and to acknowledge its felt characteristics, but people have different ways into these question, and they do not always locate or feel the image in the body. It might just remain 'in the air' or 'in the mind', so to speak. The quest to find the image somewhere is also of interest and becomes additional information to share. These are dialogic processes and somatic ones, with reciprocal utterances at their core. Alice's saw and felt a dark hole in her chest and shoulder. Later she shared with me her painting of the dark spot and how she transformed it through our dances together and in our somatic movement lessons.

Shaking, listening, balancing and standing

'I have trouble loving my father', Alice says, 'I shake. It is not that I think about him much now that he's dead', she observes, 'but his Germanic authority and rigid demands of perfection never leave me'. We continue to wait. 'If I listen to my shaking, I hear that I need to love my father now, but it seems almost impossible'. Alice says she wants to be able to trust her decisions, but lacks confidence. 'I shake so badly sometimes I'm ashamed', she says.

Alice became aware of her tremors at age nine when her mother asked the doctor what to do about them. She does not know when they really began to takeover her awareness and to make her feel so inadequate and guilty. She is in her 40s now and just beginning to talk to her tremor. She now knows how to bracket the tremor – set it aside and distance it from herself enough to acknowledge that the tremor is not who she is, not even a candidate for shame. Is the tremor something or someone other, then? 'Maybe it's a friend', she speculates.

Together we are talking to the tremor. She is calling it: 'tremor as teacher'. In the quiet intervals of not judging the tremor or herself, she lets it move and talk as she listens. Together we reflect on what she hears and the images that arrive, I as a guide, merely doubling the listening process. Then through touch, in matching the tones of the tremor with my hands as nearly as I can, I assist the movement of her breath in hands-on table work. Eventually, I hold the occiput at the base of her head until we both feel stillness and a relaxation of her central nervous system.

In standing, we balance one side of her body with the other, patterning movement symmetrically, or testing asymmetrical edges. With my feet, I plant her feet softly but firmly on the floor for support, as I wait for shifts of tone and tonus to occur in her body, all the time listening in places where the tremor shakes. We walk together in this vulnerable place with a feeling for breath and lightness; then wait for calm. And when it comes, the shifting landscapes of the soma repair us, both of us, in the silence. The spaces in-between others and ourselves are not dead spaces; they are charged electrically with energy, with embodied distance and magnetic closures that morph through time. Movement creates many tensional varieties and emotional valences of spacetime and silence. When we relax our attention in order to be congruent with a still point – or the chosen space of an extended stillness where we are neither moving nor thinking about moving – we have the possibility of listening to others and ourselves outside of time's momentum, to experience the infinite moment exposed in stillness.

Feeling crushed: Kinaesthetic utterance and phenomenology

Phenomenology is useful only when it produces insight and positive change. When we ask, 'what is this?'. We articulate the basic, simple question of the phenomenological method. 'This' *unknown* is the phenomenon (the thing) we seek to know, and we do not know how it will come to us. Thus, phenomenology in practice is further qualified by the express use of intuition and trust, not assuming anything and getting out of our own way to let the answer arise impromptu. I understand my work with Alice through the lens of phenomenology and more specifically dialogics – as a multifaceted genre of communication that can account for reciprocity of feeling, movement, and spoken dialogue in somatic movement therapy. Dialogics uses language, but at the same time, moves beyond it, acknowledging a variety of extralinguistic communications that operate together.

As an aspect of our work, Alice and I developed the dialogical element of kinaesthesia, dwelling in somatic sensations as such. We could also think of these as *somata* or somatic phenomena (a phenomenon is a thing, an appearance or a perception). Eventually, Alice described a range of sensations and emotions. The last session I had with her concerned her feeling that the right side of her body was 'crushing the left', and that the right side lacked feeling.

Of course, she was not paralyzed. She was functioning okay, even with the erratic coming and going of the tremor, but she was experiencing loss of feeling in places that felt 'dead'. Along with feeling crushed, the shoulder and heart space on the left felt tight and sometimes painful. Alice explained how she lacked security in her life, both financial and personal, that her self-confidence seemed manufactured daily. She was divorced with two children, now grown, and she had worked hard for many years to make ends meet. Since the beginning of our work over several months, she had been experiencing gradual progress and seemed most fascinated with what she called the 'magical' hands-on somatics we undertook together. At the same time, she often felt 'raw' through the changes that were occurring. She was practicing the movement explorations I gave her at home, and also creating a space for silent listening in being her own witness and keeping a journal as a means of self-listening and for self-dialogue.

When we talked about her progress as a whole, Alice spoke of how she was changing and of her fears. 'Last week I felt the two sides of my head coming together, almost like two halves of the same thing', she said one day:

> My life is being basically 'unearthed', and this is frightening, because I wonder if I will be able to sustain this progress without reverting back to my habitual self. The moments of physical and mental strength I've not had before are exciting to me, but at the same time, I continue to question. I want to base my life on security, even within my struggle for financial resources. I have the feeling that I can shift everything. I'm now beginning to see better how my personal relationships work and my part in them. When you feel a new aliveness in your body, everything changes in how you are programmed to live.
>
> (Alice)

Three lessons to do

After my initial focusing and hands-on work with Alice, I created a sequence of simple interrelated movement lessons for her. She could also repeat these at home. These lessons might be also taught in class settings, and at a pace that works for the class. They could all be taught in one session, for instance, or integrated with other somatic sessions. They are easy lessons to embody, but the kinaesthetic value develops more deeply with repetition and more time. These lessons are most useful as structures to explore, and they lend themselves to adaptation.

Lesson 1: Starfish, spinal rooting of the head and limbs

I thought it might be valuable to work on security very physically at a certain point with Alice, since she was excavating the issue of security in 'talking' to her tremor. I decided to help her find the root of her limbs in her spine. I considered the limbs to be her arms and legs, also the complex relationship of the neck and head, extending this to a starfish image, including the coccyx as a sixth limb – or small tail – capable of extending in the imagination.

I taught Alice how to balance her spine by lying down, vertebrae by vertebrae, along a very firm 3-inch-thick-styrofoam roller, leaving her head on the floor with the neck gently but noticeably extended. A rolled up towel also works, but the firmness of the roller aids greater change. Some people respond better to softness, however. So I experiment. Some people might need a small towel for support under the head if the head (in hyperextension of the neck) falls back too far. I helped Alice lift one leg after the other, slowly and just a little, while she maintained balance, eventually reaching one hand, then the other, across the body to connect with opposite knees while maintaining balance on the roller. The extension of her neck and head lifted her chest and let her feel how dramatically the arms are rooted in the spine through their connection with the clavicle and thus the sternum. One feels the muscular lifting of the arms in-between the scapulae and behind the heart from this position. In balancing precariously on the roller, the legs are challenged to find their connection to the low back through the iliopsoas and to the breath through the interdigitation of the psoas with the primary breathing diaphragm.

Lesson 2: Steady hands

After this first lesson, I let Alice rest lying down on her back on solid ground while I opened and closed her hand very gently like a flower bud, opening and closing. The large movements of the first lesson initiated a 'balancing act', while the comforting articulations of the hand reassured her body, and taught her neuromuscular system that with support, the tremor could subside. This opening and closing of the hand seems simple to the adult, but is by no means easy in the developmental spectrum of movement. It takes the baby a long time to be able to control the hand in finite ways, opening and closing at will, grasping things, maybe a rattle, and holding steadily.

Lesson 3: Magic breath, exhausting exhalation and flooding inhalation

I helped Alice internalize support for the 'steady hands' lesson (or choreography) by bringing her attention to the residual effects of the core work we did with the nervous system in balancing on the roller. In the third lesson, I placed a 6-inch-thick roller horizontally under her pelvis to lift it from the floor, allowing her to rest her body on the floor, sloping the torso diagonally down towards the head from the pelvic lift. (This can also be accomplished with two big towels rolled firmly together.) This required that the feet be planted for support. From here she played with sending her breath into the abdominal cavity. From this position gravity aids the exhalation (as the diaphragm moves towards the chest and head, now on a down slope), reversing the habitual dynamic of the diaphragm. The exhalation is easy to exhaust completely, so during inhalation, the breath floods in as a response.

We finish through matching stillness

As we finish, we walk together, she finding her natural horizon, and I matching her by finding my horizon in relation to hers. In walking together, matching can be a powerful impetus to double the breath in the security of movement. Of course this is a special kind of walking, fully aware, and full of stillness. I make sure to keep an ease and balance in my walk, so Alice might match these in her walk. We complete our session in standing meditation, giving ourselves a chance to assimilate the three lessons and feel secure as we attend to the ease of the breath moving smoothly on its own without interference of the will. When we meditate in motion, we find stillness there and cultivate a capacity for passing through difficulties with calm.

> *Tipping a subtle balance to pause and hold a shape, or gathering momentum for a leap, the dancer claims a quiet moving center that goes with her through the air. She can also sit in the middle of stillness, close her eyes and pay attention to the vast inner space of herself. Somatically, she might clear a place for insight (literally 'seeing inside') that she might experience her power to adjust in self-healing directions or understand something about her life that has heretofore escaped her attention. The mysterious as unknown can unexpectedly become known in uncluttered spaces of movement consciousness: This, for the intrinsic dancer in everyone.*

Reflections on ideal listening, and becoming your own teacher

As the guide, I am involved in several ways while holding presence for Alice's process. I do not get wrapped up in the tremor, I remain as objective as I can in facilitating the tremulous path of self-healing in another. I differentiate *empathy* as 'following and feeling with' from *sympathy* as 'feeling sorry for or in favor of'. My role is that of a catalyst. I do not interpret Alice's experience as a final authority. Rather, I listen to her interpretations, and I do not directly analyze or advise. I do not judge; rather

I listen to the process and guide it dialogically.[3] I cannot pretend to be neutral, however, as Bakhtin makes clear in his translinguistic phenomenology. Every genre of speech from literary to everyday language is a living dialogue vested with the individual imprint of the speaker, oriented towards the response of another and positing communication with an ideal listener, someone who can try to understand.

In the latter sense that Bakhtin develops, we model an image in the belief of understanding. The image moves past the immediate encounter, and it might weave back. Through the dialogical interplay of self and other in somatic movement therapy, I sense an amorphous third presence, not necessarily a person, but the inexhaustibility of the not-already-known that lies waiting in our imaged, spoken and danced communication. Some might choose to call this kind of waiting a spiritual sensibility. It occurs to me that I am not only guiding a lesson/session, but that I also invoke guidance. This is a subliminal wish, however, and I do not want to depend on it. It is sufficient that I clear a place for guidance while calling on my somatic skills and the dancer in me – waiting and listening for the as-yet-unknown to arrive. In one sense it is not mysterious, but rather a composite experience of sharing and trust. We speak to be understood, to hear and to learn.

Alice and I had a few more sessions together, but she was rapidly incorporating movement and stillness techniques along with self-dialogue through journaling to internalize her own support without me. She is not insisting that the tremor leave, she says. She just hopes it will get bored because she is not giving it undue attention, and will go away on its own. When the tremor comes around, she realizes that she can greet it with conversation, not fear. 'I have had such a need to get things right', Alice says. 'It's new to me not to have to work so hard. Now to hold on to this kind of ease!'

As Alice becomes her own teacher, she also activates the ideal listener in herself. She initiates movement and dialogue in the first place, listens in the second, and in the third place, she hears. Hearing is certainly a basic sensing, but it is also a choice to pay attention to the world of sensation dwelling in sound and silence. In the process of simple movement tasks, Alice and I ask what ease fells like, and what it sounds like. We become familiar with the not-already-known feelings and words waiting in stillness. As a guide, I call on my best self in waiting, and I notice that I am better able to assist others dialogically when I can move from a place of silence and non-expectation. In this place I know that I do not know, but I trust that a useful way forward will become known to me as I go forward. Or if I go backwards, I can attune to options opening up from there.

I gave Alice six more written movement lessons to take home. These are all related to walking and to rooting the limbs through the spine; thus, she can continue to practice the lessons we experienced together and add these new ones on her own. These six easy lessons can be found on the Eastwest Somatics website: www.eastwestsomatics.com.

NOTES

1. This is the thesis influencing the somatic psychology and practices of Eugene Gendlin in *Focusing* (1987).
2. The phenomenology of Yuasa Yasuo, based in Buddhist thought with precedents in Heidegger and Merleau-Ponty, posits a bright and dark consciousness. The dark consciousness does not correlate exactly to Jung's collective unconscious, but does approach his views on the intuitive core of consciousness (see Yuasa Yasuo 1987).
3. Not analyzing and not judging are communication strategies I learned in seminars with psychologist Selwa Said in Monterey California when I studied 'Effective communication and relationship building' with her in 2001.

REFERENCES

Bakhtin, Mikhail M. (1986), *Speech Genres & Other Late Essays* (eds C. Emerson and M. Holquistk and trans. V. W. McGee), Austin: University of Texas Press.

Damasio, Antonio (1999), *The Feeling of What Happens: Body, Emotion and the Making of Consciousness*, London: Heinemann.

Damasio, Antonio (2003), *Looking for Spinoza: Joy, Sorrow, and the Feeling Brain*, Orlando: Harcourt, Inc.

Gendlin, Eugene (1987), *Focusing*, Toronto: Bantam Books.

Heidegger, Martin ([1928] 1962), *Being and Time* (trans. J. Macquarrie and E. Robinson), New York: Harper and Row.

Heidegger, Martin (1971), *'The origin of the work of art'*, Martin Heidegger, *Poetry, Language, Thought* (trans. Albert Hofstadter), New York: Harper and Row, pp. 15–86.

Williamson, Amanda (2018), 'Falling in love with language', in S. Fraleigh (ed.), *Back to the Dance Itself: Phenomenologies of the Body in Performance*, Urbana: University of Illinois Press, pp. 78–98.

Yuasa Yasuo (1987), *The Body: Toward an Eastern Mind-Body Theory* (ed. T. P. Kasulis and trans. N. Shigenouri and T. P. Kasulis), Albany: State University of New York Press.

8

Back to the Dance Itself:
In Three Acts

BACK TO THE things themselves I cry, or else philosophy will die. My cry is an onto-logical one, asking, as constitutive phenomenology does, 'what is this thing called "dance" made of'? How do we live consciousness in dance? Let me count the ways. In its aim to rescue consciousness and experience as key concerns of philosophy, phenom-enology is no stranger to conceptual analysis, but not as a science. At the same time, definitional work is key in the performance of phenomenology, with the experiential study of things (anything) being basic. How does meaning arise in dance, for instance, and why is intentionality important? What is the difference between movement and action? What are the materials of dance? Or shall we assume that dance is wholly immaterial? These are fundamental questions of philosophical enquiry in phenomenol-ogy that interest me deeply in this essay, even as I have engaged phenomenology for 49 years and am still learning. Phenomenology is not a philosophy of closure, and in this spirit, is being developed on several fronts in dance, as recent Intellect journals show, *Dance Movement and Spiritualities*, 2:2, and *Dance and Somatic Practices*, 8:2. I hope to contribute further in this endeavour. When I first encountered non-dual discourses of 'the lived body' and 'pre-objective world', I realized what a goldmine this represented for bodily oriented studies. I barely scratch the surface here, or in the wider scope of *Dance and the Lived Body* (1987) and *Dancing Identity: Metaphysics in Motion* (2004). Since Edmund Husserl's initiation of phenomenology, questions regarding normative understandings of body, self, materiality and subjectivity continue. Consciousness is shaped, or we could say 'intended', in countless ways. This has consequences for understanding somatic movement arts as a field of study, as we take up.

Prologue

This essay is conceived as a conceptual play, portraying several key players in phenomenology and applying their work to dance. The motivation for using play as a metaphor is wider than concerns for dance productions; it includes somatic processes, and sees the possibility of artful values in all dance. Tracing a line back to Husserl's founding of phenomenology in 1900, we focus on the concepts of intentionality, which Husserl considered to be the primary topic of phenomenology. From these considerations, we explore how intentional actions of dance can renew bodily responsiveness, assisting participants to realize greater potential and surpass perceptual habits, aligning with the hope of somatic methods.

The doing of phenomenology is a performance that involves insights of the author. This is the difficult theoretical work, which may include intuitive descriptions, but does not depend on these. As a philosophical investigation of experience and study of phenomena (things in themselves), a phenomenology of dance will always be ongoing. We can write about phenomenology through explaining it, or we can do phenomenology, mining its concepts and descriptive/definitional methods in application to specific questions. This essay involves both approaches, but emphasizes the latter through the lens of intentionality. It takes an *intentional* stance towards dance rather than an *instrumental* one, holding that the body is not an instrument to be trained as a tool for choreography because it is alive with subjectivity, and cannot exist as an object or unmapped channel. We are studying how 'wanting' and 'choice' move us, and considering the layers of consciousness involved in going back to the dance itself – back and back, towards experiential foundations. Dancers get to practice intentionality in extraordinary ways. How lucky are we?

Characters (Players) in order of appearance

Maurice Merleau-Ponty (1909–61), French philosopher, strongly influenced by Husserl, the arts and psychoanalysis; textured Husserl's model of intentionality with imagistic concepts of 'flesh' and 'reversibility'; important background of ecophenomenology.

Edmund Husserl (1859–1958), German philosopher who established phenomenology as a school of thought; remains a key figure in contemporary developments of phenomenology; root of ecophenomenology.

Paul Ricoeur (1913–2005), French philosopher with a square in Paris named in his honour; noted for advancing understandings of hermeneutic phenomenology and showing how translation occurs not just between languages but also within them.

Jane Bennett (1957–present), American professor of political science, vibrant materialist and widely quoted political ecologist.

Francisco Varela (1946–2001), Chilean biologist, philosopher and neuroscientist who developed influential theories of embodiment and enactment in neurophenomenology.

Moshe Feldenkrais (1904–84), Israeli physicist and international teacher of somatics; studied how thought, feeling and perception relate through movement; invented a widely known method of movement and touch for the improvement of human functioning.

Author as conceptual dramaturge (1939–present), American dancer with an international focus, professor, phenomenologist, somatics teacher-practitioner and ecological advocate.

Act 1. Symbiosis

Scene 1: Made of movement, shone in light

This morning, I sat by my favourite pond as light dawned in diagonal ripples on the tall green reeds and common cattails lining the marsh at water's edge. I had never seen this particular phenomenon before, the grazing and flickering light illuminating water and plant life amidst shadows of spreading trees on the opposite bank, the ducks and swans floating quietly by. The pond enveloped me in peace, that most elusive of qualities, and it became meaningful to me in that sense. Sometimes I think about death when I meditate by the tranquil pond, not dwelling on it, but imagining it as a performance. Can I move towards death with equanimity? Might my daily dances assist this? If so: when I die, I still want to be surprised. Pond is cosmos.

Watching the pond, I remember the purpose of phenomenology as it first captured my imagination – to light the hidden truths of experience. I think how performers trust Aletheia (*personified truth in ancient Greek*) and sometimes inspire their audiences with psychosomatic, surprising and even unwelcome truthfulness. But truth in dance can also arrive in unassuming developmental contexts. The simple act of moving spontaneously in open-ended improvisations encourages the flow of *Aletheia*, and so does dance in the service of community – in programmes for children at risk, for cancer recovery, in elder care – to name a few examples. With a shift in attention, some specialized study, and a focus on playful and developmental processes, dance can be shared widely beyond stage productions. The body, whether still or dancing, is our common bridge to consciousness and states of change.

In its processes and performances, dance can reveal what lies hidden in the psyche of the body, its somatic truth in affective terms. In coming forth from vibrant yielding matters, the affective mien of dance takes on playful, beautiful and sometimes terrifying forms. I have seen many people dance through flowing tears of relief – moving in torques, away from trauma, letting go of worry and shame. Relief is activated in dancing, often enhanced and shown in performance. Dance seeks *experienced truths*, which are not defensible in objective terms. It draws together what might be split as objective matter and subjective truth in a single flow of matter and mind. Such nondual flow of consciousness is a potential in dance experiences of many kinds. But attentional splits can also appear. Husserl defines consciousness widely as 'awareness of one's own psychic experiences [...] a comprehensive designation for 'mental acts' or 'intentional experiences' of all sorts' (Husserl [1900] 1970: 81).

Scene 2: Advancing basics of intentionality and reciprocal play

Merleau-Ponty finds symbiotic flow in 'the thing' that presents itself to sight and touch. Light guides his description of sight, while qualities of density and surface texture his description of touch:

> In so far as my hand knows hardness and softness, and my gaze knows the moon's light, it is as a certain way of linking up with the phenomenon and communicating with it. Hardness and softness, roughness and smoothness, moonlight and sunlight, present themselves in our recollection, not pre-eminently as sensory contents, but as certain kinds of symbiosis.

Envisioning motor intention at the heart of what he calls 'inter-sensory' experience, Merleau-Ponty continues,

> The object which presents itself to the gaze or the touch arouses a certain motor intention which aims not at the movements of one's own body, but at the thing itself from which they are, as it were, suspended.
>
> ([1945] 2002: 369–70)

He leaves us 'suspended' between our own body and alterity, 'the thing' of our seeing and touching. His skilful description brings sight and touch into a symbiotic space between self-sensing and other-sensing with movement as the link. His is the linguistic of perception and intention, which does not get trapped in normative terms of body and mind. *The language of perception and intentionality is non-dual.* It brackets body and mind (sets these aside) and reorients. 'When I fall, I let go'. It is not that my body falls and my mind or psyche lets go. Everything falls, and my consciousness changes in an instant. This speaks to what is happening in time, movement and affect, and not to the body or mind as instrumentally causal. Uses of language reflect intent. For instance, 'mindful body', 'embodied mind', 'intentional body', 'expressive body', 'dancing body', 'lived body' and 'kinaesthetic consciousness' are non-dual constructs, singular and symbiotic descriptions that foreground phenomenology.

In developing a symbiotic philosophy of the lived body, Merleau-Ponty builds upon the earlier work of Edmund Husserl, who conceived kinaesthetic consciousness in terms intentionality and lived body phenomena of perception in *Ideas 2* ([1952] 1989). In this work, first pencilled in 1912, Husserl also delineated intentionality more broadly as oriented through 'attention' and 'the comportment of acts' ([1952] 1989: 60–93, 291), a fundamental insight that propels the momentum of this essay. Intention and action coalesce as *singular* in experience. Unless I stop to work it out, I do not think to act, and then act. For the most part, I orient my attention in action, attending to 'what' I'm doing – as in falling, dancing or cutting an onion with a sharp knife.

Husserl explains that motility and kinaesthesia (movement perception) relate to his construct, 'I can' – as crucial components of the ability to move spontaneously and responsively ([1952] 1989: 273–77). 'I can', as basic capacity, is enriched experientially through bodily cultivation and in learning new skills. Movement abilities can also be compromised by illness or injury, and are subject to variables in individual responses.

Existing in the 'I can', kinaesthesia is apparent through the gift of embodiment, given in being born. Yet, embodied motility develops through the use and ongoing access to the world from the time of embryonic life. *We learn through doing.* At every moment, we embody our lives interactively and psychophysically – whether reaching, resting or dancing. Motility is connective, taking us from here to there, and relating the senses – as when kinaesthetic systems of balance work together with seeing, hearing and walking in coordination that we take for granted. There is ground swell for this. Motility and all of the abilities of bodily life are founded in perception. Perception is 'always already there as the foundation of everything else' (Husserl [1925] 2005: 14).

Motility grows through exercise of agency, and the spectrum of movements available through kinaesthetic awareness also grows. But the operations of kinaesthetic awareness are not always straightforwardly apparent. Existential phenomenology textures understandings of voluntary and involuntary aspects of movement, particularly through the early work of Paul Ricoeur ([1950] 2007). We learn through this work and the Feldenkrais Method of movement awareness that we do not move in isolated instances. Even when we isolate small gentle movements, these resonate through kinaesthetic consciousness, or movement awareness as a whole, evoking affectivity and body memories.

What guides such evocations? For that answer, we look more closely at our central topic of *intentionality*, which Husserl studied as the fundamental property of consciousness and the primary theme of phenomenology (McIntyre and

Smith 1989). His first major publication in 1900 studies intention as a property of mental activity. His later works expand towards *intentional experiences* of all kinds, accounting for motility, kinaesthetic consciousness and lived body consciousness as inseparable from the larger world of nature and culture ([1952] 1989, 1995; [1925] 2005).

His integrative view of intentional experiences applies to phenomenologies of dance through articulations of non-dual awareness, which we have touched upon, and through related concepts of *creative intent* and *reciprocal play*. Husserl sees creativity as a link between individual intentionality and the larger productivity of culture, further delineating reciprocity and receptivity as central to creativity. *Receptivity* is an overlooked constituent of *productivity* (Husserl 1995: 51). This idea expands still further through Merleau-Ponty's notion of 'the flesh' in *The Visible and the Invisible* (1968). 'Flesh' in this work is an image for reciprocity of the sensate and the sensible, particularly their potentials of 'reversibility' and 'folding'.

Intentionality is reversible when *activity* folds inwards and moves back towards *receptivity*. As we move our senses out towards the world, and a sense of the world returns to us, there is folding *reciprocal play* in consciousness – an action and return within. This is *the same play* that sustains creative consciousness. Merleau-Ponty described this play as a 'chiasm' or 'intertwining' of the visible and the invisible (1968: Chapter 4). In terms of self-evidence, I understand that I am affected by what I set in play. In bodily changes and becomings, I become the durational time and affective trace of my dance. In the paint between my toes, my dance speaks back to me (Figure 8.1).

Scene 3: On extraordinary intentions, actions and agency in dance

Because they are creative reciprocal actions, performed for themselves and chosen in the doing, the extraordinary acts of dancing give us a way into the workings of human intentionality in its interactive agentic aspects. Indeed, there is no way to escape intentionality in oriented movement of any kind. We decide to dance, even when the dance seems to happen of its own accord. Intentionally committed and set apart from utilitarian actions, dance is not just any random movement. It is extraordinary movement, even in unspectacular instances. It does not accomplish anything of functional use outside of what it is, and its countless appearances go nowhere but in the dancing; it shares this in common with play. 'Uselessness' can be useful in extending a play of consciousness.

Here we come up against 'movement and action' without providing clear distinctions. If we understand dance as *consciously oriented action*, then we can see a distinction – in understanding that *movement powers action*, and *affectivity*

FIGURE 8.1: Squishy Toes in Reciprocal Play. 'Selfie', 2017. Copyright Ashley Meeder. Courtesy: Eastwest Somatics Mexico, principal teacher, Ashley Meeder.

is an indivisible qualitative (aesthetic) part of movement powers. Acting is intentional doing that constitutes an event, not necessarily a performative one, but an event nevertheless, one we can *name* – like visiting a friend, throwing a ball, performing a part in a play, dancing onstage or in the environment.

An act can also be singular and simple – like moving from 'here to there' or performatively lowering an arm in a smooth undulating rhythm. *Action has an object and purpose; movement is change and process.* Action assumes agency. As the author of an event, I act (as in lowering my arm). Movement is the power that enables my actions: affectively (in smooth undulation), temporally (slowly) and spatially (descending). Human movement holds varying degrees of intention and agency and is not always volitional. Action is a 'doing' on purpose. Actions often accomplish a plan or fulfil an idea. Dance is action (event) and also movement (change and process). Dancing as acting and moving weaves a continuum; we can make separations only through definition and by abstraction.

In his studies of 'acting and moving', Ricoeur holds that actions culminate in some kind of realization ([1950] 2007: 201–30). If we look behind this linear analysis, we notice that movement and action hold reciprocal possibilities. Movement by definition is ongoing and basic; it underlies *actualization* (relative to acts and the actual). *Movement needs a body; acts need a situation, orientation, project or performance.* In dance, bodies, actions, movements and performances fold one into the other at crucial points of realization. They become actively embodied in other words. As we saw earlier, Merleau-Ponty, in *The Visible and the Invisible*, describes this relational and crucial point as a 'chiasm' or perceptual 'intertwining' of subjective experience and material existence in the lived body.

Scene 4: Texturing intentionality with people dancing

What happens when people dance? Maybe it isn't just one thing – but many kinds – cerebral, physical, radiant and illusive. As affective action, dance is more than movement; and yet, movement powers it. I love to witness people dancing, especially in events that are conceived in light of possibilities. Dancing connects people in a play of consciousness that illuminates the world we live in, or possible worlds we can only discover and imagine.

Dance relates people to an external world at the same time it occurs internally in the body. The extraordinary, inventive activities of dance ignite mental and affective life, while intentionality orients the ongoing flow and stutter – mobilizing the sentient content in the responsive process. *To grasp intentionality is to comprehend the play of consciousness and meaning in action.*

Intentionality, as we study it in phenomenology and somatic perspectives, concerns *the whole course of intentional activity*. 'To act intentionally' is to orient a movement, plan or purpose. The ability to do this can represent the difference between health and insanity. Dancers get to practise creative intentionality in all its variables. Intentions are embedded in repetitions of practice and embodied in *how* dancers orient themselves in relation others and the world. The particular manner or disposition of intention reflects individual personality and agency, creating much of what engages us in dance processes and performances. This would certainly include all kinds of dance, each according to its purpose: as theatre, entertainment, art, therapy and sociopolitical or somatic expression.

But what about accidental – may be unintentional – dance made through 'chance' processes, as Merce Cunningham taught, for instance? When I studied with Cunningham, I found his teaching of chance procedures was not about moving without intention. One had to be highly observant and memorize myriad patterns that would later coalesce in a dance discovery. To choose chance is a choice to work with elements already present in receptive and sometimes chaotic phases of consciousness but still in a general mode of attentiveness. To choose to dance is to exercise agency, whether the process involves chance procedures, improvisation, structured play or highly structured choreography. But agency as wholly individual may be a fiction, as we explore next.

Scene 5: 'Thing-power' and agency of assemblages

In her political ecology of things, Jane Bennett shows that *agency*, the power of choice in action, depends on the interactive power of humans and other material bodies and forces (2009: 21). Her question is whether humans will begin to work from a place of equality and cooperation for the good of the whole. Bennett relates her current work to phenomenology in considering how agency arises *symbiotically*, not simply in the self, but through the embodied self as an assemblage of vibrant materialites of the world (2009: 115). Merleau-Ponty's ecological view is similar: 'Our own body is in the world as the heart is in the organism: it keeps the visible spectacle constantly alive, it breathes life into it and sustains it inwardly, and with it forms a system' ([1945] 2002: 235).

Neurobiologist Antonio Damasio reminds us that the self is always developing on several levels of consciousness; 'it is a dynamic process' (2012: 175). It exists for Bennett as an assemblage of myriad material 'things' – metal, flesh, water, mineral, parasites and much more. Morphically, the bodyself is in process like nature itself. Bennett acknowledges that she follows in the tradition of Spinoza, who was one of the first philosophers to see unity in nature and culture, divinity and humanity, rocks and flesh, physicality and affect. She also draws upon Deleuze and Guattari and their more recent philosophy of morphic continuities, where human potential becomes part of the dance of material nature (Bennett 2009: 117). Bennett discovers life in the creativity of nature, one that links humans and non-humans in a continuum that is increasingly important to recognize:

> All forces and flows (materialities) are or can become lively, affective, and signaling. And so an affective, speaking human body is not radically different from the affective, signaling nonhumans with which it coexists, hosts, enjoys, serves, consumes, produces, and competes.
>
> (2009: 117)

Japanese butoh – a crazy post-Second World War assemblage dance – does not side with one life form over another. Butoh is crazy in the best somatic sense, pursuing the originary *phusis* (the arising) of all life and including dancers of varied abilities in performance. Now a global phenomenon, butoh breaks with visual distance, becoming solid earth and bugs, letting go of the past and morphing through material object life, from organic biotic matter to imagined body parts – hidden arms (more than two) waiting to emerge, for instance. Does it matter whether the arms appear or not? It depends on the dance and the performance. What matters is the morphic attempt to materialize anew. Butoh dancers move a consistency of human life with other kinds of life. In their dances, 'everything' is alive in the dance, puffing and decaying in human continuity with other 'things'. As in Zen, nothing is pushed away, neither pain nor suffering. Disease, disintegration and repair might propel a dance as well as opulence. Nor does butoh require a traditional theatre space. It can take place in prison camps to remember the dead, in the rubble and ruin of earthquakes or in pleasures of beautiful landscapes. In tending darkness, rejected materials also motivate butoh.

How do you dance unwanted material? In butoh, I try. I dance my 'unwanted body', my inept flesh and uncertainty. Could I possibly be something else? Can I be rotting bark on a tree? Shall I cast myself away? Recycle? I explore related themes in 'Butoh translations and the suffering of nature' (Fraleigh 2016). As in Zen, material form in butoh comes from and returns to emptiness. Butoh presents the riddle of the material body through the threshold of movement and action, coming and going in constant translations.

Act 2. Somatic habitus

Scene 1: Sediments slink and play

I live my habits. As my characteristic style of moving and dancing, these become somatic habitus. Habitual acts *sediment* in the body. Do they settle like rocks? Not quite. For the most part they escape notice because they become part of habit or maybe a rehearsed skill that we eventually take for granted. We can also think of sediments in terms of cellular consciousness alive in the workings of the nervous system, whether smooth or static in affect. Dance sediments or settles in the body as it becomes embodied. Danced movement has the advantage of being consciously embodied, sometimes recalled and performed, or it might be spontaneous and playful. What we have not said is that movement creates 'maps' in the brain body and full body responsivity through motor patterning in its intentional, affective character.

As past, intentions have already been embodied or mapped in somatic responsivity through practice or habit. Are we, then, stuck in our past? How do we recognize and move past habit? How do we renew? In dance, we learn new skills through movement and practice, and we have novel experiences in community. We seek to move freely in the ways we want to. In the meantime, we encounter all manner of questions concerning concentration and confidence. What do we let go of in order to develop? What do we keep? Can we 'voice' our dance in a group?

How do we move past self in a self-involved art? It is the province of movement somatics and dance studies to ask such questions, and to be concerned with how practised activities become affective in our lives. Intentionality is formative.

Husserl speaks to this:

> All personal 'intentionality' refers to activity and has its origin in activities. For it is either an intentionality which has arisen originally and is then active, or it is a 'sedimentation' of activities, which as such are meaningful and in their 'sense' refer back to the active or constitutive nexuses, and that by means of many levels built one on the other.
>
> ([1952] 1989: 344)

When we dance, we orient our movement consciously, even if we sometimes surrender to liminal consciousness and forgetfulness. This can be a choice. The internal time consciousness of intentionality in dance is curious. We do not think about what we will do in a performance beforehand and deliberately intend each part as a separate act. The intentionality of a dance we know how to do has already sedimented in movement memory.

We perform the parts as we know them, or in the case of improvisation, let the whole flow into the present. But somewhere in the past-made-present we have intended a path, tried it out and perhaps succeeded. The brain and nervous system register the kinaesthetic and sense-responsive matters involved in success and failure and lay down associated neural tracks. Sometimes we speak of second nature in terms of movement that has sedimented and become natural, as we noted with Ricoeur. We do not have to think about it. Good performers learn how to use movement and dance practices as ingrained intentionality in the involuntary nervous system. They also court past failures and future renewal through intentional awareness. Ohno Kazuo-sensei, my butoh mentor, read his dance poetry aloud before a performance in order to bring it to mind imagistically, and through poiesis, renew his relationship to life and art in the making.

Phenomenology through Merleau-Ponty (and those who followed) has held that movement, expression, cognition and body are part of each other, and cannot be separated (1964: 66–67). Like Husserl before him, Merleau-Ponty reiterated the collaborative nature of consciousness: 'our gaze prompted by the experience of our own body, will discover in all other "objects" the miracle of expression' ([1945] 2002: 230). Embodied movement does not contain consciousness; it is consciousness in action. Movement is not merely something we do; more, it extends towards expressive activities of relating and remembering – as such, *movement makes meaning*. Sedimented unconscious habits and practised skills play a role in this hermeneutic. Somatic (psychophysical) habits and skills sediment through practice, and subsequently can be made conscious through mindful movement and somatic dance practices, where excavation of body memories is a major purpose.

Dance somatics in its concerns for sense in action explores how activities and ways of performing become persuasive in life and considers each person as an individual. Husserl identified 'sensuous dispositions' with 'individual *habitus*' ([1952] 1989: 308). He speaks to 'the *total style and habitus of the subject* [...] all his modes of behavior, all his activities and passivities, and to which the entire psychic basis constantly contributes' (1989: 290, original emphasis). Teaching dance somatically involves respect for individual habitus and movement styles, but not in a vacuum. We exist in a world of others, and our individual styles have a collective history.

Scene 2: On histories in bones and dance materials

Our bones have a history, not unrelated to the history of other species. How our ancestors behaved shaped the neural structures of our present brains: 'Biology and culture are interactive', as Antonio Damasio shows (2012: 312). Attempts to enhance the neural networks of our brains through dance experiences matter. Consciousness and awareness expand through use. In this, dance matters. All of the arts matter. *Mattering* is a way of becoming *material*, of validating *the maternal* – flowing linguistically from *materia* and *mater, the mother*. Mattering carries affective histories of caring and empathy, of neglect and recovery – to name a few existentials that contribute.

Consciousness is the originary part of the *material* of dance, particularly as consciousness involves affectivity (feeling) and imagery (form). Empathy, as a felt resonance with the world, motivates much of my dance. I am aware of being somatically changed in encounters with the natural world.

The materials of my dances come from many sources, however, being influenced by music, ideas, narratives, material nature, and movement potentials. *Foot Falls and Free Falls* (1985) is made of odd stamping rhythms, inflected with rapturous falling and rebounding. *Split Second* (1988) expresses speed in partnering. *The Circus of Dr. Lao* (1967) is influenced by a book of the same title, and includes a 'snake goddess' handing (adapting to) a large live snake (chilly but not poisonous). *Meditations* (1990) explores 'the poetics of everything' – emergence, difficulty, chaos, arrival and dwelling. I like making dances interactively, including ideas and movements of the dancers, and I do not hold auditions but encourage dancers who commit to show up. I value process over mastery. The reach for excellence under this circumstance brings special challenges and rewarding performances. For dancers, moving beyond perceived limitations is possible on variable skill levels,

FIGURE 8.2: Sondra dancing in Snow Canyon, 2015. Copyright Robert Bingham.

as they become unselfconsciously absorbed in making dances together. I think of this as a somatic process.

Extending a somatic process approach, I made *Blue Muffins* (2015–ongoing), a dance for one or more people, using four singular movement patterns and Eugene Gendlin's focusing process, all of which can be assembled on the spot and improvised in various settings by dancers with varied abilities. Three veteran dancers performed a version in the sandstone cliffs near where we live (Figure 8.3). Here is a video link to a version for four, adding Robert Bingham and my original music, 'Pulsing Slumber' (Fraleigh on YouTube 2015a). I joined them for an imagistic, gestural version, shown here in a video link: 'Blue Muffins in Snow Canyon', performed with my 'Sky Glacier' music (Fraleigh on YouTube 2015b).

These are a few examples from 59 years of making and performing dances, in which are embedded myriad intentions. These dances are not lost in time. They still exist in the 'material me', in those who danced with me, and those who witnessed our good intentions.

Intentionality grounds and gives flight to meaning, as we find in the work of Chilean philosopher and neuroscientist Francisco Varela. Along with Evan

FIGURE 8.3: Three Blue Muffins in Snow Canyon, 2017. Dancers: Megan Brunsvold, Sara Gallo, and Denise Purvis. Photograph © Tom Gallo.

Thompson and Eleanor Rosch, he produced a study of embodiment of mind (Varela et al. 1991), explaining that human beings create their own domains of knowledge and meaning. He sees that that the nervous system generates meaningful patterns, and that cognition is a form of thinking arising through embodied movement. Like the perspectives of Husserl that we considered earlier, Varela's studies show that what we commonly call 'the world' is not an external fact represented internally by the brain, but arises in relational modes of consciousness (Varela et al. 1996).

Scene 3: Emergent states and past debris

Phenomenology studies consciousness and meaning as incomplete and emergent. Likewise, somatics innovator Moshe Feldenkrais considered the body a work in progress where human experiences of different kinds – sensations, feelings, motor experiences and memories – are imprinted. The malleable body bears imprints of its history and meaningfulness. We took this up through sedimentation. Habits live in the debris of past actions and practices, weaving through players' predispositions, but they manifest in flesh, not in stone.

We learn more about change and the body from Ricoeur's hermeneutic study of the relationship between freedom and nature in movement ([1950] 2007). He shows how movement and knowledge are bound together in voluntary effort, as the mental and physical bring about 'an undecipherable unity, beyond effort' (Ricoeur [1950] 2007: 249). Movement that once required effort ceases to be an effort; then bodily spontaneity and freedom can emerge. In learning a new skill, for instance, there comes a time when I no longer need to exert myself beyond the necessary effort of the movement. Ricoeur argues that the voluntary and involuntary dimensions of human existence are complementary. I like to think of 'matching' my dance, becoming one with my world and myself. Then the dance has become second nature. The dance is natural to me now; there is nothing to remember. I can be absorbed in the flow of my movement. My dance is somatic knowledge, attained through bodily adaptations and attunements that can be revisited consciously and with ease.

Habits, on the other hand, avoid attention. Habits are dim, as embedded in automatic behaviours. But they are not beyond the reach of intentionality. I can become aware of my habits and transform them, especially as I pay attention. It may be that I identify a debilitating habit, or simply that I dance into the moment

FIGURE 8.4: Matching Hands, 2017. Photograph © Ashley Meeder and Eastwest Somatics Messico.

with trust. Dancing playfully, improvisationally, is one way of transforming habits – by entering processes that present new movement potentials and ideas. I can dissolve stubborn habits in watery movements, or burn them away in fierce dancing, and I can work consciously with individual habits (mine and others) through hands-on somatic bodywork.

In somatic practices, we may even attempt to work with and transform negative effects of past actions etched in the nervous system. Earlier, we considered 'flesh and folding' from Merleau-Ponty. This is his image for 'reversibility' of intentionality, also an important concept for Moshe Feldenkrais, who taught that integrated movement should be able to 'reverse'. For me, reversing a short movement pattern is much like retrograde in music composition, but there is more to going backwards. Feldenkrais states this eventuality in terms of identity and time consciousness:

> Do not try to forget the past; it is impossible to forget the past without forgetting oneself at the same time. You may imagine that you have forgotten one or another unwanted detail, but it is stamped in some part of your body.
>
> (1985: xxxv)

His outlook applies to reversibility in somatic repatterning. Liz, I will call her, provides an example. Recently, I worked with Liz, using my experience as a dancer and Feldenkrais practitioner along with my somatic development of hands-on contact repatterning. She had a history of surgeries: a back surgery, which resulted in fusions of the low back, a hip replacement and a knee replacement. She sought me out for help with her foot and was considering having surgery on her big toe. We discovered that she couldn't bend her toe because she avoided using it. Using the toe caused pain in walking, and thus she rolled her weight through the little toe instead, stressing the outside border of her foot, which created an odd and dysfunctional gait that was throwing her whole body off-balance.

We worked for several weeks to reorient her gait. The process involved listening, matching and 'talking' gently to pain while teaching the big toe that it could bend. Working with her to include whole body consciousness, I discovered that her body would 'quake' when she lay down on her back. I thought it was a protective reaction to her back surgery, and taught her how to release her low back to gravity and float her head through a gentle breathing pattern that I call 'seahorse float'. (This dance-inflected bodywork method of Eastwest Somatics is shown here in a music video demonstration [Fraleigh on YouTube 2013].)

Over time, more of Liz's history came forward, as she disclosed how she felt her body was 'wrong' in so many ways that she sought surgery to correct it. Together we constructed a new vision and body imaging process: one of seeing herself as whole, well and beautiful. She had not studied dance; nevertheless we sometimes danced together in an easy rhythmic way that most anyone could do. The movements were easily reversible, balanced and fun, moving mostly in 'seesaw' back-and-forth patterns. She continues to improve and likes thinking of herself as 'free'.

I cite this case as an example of body history and simple means towards transforming attitudes that show how the physical and psychological are entwined. Liz 'reversed' her intentionality from one of constant self-correction to one of self-affirmation. I was able to involve her in enjoyable activities, including movement and dance explorations related to self-image and body image that she could return to and explore at home.

Instances of intentionality and body image in contexts of dance are not so different from my short case study above. Dancers can constantly self-correct in being told or thinking that they are 'wrong'. So how do they progress in difficult technical work without constantly correcting themselves? This is a matter of consciousness in direction of intention. It all starts in the learning environment. Teachers set the stage by keeping the learning full of *curiosity* rather than *fear*. I have witnessed a lot of fear-based dance training. Instead, the whole intentional orientation of skill acquisition can proceed from the understanding that people learn at different rates. Approximations towards the desired movement can work better than insistence on immediate perfection. Over time, dancers can improve at their own rate and without fear of censure. Capacity can build along the way and with pleasure in the process.

Act 3. Attention

Scene 1: Beginning with a question

How can movement have meaning? *Meaning*, as we know, has *several meanings*. Meaning is that which is expressed. Meaning is import, pointing out, sense, signification, substance and worth. All of these meanings of meaning apply to dance and somatic studies. Phenomenology shows how meanings arise from experience, including tactile-kinaesthetic (felt) experiences of movement. In this perspective, possible meanings of dance are lived and created in aesthetic/somatic (affective) terms. The sense of 'sense' is lived in dance. Still further, the lived ground of meaning can be formalized in language. Merleau-Ponty speaks of this. 'The spoken word is a genuine gesture, and it contains its meaning in the same way as the gesture contains it. This is what makes communication possible'. He explains that meaning is based in common understandings. 'In order that I may understand the words of another person, it is clear that his vocabulary and syntax must be "already known" to me' (Merleau-Ponty [1945] 2002: 213).

When I perform a dance and understand something in the process, my dance has meaning for me, and perhaps it communicates to others through the bodily life we 'already know'. I do not suggest direct kinaesthetic correspondence or always-harmonious communication, but rather embodied intra-human responsiveness involving all the senses. Creative intentionality is vast in variety; dancers establish diverse communications with audiences and places.

Senses sharpen in dancing, and thoughts leap as movement distils and becomes more potent. Walking becomes more apparent for itself, as the foot in rolling from heel to toe is suddenly more alive and sensible. Meaning can arrive through sense and making sense. It is fascinating to make sense of dancing, because it involves all the bodily senses, particularly kinaesthesia – for many, the forgotten sense of what it feels like to move and feel vital. And let us not forget meaning as worth. What does it matter whether I dance or not? It matters because my sense of being alive expands when I dance, and I remember myself as related to a broader world. Some narrative of my life often arises, possibly a story or memory, or a suggestion of someone I love. Dance represents my vitality, even when I am devolving and going very slowly as I become 'a stone' or morph towards 'rust' in butoh. Then my imagination can roam freely. Dancing with others pushes meaning further: when I dance with or for others, possible meanings double.

Pause the play

Phenomenology is itself a practice in observation and meaning-making. It teaches one how to pay attention to movement and its innate meaningfulness. Dance processes are telling in this respect; they provide the potential for meaning-making by directing intentionality in particular ways – in discovery modes of improvisation, for instance, or in refinement of choreographic practice, for another. Somatic dance strategies pay attention to affective states of our everyday bodies of movement in non-judgemental processes, and they often include community participants along with veteran dancers of various styles. But this does not mean that the extraordinary aspects of dance will be lost in somatic processes. These will arrive as meaningful to participants, and sometimes be emotionally challenging.

Professional dancers and performers learn how to think in dance as they train their attention to the tasks and pleasures of dancing. Those who undertake somatic dance processes for the purpose of personal development think in dance also, but less technically in terms of tradition, with exploration and transformative potential guiding movement intentions. Key for phenomenology in somatic explorations is *how attention is oriented (intentionally directed) in the course of the movement*.

Scene 2: Moving beyond impoverished individuality

When I dance, I lose myself – yield and seize space; I feel more alive. Time expands. My flesh quivers and falls like water. I seldom dance alone, but when I do, I am not lonely. I like dancing with others in evocative environments where we pay attention to each other and a sense of place. We make meaning in the interactions of dancing, and we express these, not as separate properties of the dance, but arising from decisions of dancers in the mix. In dance, we practise our *possible-selves-in-a-world* (a term from, Arturo Fallico, my first teacher in existential phenomenology in 1968). Through paying attention to interactive potentials, we take part in the material assemblage of dance and place.

The study of dance as experience not only illuminates consciousness, *as a practice of paying attention, it lights a path towards expanding awareness of self relative to the world and others*. Ricoeur, like Husserl before him, holds that we belong simultaneously and inescapably to both self and otherness. As an act of expression, dancing brings this to attention in an extraordinary way. In Ricoeur's late work, *Oneself as Another*, he explains that we extend relationality through acts of expression: 'the lived body extends from the subject of utterance to the very act of utterance' (1992: 55).

(Players leave for a moment.)

Scene 3: Light floods the empty stage

In Heidegger's philosophy, a phenomenon is an appearance by definition, 'that which is bright', any visible entity that which is made to 'stand in the light' ([1927] 1962: 51). Yet, we can also sense things in the dark and through touch. The 'things' or appearances of phenomenology are not simply visual or tactile things, but extend to all of the senses and bodily capacities. Light and dark both inform us.

Phenomenologists seek to shed light on phenomena by paying attention to the meaningful things of intentional awareness, whether dances, fears or dreams. In aspects of forethought, intention has an internal time meaning that binds us to the future, but the overarching matter of intentionality is bigger. *Intentionality*, as we have seen, is the broader category of phenomenological study. We have already embodied millions of intentions throughout life, carried in human motility and will, and eventually in cellular memory. In dance, we practise and embody intentionality as attention and orientation – location, momentum, position, arrangement, energy, responsivity and more. For instance, 'facing' in dance performance carries intentionality. 'Where does the movement face', we sometimes ask? Do performers face each other? Do they wear masks? Bind themselves with ropes? Face a crumbling building? These are choices of intentional orientation.

When dancers think in dance and move in meanings, the phenomena of consciousness come into play in an extraordinary way. Movement signals intentionality, particularly as it tends towards conscious actions and events. We discern its purposes, whether unpredictable, serene, lackadaisical or agitated, etc. Such intentionality signals meaning, what movement is about or maybe what a dance or danced event is about. Meaning is intrinsic to dance, appearing in the experience of the dancer and also what the dance brings to mind for others. Meaning multiplies in alterity. It is not essentially immanent or external; it is both-and. And as we grasp aesthetic intentionality in broad strokes, meaning can also take an historical mien. Looking back to the choreography of women in the last century, modern dance in Europe and America evolved a period commensurate with modern art, revealing hotter qualities (Martha Graham), expressive courage (Mary Wigman) and lyrical, orchestral intent (Doris Humphrey).

We have said that context matters in dance practices. Performative and somatic contexts are both action frameworks for the play of intentionality. I often advocate *intuitive contexts* for dance because of their participatory and experiential potentials. We can direct consciousness intentionally by paying attention to intuitive choices in dance processes. Somatic modalities and methods, as they enter into dance studies, *generate practices of self-reflective attunement and attention to others*. They are generally not oriented towards theatre performance. But all forms of dance pay attention to movement, and technical settings for learning can also be mediated with care for self and others.

We cannot perform dance movement, whether choreographed or improvised, without paying attention to what we are doing. A performance is 'a way of doing' that focuses attention on specific actions. Paying attention, more still, practising attention, is a key phenomenon of dance processes, creative, performative and therapeutic. Dancers pay attention on multiple levels – to choreographic structure or improvisatory unfolding, to self-moving, to sonorities of place, to tactile cues, to other dancers and the environment. These are entwined phenomena of moving consciously in dance. Our intentions shine through – arising fully in the whole course of the dance – when we are completely absorbed in the dance.

Attention aids perception, which is alive with motility and receptive phases in dance processes. In an ideal universe, *the practice of attention* would shape easily, not encountering distraction or stress. These are somatic matters. Dancers and teachers of dance contextualize dance experiences through orientation of attention. Writ large, these become attentional narratives for interactions. We can orient dances in life-enhancing ways, or destructively. We have choices.

We can promote rule-bound linear dynamics, open-ended discovery modes, chaotic systems, ordered ones or ones in which order arrives amidst chaos. In the play of undistracted consciousness, dancers find the order available to them at the time. They find meaning in their stride.

Scene 4: Mythos returns from the beginning scene

We are living and dying in every moment, embodying our unfinished natures in the process. Each new day offers naked potential, and every dream its strangeness. I have a chance re-embody consciously if I yield to it. The act of dancing, in particular, brings auspicious possibilities. And it also augurs risks. In the play of dance, I develop my capacities for risking embodiment. In dancing with others, I have still more opportunities to risk periods of heightened performance, both of difficulty and interpersonal synchrony. I risk possible failure, but also muster cohesions in togetherness with others. As a perpetual beginner, I learn through failure.

Phenomenology affirms that we are not alone; rather, we are embedded in the world with others and the flowing present that escapes our attention. Husserl called the unquestioned bias that the world pre-exists and is sepa-rate from you and me *the natural attitude* (Husserl [1900] 1970, 1995: 166). What seems natural may be an inherited belief, a perceptual habit, or in dance, the doxa of an ingrained movement habit. It is the task of phenomenology to question habits, especially those that propel ego as an isolated consciousness. Husserl sees how ego, even that of self-awareness, shifts into obscurity in 'every act-performance':

> For it pertains irrevocably to the essence of consciousness that every act have its horizon of obscurity, that every act-performance, in the shift of the Ego onto new lines of cogitation (action) sink down into obscurity. As soon as the focus of the Ego is withdrawn from it, it changes and is received into the vague horizon.
>
> ([1952] 1989: 114)

We are unfinished in moments of self-becoming (ego formation) and relational becoming (ego loss) as belonging to the world's body. It matters especially that we grasp relational becoming, that we understand our entwinement with all life, and that we bring our actions out of vagueness to become aware of them. It effects how we treat each other and the earth as material and ecological home. This belief powers the politics of my dancing. We dance to bring our acts out of obscurity, to generate the person we can become, to regenerate each day and to face death with equanimity and trust. Dance is oriented in letting go, letting go of the self and the contracted ego, even letting go of pain in admitting it. The body folds towards disappearance in letting go, transforming into the material event of the dance.

When we dance, we muster *Eros*, the erotic vitality that produces life while dying into that same fountain. *Thanatos*, the ancient Greek God of non-violent death, has a gentle touch like that of his twin brother *Hypnos* (sleep). These are the tender gods who bring the gift of forgetfulness. *Aletheia*, the Goddess of Truth who set the scene for our play at the beginning, balances this in remembering.

REFERENCES

Bennett, Jane (2009), *Vibrant Matter: A Political Ecology of Things*, Durham: Duke University Press.

Bruzina, Ronald (1995), 'Translators introduction', in E. Fink and E. Husserl (eds), *Sixth Cartesian Meditation* (trans. R. Bruzina), Bloomington: Indiana University Press, pp. vii–xcii.

Damasio, Antonio (2012), *Self Comes to Mind: Constructing the Conscious Brain*, New York: Vintage Books, Random House Inc.

Feldenkrais, Moshe (1985), *The Potent Self: A Study of Spontaneity and Compulsion*, Berkeley: Frog Books.

Fraleigh, Sondra (1987), *Dance and the Lived Body: A Descriptive Aesthetics*, Pittsburgh: University of Pittsburgh Press.

Fraleigh, Sondra (2004), *Dancing Identity: Metaphysics in Motion*, Pittsburgh: University of Pittsburgh Press.

Fraleigh, Sondra (2013), 'Seahorse Float in Shin Somatics Bodywork', music video, YouTube, https://youtu.be/isXvWyAlg8E. Accessed 27 March 2017.

Fraleigh, Sondra (2015a), 'Pulsing Slumber', music/dance video (videographer T. Gallo), YouTube, https://youtu.be/qaI5BjGpHDQ. Accessed 27 March 2017.

Fraleigh, Sondra (2015b), 'Blue Muffins in Snow Canyon', music/dance video (music 'Sky Glacier', S. Fraleigh and videographer T. Gallo), YouTube, https://youtu.be/PREImPoEhqE. Accessed 22 March 2017.

Fraleigh, Sondra (2016), 'Butoh translations and the suffering of nature', *Performance Research*, 21:4, pp. 61–71.

Heidegger, Martin ([1927] 1962), *Being and Time* (trans. J. Macquarrie and E. Robinson), New York: Harper & Row.

Husserl, Edmund ([1900] 1970), *Logical Investigations* (trans. J. N. Findlay), vol. 2, London: Routledge & Kegan Paul Ltd.

Husserl, Edmund ([1952] 1989), *Ideas Pertaining to a Pure Phenomenology and to a Phenomenological Philosophy* (trans. R. Rojcewicz and A. Schuwer), Book 2, Boston: Kluwer Academic Publishers.

Husserl, Edmund (1995), 'Appendices', in E. Fink and E. Husserl (eds), *Sixth Cartesian Meditation: The Idea of a Transcendental Theory of Method* (trans. R. Bruzina), Bloomington: Indiana University Press, pp. 163–98.

Husserl, Edmund ([1925] 2005), *Phantasy, Image Consciousness, and Memory (1898–1925)* (trans. J. B. Brough), Dordrecht: Springer.

McIntyre, Ronald and Smith, David Woodruff (1989), 'Theory of intentionality', in J. N. Mohanty and W. R. McKenna (eds), *Husserl's Phenomenology: A Textbook*, Washington DC: Center for Advanced Research in Phenomenology and University Press of America, pp. 147–79.

Merleau-Ponty, Maurice ([1945] 2002), *Phenomenology of Perception* (trans. C. Smith), London: Routledge Classics.

Merleau-Ponty, Maurice (1964), *Signs* (trans. R. C. McLeary), Chicago: Northwestern University Press.

Merleau-Ponty, Maurice (1968), *The Visible and the Invisible* (trans. A. Lingis), Chicago: Northwestern University Press.

Ricoeur, Paul ([1950] 2007), *Freedom and Nature: The Voluntary and the Involuntary* (trans. E. V. Kohak), Chicago: Northwestern University Press.

Ricoeur, Paul (1992), *Oneself as Another* (trans. K. Blamey), Chicago: The University of Chicago Press.

Varela, Francisco, Thompson, Evan and Rosch, Eleanor (1991), *The Embodied Mind: Cognitive Science and Human Experience*, Cambridge: MIT Press.

Varela, Francisco, Thompson, Evan and Rosch, Eleanor (1996), 'Neurophenomenology: A methodological remedy for the hard problems', *Journal of Consciousness Studies*, 3:4, pp. 330–49.

Whatley, Sarah (2016), 'Editorial', in S. Whatley (ed.), *Journal of Dance & Somatic Practices*, 8:2, pp. 113–14.

Williamson, Amanda (2015), 'Special issue: Dance, spirituality and phenomenology', in A. Williamson (ed.), *Journal of Dance, Movement and Spiritualities*, 2:2, pp. 92–217.

Williamson, Amanda (2016), 'Reflections on phenomenology, spirituality, dance and movement-based somatics', in S. Whatley (ed.), *Journal of Dance & Somatic Practices*, 8:2, pp. 275–301.

9

Phenomenologies in
The Flowing Live Present

PHENOMENOLOGY IS A popular qualitative method of enquiry, but not all phenomenology is the same. There are basic differences, and, at the same time, common threads that define an approach as phenomenological. Outgrowths of phenomenology are rooted in Edmund Husserl's philosophy, now differentiated and widely applied in the arts, social science, psychology, somatic fields of enquiry and religious studies. Husserl's foundational ideas return throughout this essay. In Part 2, I engage connections between phenomenology, spirituality and dance. My hope is that practitioners and scholars of dance who are drawn to phenomenology will find themselves somewhere in this study.

Part 1

Phenomenologies

Phenomenology is a popular qualitative method of enquiry, but not all phenomenology is the same. There are basic differences, and at the same time, common threads that define an approach as phenomenological. Outgrowths of phenomenology are rooted in Edmund Husserl's philosophy, now differentiated and widely applied in the arts, social science, psychology, somatic fields of enquiry and religious studies. Husserl's foundational ideas return throughout this essay. In Part 2, I engage connections between phenomenology, spirituality and dance. My hope is that practitioners and scholars of dance who are drawn to phenomenology will find themselves somewhere in this study.

Here, I identify at least six major forms of phenomenology: philosophical, transcendental, existential, hermeneutic, heuristic and ecological. As basic, *philosophical phenomenology* suspends presuppositions by design, draws upon

165

FIGURE 9.1: The Flowing Live Present, a somatic improvisation directed by Sondra Fraleigh at Southern Utah University in Cedar City, Utah. Dancers: Megan Brunsvold (top) and Denise Purvis (bottom). Photograph © Sondra Fraleigh, 2015.

the history of philosophy and seeks to understand consciousness of phenomena – or the contents and operations of conscious awareness. It also refutes dualistic language, showing that perception relates to intention, that without feelings there is no consciousness and that the brain is not an engineer but part of the entire symphony of conscious embodiment. Neurobiologists, like Antonio Damasio, who write for audiences outside the quantitative confines of science, advance the philosophical themes of phenomenology, as he did in *Descartes Error* (1994) and more recently in *Self Comes to Mind* (2012).

Phenomenology with autobiographical aspects is often identified as *heuristic*, encouraging discovery by following the author's subjective threads and possible ties to others in the study. Like all phenomenology, it aims to awaken a sense of wonder about the phenomenon of interest and employs experiential description. Towards the end of this essay, I write concretely in the discovery mode of heuristics, which I explain in more detail, and because I teach with insights from phenomenology, I touch upon this also.

Transcendental phenomenology is defined in Edmund Husserl's life work, and provides the root of phenomenological enquiry. It accepts 'the self-knowing I' of the 'normal mode' of awareness, and seeks to go beyond this through 'stepping out of the darkness', awakening the luminosity of 'transcendental subjectivity'. In this endeavour, Husserl seeks to go beyond accepted norms through a bracketing or reduction of the normal mode or 'natural attitude'. Bracketing is the act of suspending judgment, also called epoché and phenomenological reduction. Husserl's goals are defined in abstract and lofty terms: 'In the phenomenological reduction there occurs the awakening of the transcendental constitution of the world' (Fink and Husserl 1995: 13–14). This awakening is a key term for this essay.

Mention of 'transcendence' might direct the reader's attention to divine essence, but Husserl doesn't mean this. Rather, he directs attention beyond habit like a somatic healer, 'inhibiting' (his word) norms by bracketing ever further towards a renewal of the human person (he also uses 'soul' for 'person') in recognition of the 'flowing change of the world' (Husserl 1995: 182–86). In shedding limiting habits, we reach Husserl's vision of a flowing 'transcendentally constituted world'. I read Husserl's work as a spiritual odyssey in dedicated philosophical thinking. His ideas influenced generations of phenomenology. Yet, because he was Jewish, the notorious race laws in Germany of 1933 stripped him of his academic standing and privileges.

Existential phenomenology is a branch of philosophy grounded in Husserl's ontological insights on the nature of being, but takes them in a less abstract and often poetic direction. This includes existentialism's literary iterations in novels and plays by such authors as Jean-Paul Sartre, Simone de Beauvoir and Albert Camus. On Husserl's terms, *transcendent consciousness* moves between *transcendence* and *immanence* (Fink and Husserl 1995: 158). What seems outside and objectively independent also has an elusive inside, as demonstrated in psychology. Because initial observations are naïve and full of assumptions, moving towards a pre-reflective intuitive grasp of phenomena (the 'things' of consciousness) requires letting go of bias and prescribed theory. With this in sight, existential phenomenology develops descriptive accounts of lived experience.

For this reason, I use it to speak to the dancer's experience in *Dance and the Lived Body: A Descriptive Aesthetics* (1987). In this, I appeal to my own experience, but not autobiographically. I seek to say something fundamental about dance experiences. Most aesthetic treatises are not written from the first person point of view. Study of phenomenology and a life in dance allow practitioner scholars both an inside and outside glance. In my case, I look inside towards the expansive experience of dance relative to *self and other*. From outside, I look towards *the dance itself*, defining its objective status (its ontology or identifying features) through bracketing normal taken-for-granted definitions. This leads towards a descriptive aesthetics in delineating aesthetic models that sustain classical and modern/postmodern dance forms. Along the way, I describe many contemporary and classical works, including examples from Graham, Balanchine, Tharp, Cunningham, Streb and many more.

Thus, I draw upon historical elements in both philosophy and dance, but with a focus on existential approaches. My lens and scope of enquiry is dance as theatre art. Had I taken into account more dance phenomena, my view would have been wider, including descriptions of folk and social dance, as well as dance conceived in somatic contexts. Moving forward, I continue to explain the aesthetic as the affective, and to define dance as aesthetically constituted movement of our own doing, making and perceiving. *Dance is human movement created and expressed for an aesthetic purpose* (1987: 49). Aesthetic purpose is also foundational in somatic dance, which emphasizes affectivity, and in social and folk dances, enhancing social and community values.

FIGURE 9.2: The Flowing Live Present, a somatic improvisation directed by Sondra Fraleigh at Southern Utah University in Cedar City, Utah. Dancers: Devise Purvis (top), Megan Brunsvold (middle), Robert Bingham (bottom). Photograph by Sondra Fraleigh, 2015.

Existentialism as a philosophy develops the concept of 'the lived body' with a debt to Husserl's view of 'the life world'. It further grounds phenomenology in theory concerned with perception through Maurice Merleau-Ponty's *The Phenomenology of Perception* (1962), and it develops ontology of art through Martin Heidegger (1971). His post-metaphysical phenomenology, a deconstruction of traditional metaphysics, came to fruition in *Contributions to Philosophy* (1999). Several strands from Merleau Ponty and a critique of Heidegger assist my work in *Dancing Identity: Metaphysics in Motion* (2004), which involves heuristic fieldwork in dance, this along with feminist existentialism from Simone de Beauvoir to Judith Butler. And it develops more explicit themes from ecology, which were latent in my earlier publications, especially 'Freedom, gravity, and grace', published in two parts (1999a, 1999b).

Dance, as something humans do, offers both embodied and linguistic ways of knowing. All forms of phenomenology are concerned with lived experienced, and thus are ripe for researching dance as knowledge. Hermeneutic analysis makes use of interpretation and admits that the author and researcher are involved in making and articulating meaning. Traditionally, hermeneutics is aimed at deriving meaning from textual analysis. But *meaning making itself* can be the subject. Meaning arrives through interpretation as ongoing in perception and cultural inscriptions. In her chapter on hermeneutic enquiry, 'Dance in the hermeneutic circle', Joann McNamara explains that *phenomenological hermeneutics* emphasizes the value of subjective understanding within various settings. Dance in its aesthetic and cultural processes provides unique opportunities for human understanding, but it is significant that the 'meaningfulness of language' is central in hermeneutics of dance (McNamara 1999: 164–78).

Phenomenology is closer to art than science, even as Husserl projected it as a transcendental science. He produced *Logical Investigations* (1970), the root text of phenomenology – originally published in 1900–01 – but he did not consider his philosophy complete, even in subsequent writing. In his old age, he designated his trusted assistant Eugen Fink to the task of furthering his 'transcendental method'. Husserl himself provided notations and additions (Fink and Husserl: 1995). Still, Husserl considered his philosophy an unfinished project. Even Fink's attempt to explain the phenomenological method of reduction remained provisional. Fink considered his extensive work on Husserl's philosophy 'a draft' (1995: xlvii–viii). Phenomenology, in its genesis with Husserl and its later philosophical expansions in existentialism, emerges with general and inspiring outlines, but not with an exact methodology. There is no single phenomenological method.

I learn central lessons in phenomenology from Husserl. He taught that we constitute the world in our disposition towards it: 'human subjects are only in the world by the fact that, as bearers of world-consciousness, they produce the sense, world, for themselves at every moment' (1995: 166). His use of 'at every moment' indicates the importance he placed on temporality as internal time consciousness. Internalized time is not necessarily linear: as in dance, it can be poetized and lived – through slow, sustained movement, for instance – or seem to split seconds into movement fragments. I call all phenomenological reflection *tabula rasa thinking*. This is the kind that begins with a clean slate. Phenomenology of any kind is a study of oneself in transition, as in a dance. Still more philosophical foci entail how we humans are situated in the world together, intersubjectively, even in lonely moments. Philosophical phenomenology envisions the life-world of human and non-human entwinement, and it situates phenomenology in the historical stream of philosophy. Placing dance in this glorious stream has been one of the goals of my writing.

We-life: Dance, spirituality and ecology

David Abram is a good example of a philosopher who develops an *ecological phenomenology* in support of human communion with sentient non-human life and nature. In his early work, *The Spell of the Sensuous* (1996), he credits Merleau-Ponty for sending phenomenology on its way towards ecology, but looking still further back, we might see that Husserl provides the backdrop for Merleau-Ponty's world-friendliness. Envisioning the future through Abrams, I understand the necessity of celebrating my earthly senses and finding joy in my dancing body. In *Dancing Identity* (2004), I take a somatic perspective on sentience, which interprets embodied life as arising through the relatedness of nature and culture. Post-structural views often see culture as all pervasive, but I believe we ignore our relationship with nature at a great cost. From Husserl, we gain a profound appreciation of the world we take for granted – as being larger than scientific observations can reveal or normal everyday attention can perceive. Stated even further, this is a shared awareness 'with every mundane real thing, and all mundane truths'. It leads 'to the ego that embraces all being in every sense' (Husserl 1995: 167). I especially like Husserl's expansive term, *we-life*: 'Human life is we-life' (Husserl 1995: 192).

Husserl's quest for what he calls 'Absolute Spirit' leads towards spirituality and ecology in dance. At the outset of this study, I did not expect this, veering towards transcendence in the 'everyday' with Heidegger and perceptually concrete matters of 'the lived body' with Merleau-Ponty. Heidegger delineates time in experiential tones with subjects such as 'care' in *Being and Time* (1962), while Merleau-Ponty develops themes of depth and thickness in 'Eye and Mind' and in his essay on art in 'The Primacy of Perception' (1964: 159–90). He believes Descartes's error is in placing space beyond depth and thickness. Merleau-Ponty conceives space as bound to existence through such lived qualities as orientation, spreading, polarity and envelopment. Furthering this insight, we observe that dancers imbue form as they give flesh (depth and thickness) to these qualities, as to space–time phenomena in all their embodied specificity.

Merleau-Ponty and Heidegger both depended on their teacher Husserl's elucidation of 'the life world' in its array of appearances. Answering the question about what phenomenology is involves in part answering the question of who is speaking and writing it (Bruzina 1995: xxviii). Phenomenology is a joint project, still ongoing, and not linked to a single perspective or person. But its philosophical strain did begin with Husserl and his impossible goal of describing how the attempt to understand the structures of being deepens the spirit. All roads in phenomenology lead back to Husserl. I see in his enquiry a way to excavate spiritual love of knowledge and respect for humans as part of the natural world. Involving interactive modes of 'we life', the embodied enactment of dance offers all of this as potential.

It would be pretentious to speak for nature, but in belonging to its vastness, we can certainly attend to our envelopment in it. Site-specific somatic dance presents opportunities for *experiences of belonging* when the focus is on connecting with elemental phenomena like water and moss, rock, sky and wind – inviting transformation through letting go of self.

Husserl's use of the term 'transcendence' in reference to nature gives me pause, and I have sought to understand his meaning. His transcendental project is to produce a new way of doing philosophy with the goal of reaching transcendental spirit through successive 'reductions'. Husserl envisions 'purity' there. Reducing one's habitual attitude towards phenomena (objects of awareness) through shedding presuppositions promises to take intuitive reflection towards the untrammelled contents of consciousness. I receive from Husserl and my teachers in existential phenomenology the incredible gift of being able to say that in dance 'consciousness matters' (Fraleigh 2000). How we direct our attention influences our perceptions and feelings. Where Husserl envisions purity, I find transcendence in the flow of everydayness, stepping in sandy puddles and dancing in streams. This is, of course, the very stuff of somatics. I sometimes look out with awe on the canyon wonders where I live. It changes me to be near layers of geological history, its glacial particles and dinosaur tracks offering windows to eternity.

It is significant that the spirit Husserl sought to reveal was a facet of being human, and more, of being human in a more than human world, not to be taken for granted. He sought the human through what lies in and behind the human, invoking the lifeworld and shared intersubjective life. A merely subjective reduction would simply reveal the ego. In other words, it is not enough to look singularly into one's own experience of phenomena. Time and perspective make a difference also: one needs to do several reflective reductions in order to get closer to spirit, especially in view of the lifeworld and intersubjectivity.

Husserl saw that the way we direct our intentions towards the world produces, or 'enworlds', it in consciousness. At the same time, there is a core ontological form in nature. In other words, nature has a fundamental identity in itself. 'Subjectivity in its grip upon it of course changes nature, but alters nothing of the unity of nature as core in its own ontological form' (Husserl 1995: 189). If he is right, and I think he is, this means that humans can have inter-sentient relationships with nature. We can commune with nature, even as we constitute it in our own senses, throwing our consciousness towards the unifying core we sense in and beyond us. In this, we have the possibility of experiencing ourselves *enveloped in nature*, not different from, or above, all other life.

I stay with Husserl because he pointed phenomenology away from the ego and towards the spirit, as this includes the world and the constant relativity of self, world and other. I shift away from Husserl for the same reason that Heidegger and Merleau-Ponty did, as they turned towards concrete experience, even admitting its darker registers. Like butoh and Buddhism, they also make peace with the 'messiness' of life. Their phenomenology, however different from Husserl, is still connected to his themes of intersubjectivity and the constitutive function of consciousness. We sense that the world is tangibly other because we are predisposed to separate from it in our naïve, natural and unexamined relationship with it. We can, however, cast our world sense more widely.

If I consciously suspend my habituated perceptions (reduce or inhibit my habits), and I look towards the world with wonder, I might wonder whether the world stops to look at me. Do the plants and animals, the rivers and oceans care about me? Maybe, like me, they are busy doing what they do? Likewise, they might whisper their occupations when I listen, or hold me when I need to rest? Thus, I enquire into sentient reciprocity between the human and other than human world. I intuit that such reciprocity exists, especially through my affinities with canyons and lakes, with frogs and whales, as also with Annabella, my fine fury puppy. Dancing leads me to wonderings about reciprocity, intimately and directly through embodiment, an inclusive phenomenon not bounded by 'self'. Dancing is applied phenomenology, a way to study our humanness in the flowing live present, always in process in the larger than human world, not separate from consciousness.

Sociality and the blurry edges of the human psyche would not have arisen in Husserl's phenomenology of pure spirit. As a dancer and teacher of movement through somatic studies, I want to span the distance between the insights of Husserlian phenomenology and the existential themes that arise through the challenges of day-to-day life. Dancing may not seem to be so 'everyday' because it does not enter into the everyday life of everyone. Dancing is seldom viewed as universal necessity, and yet, I want to say that it is, and that there are many ways to dance, including ways that engender community and an embodied sense of wonder. Dancing, and the performative in dance, needs to expand its manifestations beyond traditional theatrical contexts and the proscenium stage. Somatic movement arts aim towards such expansions, as I explore with other authors in *Moving Consciously* (2015). Those who train to become skilful performers have

FIGURE 9.3: The Flowing Live Present. Dancers left to right: Denise Purvis, Robert Bingham, Megan Brunsvold. Photograph by Sondra Fraleigh, 2015.

my utmost admiration, but there is more that even they might explore towards unity with the flowing present and expansive world consciousness.

I suggest some initial explorations, and will say more about them later. *Dance in the environment* offers opportunities for sentient communication between the human and more than human world. Some would call this 'site-specific dance', and it is, but such explorations do not always have sentient connections with the lifeworld in mind. Husserl's spiralling towards a spacious core of being suggests that we-life is communicative and wide. *Inclusive pedagogy* also serves a broad purpose. Do we dance with acknowledgement of togetherness, for instance, or with competition and fear? Are we centred in the dance or doing it to be impressive? Intentions matter. The affective qualities of our moving together can be considered in existential, experiential dimensions, as I consider next, and in Part 2. My method includes close reflection akin to heuristic phenomenology. Practitioners and teachers tend to apply the lessons of philosophy; this is where my heart lies.

The Flowing Live Present – 2 July 2015

Patterning and focusing

I recently facilitated a trio of dancers in a group improvisation that included four movement patterns as guides towards interactive movement performance. This constituted the first half of our time together in the studio. Then we sat together in a Focusing exploration inspired by the Focusing process of Eugene Gendlin.

Dancers held presence for each other by focusing images that we then observed in dance renditions. Megan imagined a small wagon, not necessarily from her childhood, just one that came to mind. When she danced with the image, she carried the sound of the wheels into bumpy dangerous movement, riveting to watch. To improvise with the sensations of the image, and to have others reflect verbally on how they experienced it, helped her deepen the daring of her dance.

Wheels, tree, foundation

After we witnessed Megan's 'bumpy' dance, Denise became a tall tree with minimal visible motion and maximal inner distillations. Denise isn't tall, so her style of becoming tall intrigued me. I felt drawn into the butoh-like stillness of her tree and her regal standing presence. Robert imaged the foundation of a building, and then in his dance, the building seemed to materialize. It began with a low squatting foundation that made me jealous, as I once could squat that low, but not with his strength. Megan thought immediately of architecture in Robert's dance, and I added the idea of archetype from there. I asked Robert about his present study and doctoral work as laying a foundation for the future? I also witnessed the struggle of emergent form in his dance. Internalized time as lived became apparent in all of their dances.

Linking

We linked the imagistic dances with the patterned improvisation in a long flow of interactions. Now I'm making a film of this through video and photographs that I caught on camera. I title my short video/film, *The Flowing Live Present*, borrowing a phrase from Husserl. I like his phrase because it speaks to me of the inner essence of dance, especially as it is improvised so clearly in present time, and often with an awareness of time in space. Qualities of thickness and flesh echo from Merleau-Ponty. It seems that I am also a link in the whole of the dance: conceptually, bodily, and through my camera.

Noticing discoveries

The dancers and I ask about our awareness of the improvisation. Megan is often the 'glue' that holds the trio together. We notice how she likes to connect. Robert explores details of movement and originality. He seems to like surprises. Denise alternately coalesces and melts away. As a trio, they meld, becoming faithful to the whole. In our dance, we discover how to internalize the flow of time and the density of space, how interior sensations evolve with the shifting patterns, and how the group surpasses personal boundaries.

Photographic record

My camera witnessed our increasingly structured improvisation. Some photos are shown here, and the fuller documentation through video is on YouTube. [...] Our time together stands on its own as complete in experience, but could also be the first step towards a presentational performance. Whether this happens or not, the discoveries of today are enough. If we want to go back to the experience, photographs will evoke parts and the spirit of the whole.

> Postscript: Today is my birthday. I'm 76 and still dancing. Denise brought 'really gooey-good' doughnuts to the studio for us to celebrate.
>
> (Music Video of Dance Improvisation/Performance: https://youtu.be/GIWM3H3Wc_E)

Part 2

The mattering of spirit

Unlike Husserl, I have only recently begun to identify with the term 'spirit'. In fact I have distanced myself from it, probably for the same reason many people do. It is not precise in any writing enterprise, although it seems to resonate in everyday speech and understanding. I believe it is important to take up the mattering of spirit, particularly how it appears in what Husserl calls 'transcendental world consciousness'. If we do indeed have consciousness that is both given and learned, we also have the opportunity to pass into heightened and renewed consciousness deliberately and in a *tabula rasa* reduction. That is, I can clear my mind to ask how I access my consciousness of the world, including nature, in ways that are ordinary but overlooked, or even hidden to me. What if I imagine a childlike consciousness, the one of my early years? Perhaps, I can cross over from my life now and into my early life as I discover. The discovery point of *heuristic phenomenology* allows me to stay with experiential learning as method. The heuristic perspective relative to phenomenology is well developed by Clark Moustakas (1990).

Heuristic enquiry begins with a question or problem, and is often a personal quest to understand one's self in the larger world. The heuristic process is autobiographic to a certain extent, and often includes poetry, interviews, notes and photography – also drawing, painting and dance. Heuristics is aimed at discovery through self-enquiry and dialogue with others. Like existential phenomenology, it is concerned with meanings of human experiences and is not removed from subjectivity, but involves one's senses, perceptions, beliefs and summary findings. Unlike some phenomenology, it does not aim towards theoretic analysis, but stays close to experience. Like phenomenology, heuristics aims to illuminate the heart of a question. The search itself can be illuminating and also vulnerable, providing standpoints, vistas of lived experience, and not definitive answers. All forms of phenomenology look beneath the veneer of life, consider varied standpoints, and elucidate time and change. Phenomenology does not stand still, and it does not have to be 'right'. The word phenomenology comes from the Greek *phos*, meaning light. Phenomenologists want to shed light.

With this in mind, I write into the mattering of spirit. Not depending on any definition of spirit or spirituality, I begin where I am, not knowing, and without a definition. I notice aspects of life that appear in people who are fulfilled by what they do and in their associations with others. I take this as a place to start, letting virtues that are commonly called spiritual, lead me. It occurs to me that spirituality does not develop through wishful thinking, but is realized through action. But, I will bracket that thought. Maybe spirituality arrives gracefully as a simple gift, innocently in the lives of children. That would mean it is a given quality in all of us that can be tended and developed. Could it be that spirit comes to matter in adult life through virtues that we develop and also those we keep intact from childhood? We know there are many of these; I want to take up the ones that have been beacons and challenges for me. All of them have implications for dance.

Gratitude

As a child, I spent most of every day in nature. I played in the fields of Circleville, Utah, and swam in the Sevier River near Butch Cassidy's Cabin. My mother made sure I was vaccinated for rheumatic fever every year, because there were often dead cattle upriver. In springtime, I loved looking out over the spreading meadows of the valley and rolling in tall fragrant grass. My family and community went on frequent picnics in the nearby mountains, where we also played baseball – children and adults together. I went hiking as a teenager, continued the picnics and tended cattle, lambs, cats and dogs. We harvested and picked potatoes, and I rode horses. I was never afraid to go outdoors. There were no life-threatening people about. Well maybe one, but I was well warned.

> To this day:
> I love to hold potatoes in my hands,
> > the small ones and the bumpy heavy ones.
> > > I don't care if they are a starch vegetable!
> > I love potatoes, and they love me back.
> > > July, hot and pestilential,
> > > > come again as green.

FIGURE 9.4: Photograph of Sondra Fraleigh in the furrowed potato fields of Circleville Utah. Photograph © Robert Bingham.

>September now, the air sweet and clean.
>>In each of us, dances
>>>the gratefulness of dripping clouds.

My association with non-human nature has shaped my taste and perceptions. I feel lucky in this, and very grateful. Being in nature cultivates gratitude and renewed world consciousness. We have the opportunity to see ourselves as part of a larger whole and to give thanks for belonging. This can be cultivated at any age. It is not an abstraction, but a necessity in restoring health where alienation has taken hold. I believe that sentient reciprocity between humans and nature is a spiritual virtue, one that is inborn but that also needs tending.

>We come from earth and star, as angular,
>>or soft with edges far apart,
>>>not entirely owned and grouped by social strains.
>Sexuality, seemingly natural, presents paradoxes in magnetic attractions
>>>>subject to customs, clothes,
>>>and twirlings around
>>>>cosmetic gloss.

Nature can mean a lot of things, I realize. Our sustainability as humans in a more than human world depends on our effecting oneness with nature:

> Call this the blameless breath,
>> Or innocence in dancing.

We can engage with non-human nature, stepping outside of human enclosures to practise spontaneous connectivity in surround sound. I practise gratitude dances in Snow Canyon, near St. George, Utah, where I live. I like to do these dances with others. The sky overhead, the smooth sandstone caressing our bare feet holds us inside the womb of the world. Expressing gratitude through our humanness in the more-than-human world deepens spirit. If Husserl is right, we constitute the natural world in our consciousness of it. Then why not constitute the world, consciously, with gratitude? The world will echo back.

Silence

> Spirit can survive noise, but only
>> if it senses silence around the corner.

Is silence a spiritual virtue? Children do not like to be quiet, or so it often seems. But, I wonder? I spent many happy quiet hours as a child, not wanting my independent play disturbed by pesky adults. Now, I especially enjoy silence. Being alone is not lonely for me, but I do remember when it was. Much of my life as a child and young adult was lonely and clouded with dysfunction in my family. I felt dark oppressive aloneness as a weight in my chest and a hole in my being. I fantasized that an ultimate rescuer would save me, probably a man. Through the years, I got over that – finding ways forward as my own rescuer. Eventually, I learned that loneliness not pushed away deepens the spirit as part of resilience, and that silence is part of loneliness. A friend of mine is trying to decide whether to have radiation as postoperative further treatment for cancer. I see how lonely this decision is for her. No one can make it for her, and I see how much she would like to hand over this burden. The ability to make peace with silence and loneliness is a spiritual virtue. In this, we have meditation and prayer as models.

Silence is beautiful in music, as stillness is in dance. The darkness, the light, *phos*, is held in the stillness of butoh, the postmodern, surreal dance of Japan. Still faces in butoh have on many occasions carried me away, but I understand that not everyone is. The slow, still qualities in butoh take time. My question is how to conceive dance in ways that move in the silence and stillness at the heart of movement. Some butoh does this; Ohno Kazuo's did. His dancing

PHENOMENOLOGIES IN THE FLOWING LIVE PRESENT

into old age assisted this perception. Sometimes, when I watched him dance, I could sketch phrases in an outline form, so slow was his movement into stillness and spirit.

Humility

This is a difficult subject. My mother taught me to put myself last, to hold back my thoughts, not to interfere, and to be quiet. Now that I am getting old, I think she was right to caution against boldness.

> Well, there is a time for humility, but not all the time.
> Listening is more important than speaking, but the two are a duet.

We need spiritual lessons in humility these days. Worldly as we may want to be in moving wide and running far, unworldliness needs to bring us home. The body is the fascinating home for all our dispositions. Spiritual qualities are embodied. We dance them into being and sing them out. In all of our cultural doings, spirit is stirring. Humility may be inborn, and some of us try to unlearn it, only to seek its refuge and power late in life. Children suffer it, and some adults do also. Humility comes better in the choice to give up all pretentions.

> In our dances, we can support others,
> be the still point around which they ground,
> draw back so they can shine,
> and know the right time to come forward,
> inside the commotion.

Learning

This has become a favourite of mine. I see this virtue in my husband and in many friends and colleagues. Many people like to learn and go on learning throughout life. I believe it is a virtue, and one that cultivates spirit. Even as I continue to aspire to learn more, I realize that in this I am not becoming more. I simply want to be who I am, and to be able to relax into my being every day. Learning, Moshe Feldenkrais taught, should be fun and enjoyable. Learning can unfold naturally. We all have abilities that are native to us, frames of knowing and doing that fit who we are. Throughout life, we continue to learn how to be more fully ourselves; ideally, we do. Plato taught that we are born knowing everything we need to know. Good teachers help us realize what we already know (Caton 1989). Learning that is stressful and filled with fear does not foster spirituality. The natural unfolding of who we are does.

Dance can find its expression in naturally unfolding movement abilities, as also powers of expression in wide array of emotional shadings.

> It is liberating to dance toward oneself,
>   out-toward-the-world through being-in-the-world.
>   Spirit matters,
>   Materializing a body, thickening our dances:
>   Liquefying—polarizing—
>   enveloping.

Dancing towards the world and each other is necessary in the development of embodied learning. Dance can be a metaphor for any and all aesthetic activity that is developmental in the arts, as also in sports and games, especially when art and sport are undertaken playfully and with love of movement. Embodied learning is a spiritual undertaking.

Canyon dances

I said I would speak of phenomenology *as method in teaching*. Dances in the environment and on camera provide a starting point. When I take students into specific environments to dance, I am aware of the spirit of place that greets us there. I am not speaking of a particular entity or of something ghostly, but rather the whole character of place. Old railroad tracks will present unique affordances and characteristics that will differ from abandoned construction sites, for instance. When we go to Snow Canyon in Utah, we can experience the soft sandstone as a prehistoric drone, a repetitive and constant 'ground bass' for our dances and photographs.

> The spreading alluvial stone hums beneath us.
>   We know it will be warm on a warm day.
>   We can dance barefoot, but probably won't leap on the rock.
>   We can save that for the studio.
> More likely, we will bond with the smooth, grainy surface.
>   The stone invites us to ground, speaks
>   to soft flesh and porous bone, and provides interesting dwellings—for
>   standing,
> sitting, and lying down.
>   It calls bellies to earth like lizards, or spines
> to coil like snakes next to ledges.
>   It affords our bodies the comfort of spreading
>   and sprawling over big soothing rocks.

According to Husserl,
the world is already transcendentally constituted,
and it is up to us to catch up with it.

My teaching method in the environment is heuristic, or one of discovery, whether the place is wild and uncultivated, architected, gorgeous or decaying. I know I will not have to teach very much; the spirit and sense of the place will do the teaching. Dancers only need time to explore and discover themselves in relating to it. Capturing moments in video and photography extends the experience. My role will be to set the tone for discovery. That might mean a story, or perhaps an evocative poem. Making a dance map of where to begin and end will be helpful; so can we finish together and share experiences? Sometimes I ask dancers whether they would like to be aware of an aspect of sense in relation to place, like attending to breath relative to the breeze or wind. I usually remind them that they are both dancer and audience in the event, and to remember to witness the dance in order to take pictures when (and if) they want to.

Now is time to ask, 'what is phenomenological about this teaching method? Or what is P'?

What Is P?
P is not accepting beforehand that we know what to do.
P is trust that intuition can guide us.
P is letting go of what we know in order to discover something.
P is unearthing our hidden assumptions about dance.
P is unearthing our hidden assumptions about ourselves.
P is letting go of performance for an audience.
P is holding presence for each other.
P is letting go of presentational presence in favour of sharing.
P is witnessing dance experiences.
P is witnessing of place and our humanness as part of place.
P is not separating from the natural world around us and moving through us.
P is dancing as nature dances.
P is accepting unknown outcomes.
P is celebrating earth, air and water.
P is noticing the hummingbird in the thicket.
P is sharing photos.

Ephia Gbruek, whose workshops have been hosted at various locations in Europe and The United States, leads butoh-influenced environmental dances in Valcivières, France. She explains what is important in her teaching process. I read it as an attempt to bracket or reduce the commonplace:

SOMATICS IN DANCE, ECOLOGY, AND ETHICS

We open our senses and ask how can the environment change our way of being. Blindfolded exercises permit us to discover different ways of guiding and being guided. The body of our partner becomes our prosthesis: we enter into its experience and, through listening, deepen our own presence. Walking meditations invite us to play with the transformation of our quotidian. Dream symbols alter commonplace reality and provoke a flowering of poetic vision. Reflections, shadows, sounds, passages, colors, meetings, departures take on new importance as in the dream. A finger placed on the pulse of the earth touches the connection of the sub-conscious and the landscape, of memory and place.

(Gbruek 2015)

Postscript on beauty and spirit

Beauty – whether crude or elegant.

I like this word.
The very idea initiates fragrant smells,
And I feel the exquisite smoothness of dancing naked fall on me like snow.

Is beauty a spiritual quality? I suspect so. 'Every day be beautiful', my Zen teacher told me. I have been grateful for this advice, but have sometimes wondered how one can just 'be beautiful'. The more I write into the matter, the more I understand that we do not find beauty outside ourselves. It exists as a feeling – like love – that can be cultivated each and every day. It develops from the conditions of our lives and how we shape our consciousness around these. It is given to us in childhood, but we can squash it. Fortunately, it is renewable. Beauty is not absolute; it is renewed daily in adapting to the present by being present, and not reliving past regrets. There are beautiful paintings in museums, but in order to see them as such, we need an internal compass that draws us to the beautiful.

Suffering brings beauty beyond the first pangs and shortness of breath, arising when we absorb our grief and turn it into compassion. The relationship of beauty and compassion is not a new idea, of course. Buddhism teaches us to be open to life as a witness to all of it, to see beyond oneself and to care for others, to find beauty in nature and do nature no harm. Aesthetic sensibilities are associated with beauty, but we know through the study of aesthetics, historically, that its definition has changed from classical balance and proportion to wide-ranging qualities, including expression and rawness, even beautiful ugliness. Perhaps, we can look upon ugliness when we see its dry unfriendliness and malice as part of change, decay and transformation.

Most people are beautiful when they are innocently engaged in doing something they really love. Dancing gives people the promise of losing themselves in love with the beauty of movement. For me, this takes time and centring of consciousness. For beauty's spiritual flowering in me, I need to find the ground beneath my feet, and to achieve balance in surrender to flow. Meditation and dancing in nature afford this, as does also the experience of dancing with others in the studio, when we step inside the beauty of companionship and laughter.

REFERENCES

Abram, David (1996), *The Spell of the Sensuous*, New York: Random House.

Bruzina, Roland (1995), 'Translators introduction', in E. Fink and E. Husserl (eds), *Sixth Cartesian Meditation* (trans. R. Bruzina), Bloomington: Indiana University Press, pp. vii–xcii.

Caton, John (1989), 'Plato', State University of New York: College at Brockport, Spring Semester.

Damasio, Antonio (1994), *Descartes Error: Emotion, Reason, and the Human Brain*, New York: G. P. Putnam's Sons.

Damasio, Antonio (2012), *Self Comes to Mind: Constructing the Conscious Brain*, New York: Vintage Books, Random House Inc.

Fink, Eugene and Husserl, Edmund (1995), *Sixth Cartesian Meditation: The Idea of a Transcendental Theory of Method* (trans. and intro. R. Bruzina; textual notations and appendix E. Husserl), Bloomington: Indiana University Press.

Fraleigh, Sondra (1987), *Dance and the Lived Body: A Descriptive Aesthetics*, Pittsburgh: University of Pittsburgh Press.

Fraleigh, Sondra (1999a), 'Freedom, gravity, and grace' (Part 1), *Somatics: Journal of Body/Mind Arts and Science*, 12:2, Spring/Summer, pp. 14–18.

Fraleigh, Sondra (1999b), 'Freedom, gravity, and grace' (Part 2), *Somatics: Journal of Body/Mind Arts and Science*, 12:3, Fall/Winter, pp. 8–13.

Fraleigh, Sondra (2000), 'Consciousness matters', *Dance Research Journal*, 32:1, Summer, pp. 54–62.

Fraleigh, Sondra (2004), *Dancing Identity: Metaphysics in Motion*, Pittsburgh: University of Pittsburgh Press.

Fraleigh, Sondra (2015), *Moving Consciously: Somatic Transformations through Dance, Yoga, and Touch*, Urbana: University of Illinois Press.

Gbruek, Ephia (2015), 'Le Corps: SENS DEDANS DEHORS', flyer on 2015 workshop in French and English, RESOURCES, Valcivières, Auvergne, France, 9–14 August.

Heidegger, Martin (1962), *Being and Time* (trans. J. Macquarrie and E. Robinson), New York: Harper & Row.

Heidegger, Martin (1971), 'The origin of the work of art', in *Martin Heidegger: Poetry, Language, Thought* (trans. Albert Hofstadter), New York: Harper and Row, pp. 15–86.

Heidegger, Martin (1999), *Contributions to Philosophy (From Enowning)* (trans. P. Emad and K. Maly), Bloomington: Indiana University Press.

Husserl, Edmund ([1900–1901] 1970), *Logical Investigations* (trans. J. N. Findlay), London: Routledge & Kegan Paul.

Husserl, Edmund (1995), 'Appendices', in E. Fink and E. Husserl (eds), *Sixth Cartesian Meditation* (trans. R. Bruzina), Bloomington: Indiana University Press, 163–192.

McNamara, Joann (1999), 'Dance in the hermeneutic circle', in S. Fraleigh and P. Hanstein (eds), *Researching Dance: Evolving Modes of Inquiry*, Pittsburgh: University of Pittsburgh Press, pp. 162–87.

Merleau-Ponty, Maurice (1962), *Phenomenology of Perception* (trans. C. Smith), London: Routledge & Kegan Paul.

Merleau-Ponty, Maurice (1964), *The Primacy of Perception and Other Essays* (ed. J. M. Edie and trans. C. Dallery), Evanston: Northwestern University Press.

Moustakas, Clark (1990), *Heuristic Research: Design, Method, and Applications*, Newbury Park: Sage Publications.

10

On Dance and Phenomenology:
Interview with Sondra Fraleigh

Amanda Williamson

IN THIS EXTENDED essay, interview with Sondra Fraleigh I ask about her paving-the-way research in dance and phenomenology, and how the traditions of phenomenology historically and theoretically intersect within dance research paradigms. Together we cover questions and areas such as how and when phenomenological traditions started to integrate into Dance Studies, phenomenological approaches relative to somatics, and the ethical ramifications for students when phenomenology is taught and becomes a central research paradigm for dance studies students. Sondra shares her academic experience within these intersecting fields, and personal journeys and reflections within the intricacies and intimacies of phenomenological traditions.

AMANDA: *Can you tell us how and when phenomenological traditions started to integrate into Dance Studies?*

SONDRA: It happened gradually in my understanding – beginning with Maxine Sheets-Johnstone's book, *Phenomenology of Dance*, first published in 1966. My book, *Dance and the Lived Body*, came along in 1987. I didn't know about Sheets-Johnstone's work until I began to write my book in earnest in about 1977. I studied the concept of the lived body in philosophy classes on phenomenology and existentialism, and I wrote my first exploratory article in 1970. It finally expanded seventeen years later in the finished book. The intensive writing of *Dance and the Lived Body* (1987) was about a five-year project. I wrote it in long hand first. Computers were around, but not integrated into the skills of everyone. I took the hand written manuscript to my typewriter, and eventually it found its way into computer-ease. Now my family finds it difficult to tear me away from my computer.

185

FIGURE 10.1: Sondra Fraleigh leading discussion at an Eastwest Somatics workshop in Saint George, Utah, 2014. Photograph © Richard Biehl (Eastwest student).

As you know, the process of publication is quite involved. It took a long time for phenomenology as such to be recognized as a way to research dance in graduate studies. I thought my book would just gather dust on some library shelf, but a year after the first publication of *Dance and the Lived Body* (1987), I taught two summer workshops dedicated to dance and phenomenology for Ph.D. students at Texas Woman's University through the invitation of Dr Penelope Hanstein.

Later I taught a pre-conference full day workshop at a CORD Conference (Congress for Research in Dance, 1990). It was very well attended by students and professors – so I assumed that phenomenology had attained some recognition in dance studies. If I take the entire trajectory from the time of Maxine's first publication in 1966, my subsequent publications, and my international workshop in 1990, I see a long curve of 24 years. Of course there were others who contributed along the way, and it took even longer for phenomenology to gather adherents in academic dance departments. I don't think anyone writes from this perspective for fun, rather it is a way to place your topic in an intellectual and historical framework. This can be enjoyable when you make discoveries. By now, it's like riding a bicycle for me, even when I sometimes fall off!

AMANDA: *How about phenomenology in dance today?*

SONDRA: Now we have a fuller story, from 1966 to 2016, and quite a wonderful half-century-story, I would say. Many graduate students take up phenomenology in their dissertations and theses. Professors like Dr Karen Bond at Temple University specialize in the perspectives of phenomenology. Others like Dr Joanna McNamara include hermeneutics relative to phenomenology in their university teaching. She wrote an influential article in this regard (1999). As a professor of dance, I taught phenomenology as part of dance studies and published two invited articles on phenomenology for *Dance Research Journal* (Spring 1991, Summer 2000).

And this is just from the American side. As for recent work, many Europeans, Canadians, New Zealanders, Australians, Africans, Asians and Israelis are working from phenomenological perspectives in dance and theatre studies. Hillel Braude, born in Africa and now living in Israel, is a medical doctor and ethicist who writes about dance, movement and somatic practices from the perspective of phenomenology (2015). He is certified in Feldenkrais, and also studies my work, Shin Somatics. New Zealander Karen Barbour is inspired by phenomenology and feminism in *Dancing Across the Page: Embodied Ways of Knowing* (2011). Performance Studies draws upon phenomenology, sometimes through practice as research (PAR) – for instance in the dance and somatics films of Ruth Way and Russell Frampton at Plymouth University in the UK. Concerning spirituality and dance, I know that phenomenology also influences your work, Amanda. I see phenomenology as a large tent for furthering reflective knowledge in a variety of ways.

Influences from Asia have entered into dance phenomenology. I often cite the philosophy of Shigenori Nagatomo and his Japanese phenomenology, as it intersects with Buddhism. Nagatomo is available to English speakers via his book *Attunement through the Body* (1992). Phenomenology and Buddhism have a great deal in common in their trust of groundlessness. 'Not knowing', not needing to fix or find absolutes, is part of the existentialist narrative that sustains them both. 'The abyss' and 'nothingness' are spiritual images for letting go. Such radical release of controlling instincts can be scary, but we learn throughout life that not getting attached to things, whether material or conceptual, is part of transformative change. Control is not always the best solution; doing nothing sometimes is. Heidegger calls this 'letting beings be', as I take up in my article, 'Butoh Translations and the Suffering of Nature', now in press with Routledge Performance Research series.

The story of dance and phenomenology is vast and still unfolding; others could fill in what I'm missing. I have been aware of the influential work of Susan Kozel and her book, *Closer: Performance, Technologies, Phenomenology* (2007). I feature her work in my recent article on dance and technology, 'Enacting embodiment and blue muffins', just now being published with *Choreographic Practices* (2016). I do have a sense of humour, but the article is also serious. Susan was one of the students in my 1990 seminar mentioned above. Now she has a new book in the works, she tells me. In a turn toward transcendental phenomenology, Anna Pakes in the UK explores how Edmund Husserl's work can be applied to ontology of dance in *Dance Research Journal* (2011). In the same issue, Edward Warburton, in his article on dance, phenomenology and cognition, explains how cognitive theories of enaction are relevant to contexts of dancer action and performance (2011).

For students who feel intimidated by dense or highly intellectual texts, I like to simplify by teasing out a few main themes of phenomenology, such as non-judgement and intersubjectivity. The latter is an important concept for dancers and teachers, since it is about how meaning is created contextually between people. Meaning doesn't arise in a vacuum. It arrives as shared at some point, or else it remains private and eventually vanishes. When meanings are shared they double in significance. Intersubjectivity is the lifeblood of dance. Just think of it, whenever we dance together we share lived bodyscapes, and we do it wordlessly. We enter special ineffable states together. These could be states of joy, rhythm or dream, to name a few. We might not say anything about what meanings arise in the dancing, but we could if we wanted to.

AMANDA: *Can you say more about the difference between you and Sheets-Johnstone?*

SONDRA: Maxine and I are still writing about dance from perspectives of phenomenology, but not in the same vein. I have appreciated her contributions, and reviewed her work for *Dance Research Journal* (Summer 2002). I felt it important for dancers to understand her contributions, and to know about her extensive studies of phenomenology related to movement and dance. I see her voluminous work as foundational, and have anticipated each new phase. Philosophical phenomenology is not easy to understand for those who don't study it, and even for those who do. But close reading of phenomenology is well worth the time. It can change your life. It can certainly reveal what it means to suspend judgement and question assumptions. Attention directs perception. How we attune grounds perceptual processes and eventual discoveries.

Sheets-Johnstone is tied more closely to Husserlian phenomenology than I have been, and she has also integrated her study of zoology. Her work on feminist themes has inspired writers in wider fields of philosophy. Maxine has been a long-time friend and very supportive of my work, which has depended on the confluence of phenomenology and existentialism. I am informed by philosophers in this school of thought beginning with Jean-Paul Sartre and Maurice Merleau-Ponty, not to forget Martin Heidegger, Husserl's student and the primary revisionist of his phenomenology. Heidegger's phenomenology and post-metaphysics assist my work thematically (1999), as does his aesthetic treatise on origins (1971). Merleau-Ponty's conceptualizations of the lived body are particularly important to my vision (Merleau-Ponty 1962, 1964a, 1964b). Sheets-Johnstone has been critical of Merleau-Ponty's outlook.

It is difficult to see one's own work, but if I look broadly, I think it could be classified as applied phenomenology and transdisciplinary. Cross-disciplinary isn't the same, since this is more about working within disciplines and crossing over. I like to dissolve boundaries in transcending territorial turf. I draw on whatever helps to clarify or enrich my project, from neuroscience to mythology. I soften boundaries between philosophy and poetry quite often, trusting that this will peak the reader's attention and their ability to shift focus. Poetry can space out thicker texts with imagery and still be on topic. If I'm describing a dance, I make sure to reference the music, since perception is strongly shaped by music. Dance is infused with musical rhythms and colours in the sounds of various performances. It also matters a great deal whether the music is recorded or live. We know that silence also figures in performance. When dance moves with silence, the silence speaks volumes.

I often veer back to Husserl and sometimes forward to heuristics, represented well in the psychology of Cark Moustakas (1990). I like Merleau-Ponty for his psychological emphasis on the lived body as intrinsically expressive. I also make Simone de Beauvoir the hero of my book, *Dancing Identity: Metaphysics in Motion* (2004). This book updated my first efforts, taking up feminist themes and writing from a personal angle by integrating ecological life stories with phenomenology. Beauvoir is the first feminist to write a phenomenology with existentialist themes, also incorporating ethics. More recently, we have the example of Judith Butler, a feminist, linguist and phenomenologist who relates to theatre and performativity. In *Dancing Identity* (2004), I create a textual dance as theatrical dialogue between Beauvoir, Butler and Merleau-Ponty.

AMANDA: *Can you say something about how aesthetics has informed your phenomenology?*

SONDRA: Aesthetic theory is for the most part neglected in phenomenology, but has entered into my preview at every turn. I carry this forward through what I identify as 'a descriptive aesthetics', but I also take the history of aesthetics seriously. Aesthetics has been an important strain of philosophy from Plato to Heidegger and beyond. It infuses my work historically in *Dance and the Lived Body* (1987). I studied aesthetic theory intensively in the large collection of the University of London library for six months on sabbatical leave, finding common tones between aesthetics, phenomenology and somatic studies. The aesthetic is the affective; as such, it inheres in somatic movement arts. I bring this up where I can, and hope to be able to say more about it – in the future. 'Witnessing the frog pond' is my dance-specific study of aesthetic theory in *Researching Dance* (1999a). I tried to make it reader friendly for university students, and to include phenomenology.

Regarding dance as art, I have described the work of many artists, by now more than a hundred. I've lost count. These would be choreographers and dancers I have experienced in live performance. Butoh and Japanese aesthetic concepts, particularly *shibui* and *wabi-sabi*, enter into these descriptions and analyses. I've interviewed many of the artists I write about, and taken dance classes and workshops from or with many of them. Most recently, I wrote 'Images of love and power in Butoh, Bausch, and Streb' for the *Oxford Handbook of Dance and Theater* (2015b), describing dances from these highly contrasting styles. I weave these with conceptions of love and will in the aesthetic philosophy of Arthur Schopenhauer from the early 1800s, the existential psychology of Rollo May, and the social activist views of Martin Luther King Jr.

In describing a dance, I look at time and space as lived attributes, attempting to capture the poetry of movement and possible meanings of the whole. I don't believe there are discrete meanings to be gathered in dance works. Rather do audiences interact with performances from their own experience. We attribute meaning through interpretation and share the dance this way. I like to interact as one witness to the dance, and I don't think of myself as a critic. I aim to bring abstract concepts to life through dance descriptions, and take this as a phenomenological challenge.

Philosophers, unless they are also arts practitioners, examine the arts from the outside. Their objective aesthetic outlook has value of itself, but also limitations. Artists who study philosophy have a ringside seat, especially through aesthetics and phenomenology, and they can use this to advantage. I have felt a responsibility to describe dance from the dancer's point of view. If dancers don't do this, then who will? When I'm writing, I always ask myself if I can give concrete examples of what I'm talking about, either from my experience or through describing a dance I've seen or been part of. It is easy enough to write theoretically without giving any examples, but theory can be dry, when it is never applied to some concrete instance of performance or self-evidence. Concrete examples also serve as checks to theory. Examples of actual dances or experiences of dance might contradict theory and send one back to the drawing board.

When I'm considering dance as a phenomenon, asking 'what is this thing', or writing about a particular dance I have in mind, I ask myself who I am in the picture. Am I speaking from the dancer's point of view, that of the audience, or the choreographer? Am I speaking broadly beyond concrete manifestations and envisioning metaphysical essence? Is my voice coming more locally or intimately from the aura of an event? Am I defining a term in order to communicate a general principle? Just what is my perspective?

Phenomenologically, I speak to an ideal reader who can understand what I'm saying. I trust the intelligence of my readers, but I won't be able to communicate what appears to me as significant unless I say who I am in the process of my writing. I need to show my standpoint: am I dancing, witnessing, learning or teaching? What part of me am I channeling?

AMANDA: *It seems that phenomenology has gradually enlarged in your understanding of dance, Sondra.*

SONDRA: Yes, and writing 'Phenomenologies' for this issue has been part of that, providing me the opportunity to identify various phenomenological currents. Readers will be able to see where various authors fall in this collection of styles. Some authors and practitioners may even overlap phenomenologies. I was elated when I began to see a wide field of phenomenological practice, and to grasp this field as flexible. The idea that there is no single phenomenological method makes me breathe more deeply, fully, and with a sigh. Methods need to remain open and amendable in phenomenology, and likewise in somatic practices and approaches to performance. Regarding practice as research (PAR), I'm beginning to see how the *tenets* of phenomenology might also be expressed in media other than words: in dance, music and visual art, not to mention theatre, poetry and somatic movement arts. Those who enter pathways of phenomenologies in comprehending dance will find their own way through the thicket. I say, 'just wade in'. Then find out how a particular perspective supports your interests, or challenges and changes them. State the parameters of your study. Spiral in and out of your topic from different angles, to see if your original intuitions hold water. Good definitions well researched, always help, even if you finally discard them. Phenomenology does not throw reason out the window. Indeed, it wants reason on its side. This said, meaning in the arts often arrives through irrational substrata.

AMANDA: *I am interested in the intersection of the somatics movement with phenomenology, both historically and in terms of theoretical and methodological meeting points. Can you share your observations and experience with us in relation to the intersection of these academic movements?*

SONDRA: First, a personal reflection on the nervous system: like many people in the arts, I soak up a lot of perceptual information. Sometimes I'm on overload. Add to that the stressful enjoyments of teaching, and I could go overboard (on overload). I've noticed through the years that something magical occurs when I think I'll burst. My instinctive body comes to my aid. At a critical point, everything just shuts down. *My nervous system is smarter than I am!* This realization keeps

FIGURE 10.2: Sondra Fraleigh teaching a Bodywork section of an Eastwest Somatics workshop in Auckland, New Zealand in 2011. Photograph © Karen Smith (Eastwest student).

me interested in 'dance somatics', which I think of as studying and performing dance through a somatic looking glass.

I have written more technically and logically about dance and somatics in my new book: *Moving Consciously* (2015a). I see somatics as 'phenomenology in action', or one could say 'phenomenology come alive in movement' or 'experiential awareness explored in dance'. Somatics is an approach to personal and professional development, and it can be applied widely in movement arts, pedagogy and psychology. Antonio Damasio's *Self Comes to Mind* (2012) extends my theme of consciousness in context of neurobiology. I use Damasio because his science is consistent with phenomenology. Much earlier, I wrote an essay for the journal *Somatics* called 'Freedom, gravity, and grace', published in two parts (1999b, 1999c), that speaks to your question, and also includes Damasio (1994). This article is an early attempt on my part to bridge between dance, phenomenology, somatics and science.

AMANDA: *Can you be more specific about phenomenological approaches relative to somatics?*

SONDRA: In its approach, phenomenology asks one to think from a clean slate, to erase presuppositions, and a somatic practice asks for the same clarity. It may be difficult to visualize what a clean slate would mean in thinking and movement. Most generally, it means that we don't know in advance what outcomes will be. It means that we dance and write without expectations. In movement, *improvisation* is a way to clear thought processes and unsettle habits; at least this might be one of the goals. In phenomenology, *bracketing* is a way of looking at what is taken for granted, and preparing for new insight. Both encourage practices that aim toward life-giving renewal and stem from *tabula rasa consciousness*. Phenomenologists are happy to be surprised by new ideas or insights. Somatic detectives in movement are happy to be surprised when they can now perform (do) what was seemingly impossible and previously hidden from them.

'What am I not seeing that is right in front of me?' This question arises in somatic contexts and in phenomenology as an approach toward dance and life. As complementary fields of study, both phenomenology and somatics look beneath surface understandings, not accepting first impressions while still respecting intuition. In their methods, phenomenology and somatics both seek what Husserl called 'the flowing live present'. They seek present centred awareness in other words. I find daring and trust in phenomenology and somatic movement processes, since they seek truth in movement, or *the kinetic truth underlying consciousness*. Something hidden in the known but unplumbed is unearthed in their searches: learning, healing or meaning personally validated.

Dance is a natural ally to phenomenology, since philosophies of the body are at the core of both. Dance is immediately embodied on a nonverbal level, while phenomenology as a philosophy of the body rises to the task of language. I am fascinated by the intersection of nonverbal experience with verbal discourses of embodiment, especially with the addition of somatics.

AMANDA: *Inspired by Edmund Husserl's somatology, Thomas Hanna popularized the noun 'somatics' in order to highlight the subjective, first-person viewpoint, a distinguishing feature of movement somatics. Can you say more about this connection?*

SONDRA: In somatic movement studies, we may have over-simplified the term *soma* as indicating first-person perspectives. Certainly, we want to be able to say something about our immediate perceptions in terms of self. But through phenomenology, especially Husserl, I am careful in speaking from the first-person position, since it is somewhat of a fiction.

The body with its kinaesthetic systems shapes the ways in which we perceive others and the world. Husserl distinguishes this embodied fullness as *leib* (in German), or *the lived body*. This is an active state and inclusive, both *immanent* as inward looking through reflection, and *transcendent* in perception of the external world (Fink and Husserl 1995: 158–59). Husserl's mature work moved further away from the mental character of experience to his growing recognition of the *intersubjective* world of life, the *lebenswelt*, or 'life world'. It is not a private but a collective world even as our situation in it grounds our participation. Body is important in Husserl's discussions of self-awareness, other-awareness, and awareness of the world. Self is not just for itself alone, but appears in relation. 'Human life is we life' in a cultural and environing world constantly in motion (Husserl 1995: 192).

Soma, from Greek, is simply the word for body, even the dead body. What we mean in somatic studies by soma incorporates psyche as living essence, and is therefore complex and pervasive, very close to Husserl's use. What Husserl posited as soma is wholly embodied, accounting not only for human perceptual abilities, but also the ability to commit to an action. *Will and action are somatic phenomena.* Our experiences are complex in passive and active perceptual phases that weave together. *Moving Consciously* (2015a), the book I just completed with others, creates a large frame in which to consider *soma*. We also build on past understandings. Our field has a history, and will continue to evolve meanings of somatic phenomena. My own sense is that we should not depend heavily on single definitions of soma, because there are many.

What you find if you look up 'somatology' today are studies of the body as a branch of anthropology, and it is also seen as the physiological and anatomical study of the body. Husserl's view of the body is all-encompassing, including soul; he states that soul is innately of body and movement. Here is Husserl:

> Each movement of the body is full of soul, the coming and going, the standing and sitting, the walking and dancing, etc. Likewise, so is every human performance, every human production.
>
> (1989: 252)

AMANDA: *What are some common misunderstandings about phenomenology?*

SONDRA: There is misunderstanding in some 'pick up' uses of phenomenology. Those who take it as a quick fix for a study because they come across it as 'description of experience' don't understand the history of phenomenology through philosophy. It isn't just description of personal experience. Who cares about the purely personal? Well novelists and fiction writers do (sometimes), but phenomenologists as non-fiction detectives don't. Phenomenologists care about exhuming personal experience in relation to the experience of others. They care about conscience and sociality, nature and community. The tendency of phenomenology is to finally move past the personal and toward shared values. Experiential study in phenomenology is supported by an intellectual history that has branched out into various bodies of knowledge.

Phenomenology is not easy; it is 'mindboggling'. A nondualistic view of embodiment arises through phenomenology. Bodymind unity is a principle that runs throughout. In many ways, writers in phenomenology explain that body and mind cannot be integrated – as is sometimes claimed in dance and somatic studies – because they are not separate to begin with. This is a hard study, but it is an important one for dance. It will take a long time, I think, to erase the dualistic language of body and mind, body/mind, or even body-mind in the literature on dance and somatics. I am sure many don't think it is important. I do, and will continue to write about the problems of dualism. We humans are embodied as one with the world, minded and spirited all at once. We only know ourselves in context of others, embedded in a human and more-than-human world. Perhaps we are too precious about self in the self-focused processes of somatic studies. Our aim should be more comprehensive.

In everyday discourse, we might speak of body, or of mind, but as scholars of the body in motion we understand that mind is embodied in human movement. We do have words that help tease apart and explain some aspects of embodiment. I don't want to beat anyone up on topics of nondualism, since I surprise myself a lot in speaking about the body and the mind as though they were two different things. But at least I catch myself in the act! I know better, and immediately consider what I might say that would convey the same thing without using body/mind cliché. I don't want to reinforce the dualism of a rational mind in control of an obedient body – especially as mind represents the male, and body represents the female in the mythical dualisms underlying everyday language.

We have separate words for body, mind, spirit, and soul in order to voice certain aspects of experience, but that doesn't mean that the mind is the engineer of the body, or that the world of nature and spirit is separate from you and me. Soul may simply be a way to speak about depth of personality and feeling. Being in the world is all-inclusive. Take away the world, and we humans disappear with it. In Japan and China, *ki* is the invisible energy that permeates all things and unites them as one.

AMANDA: *But people do experience emotional and physical splits, sometimes feeling that the mind or spirit is not in sync with the physical body.*

SONDRA: Yes, people experience all kinds of attentional splits and feelings of separation. Existence philosophy (existentialism) accounts for experiences that eschew unification. Confusion and separateness are real in felt life. These lived realities are explained by phenomenology as *lived dualisms*, not metaphysical or discrete ones. If we say our 'mind is scattered' or our 'soul is lost', this doesn't mean that separate entities are floating in the air as scattered or lost. Feeling fuzzy, scattered or lonely is common. In the extreme, lived dualisms may be disorders of the nervous system, such as schizophrenia, or even depressive states. The mind as mental capacity cannot separate from the body, and it cannot control it, because the body has a head, and the minded brain extends throughout the physical body. The brain-mind manifests throughout the body's nervous system that begins with the skin. In a wide sense, the skin touches the skin and breath of everything beyond it.

The mind is not an invisible ghost companion; it is part and parcel of who we are materially, and how we are spiritually. People in mental hospitals have not 'lost their minds'; most likely, they are experiencing illness and loneliness, as physical and mental at once. Phenomenologists, like somatic practitioners, look at people as a whole, not as pathologies. In practicing somatic movement arts (through intuitive dance, somatic yoga, experiential anatomy, and hands-on repatterning), we look toward what is right and how to access this through the whole person.

AMANDA: *What drew you to passionately and prolifically write about phenomenological traditions in dance studies?*

SONDRA: What a great question. I seldom stop to ask it, and here I am still being drawn in the same direction from my first simple article in 1970. Its thesis still permeates my writing concerning the dialogue between humans and their creative works. We are works in process, shaped by the creative processes we undertake. Or conversely, we may be shaped by fears of failing, and never risk. Failure is just a step along the way toward transformative growth. I still believe that we are incomplete beings in process, as I notice how much my students change in their creative endeavors. Nothing is ever wasted. I like recognizing that spark glowing in everyone that wants to realize more of itself. The way we spend our time, move our thoughts, and dance our dances into being eventually settles into the way we walk and the way we live.

My study and writing takes an existentialist tact in phenomenology because, as a dancer, I'm interested in the psychic, unpredictable edges of experience, and in the poiesis of it all. I continue to learn from all the manifestations of phenomenology however, and I marvel how as a seed, it keeps on accruing more meaning for those who engage it. Phenomenology is such a great gift for dancer-scholars for all the reasons I have mentioned.

AMANDA: *What are the ethical ramifications for students when phenomenology is taught and becomes a central research paradigm for dance studies students?*

SONDRA: Another good question, because the study of experience comes into question in academe, although less and less today. The thematic of academe is 'objectivity'. But there is increasingly room for the subjective as well. Otherwise, the arts would be excluded, as would many aspects of the social sciences. How would education proceed at all without acknowledgement of subjective life? Phenomenology is a research paradigm in many fields, as I point out in this issue. Qualitative research includes a variety of phenomenologies as research models or ways of knowing. Unfortunately, 'phenomenology' and 'somatics' are often buzzwords. I think they need to be defined, and writers might locate their particular orientation within the fields of phenomenology, performance and dance studies.

Writers of qualitative research need to be clear in the design of their study, and to state what can be claimed as outcomes. Is truth a possible outcome in phenomenology? Well, I would say yes, if one is stating the truth of one's experience, and if the truth one claims comes from an intensive search. In the case of dance, I would want to know about what has been discovered through the dance itself and how this connects to wider knowledge beyond the confines of self.

Knowledge comes from varied sources, and we learn in different ways. Some of us are verbally gifted, and some of us learn directly through kinaesthetic experience. Some are musical, and others are scientists. We in dance and somatic studies cross over the arts and move into the physical sciences as well. Some of us like to discern meaning in our work. I'm one of the latter. I never want to forget the beauty of movement fully embodied in great swoops and dives, as also fine flings and shaking. My truth is discovered in movement and dance.

Quantitative research in science held the day for a long time, but quantification through employment of statistics in the physical and social domains is now considered just one way of looking at knowledge, and not the only way. *Researching Dance* (1999), the book I edited on with Penelope Hanstein, takes up both qualitative and quantitative methods. Phenomenology, to be clear, might declare its orientation and admit its limits. But this is the imperative of other research paradigms as well.

I would even say that phenomenology takes a special talent supported through interest in the personal and intrapersonal world, also looking toward the ecological body. We celebrate the study of experience, not narcissistically, but with whole bodies of knowledge to support our searches. I don't think phenomenology is simply inward looking. Human experience occurs in a world of others, and in a more-than-human world that becomes more important all the time. Phenomenology is not navel gazing. Phenomenologists care about the constitution of self relative to others, for example, and they study how community arises in the larger world of nature.

AMANDA: *Is there a pure phenomenology?*

SONDRA: Well, if so, that would be the work of Husserl himself. Later phenomenology draws upon him, finally finding its own unique way forward. In psychology, we have examples from the existential psychology of Rollo May to that of Clark Moustakas. In dance, we have those who use Husserl, but interpret him through the lens of movement, aesthetics, and ontology. Sheets Johnstone adds zoology to this. Phenomenology is applied to many fields of enquiry today. Husserl is the root of it all, and to my mind the only purist, but phenomenology would die on the vine if in every effort it tried to replicate his method, which he himself said was never completed.

AMANDA: *Who are the great phenomenologists who appreciated spirituality and integrated these appreciations into their reflections?*

SONDRA: Most immediately, I think of Soren Kierkegaard and his brooding but inspiring spirituality, expressed in all of his writing. In *Soul and Form*, Georg Lukacs says of Kierkegaard that his whole life was lived under the sign of one unmistakable gesture (1974: 28–41). I have also loved the mystical Christianity of Gabriel Marcel in *Metaphysical Journal* (1952). From American pragmatic approaches, Paul Tillich wrote his spiritual phenomenology, *The Courage to Be* (1952). Martin Buber, a Jewish existentialist and mystic wrote the classic, *I and Thou* (1958). I return to it often in my understandings of self, other, nature, and spirit.

Questions of spirituality, good and evil, and nobility of the body remained urgent for Nietzsche, especially in *Beyond Good and Evil* (1966). He was the lyrical and poetic philosopher in the background of existentialism, and one of the first literary deconstructionists. Nietzsche is accused of 'the death of God', but we cannot forget that in *Joyful Wisdom* (1924), he was lamenting the disintegration of nineteenth century foundational values. God was a symbol of these. Nietzsche was actually lamenting the death of God when he said: 'Who gave us the sponge to wipe away the whole horizon?' (1924: Section 125). He was forerunner of the depth psychology of Carl Jung, and underscored the advent of modern dance via Isadora Duncan and other pioneers. Jung's work resonates sill today in Authentic Movement Practice.

Mythologist Joseph Campbell appreciated Nietzsche. It is so interesting to me how philosophy, mythology, poetry, therapy and art develop out of many streams that make one river over time. I had the good fortune to take a few seminars with Campbell. He provided me the opportunity to revisit my previous reading of Nietzsche and Jung through his unique mythic vision, and he introduced me to the 'Great Goddess' as a transcendent all-embracing feminine divinity of pre-historic cultures. Inspired by Campbell, I write of the return of the Great Goddess in the female authorship and themes of early modern dance (*Dance and the Lived Body*, 1987).

AMANDA: *Tell us a little about eco-phenomenology and how it supports research into movement somatics?*

SONDRA: I have been reading an anthology on eco-phenomenology that explains several positions: *Eco-Phenomenology: Back to the Earth Itself* (C. Brown and Ted Toadvine, 2003). Husserl presented 'back to the things themselves', as the clarion call of phenomenology. His philosophy of 'things' needs explanation. When we define or describe 'anything', we look into its 'thingness', or that which makes it tick, so to speak. We ask, 'What is this thing', as though we didn't already know. This allows us to explore it for the very first time, even if we already know a lot about it. We therefore suspend our presuppositions about the phenomenon (anything that appears to consciousness). What if the thing I enquire into is teaching, more specifically 'teaching dance somatically'. I have often enquired into teaching as an unknown phenomenon, because I don't want to assume in advance that I know how to teach dance somatically.

AMANDA: *Can you explain more about this, Sondra? Then we can move back into the topic of eco-phenomenology.*

SONDRA: My recent book, *Moving Consciously* (2015a), evolved out of phenomenological enquiry into teaching somatically. If I can grasp somatic approaches to teaching dance, yoga and touch in *tabula rasa thinking*, then I will also be speaking about a somatic style of learning. Moreover, I will be required to define the things I'm speaking of without resorting to extant work. I can't just talk about what prominent practitioners teach. At the same time, I want to acknowledge the entire field of somatic movement studies, or what I now call 'Somatic Movement Arts'. Somatics exists in contexts of art when taught with aesthetic outcomes in mind. Somatic narratives and principles remain and overlap, or they wouldn't be 'somatic'. Phenomenology keeps us curious about somatic principles and pedagogy.

It is very interesting to me how one arrives at somatic principles by looking widely past one's own practice. Seeking a clearing, I ask what common threads define anything called somatics? I can't go back to the definition of Thomas Hanna, as many do, or I will just repeat the past. If after digging beneath his definition, I come to agree with it, then I have enriched the search and the definition. If in my search I find something new, I can still build newness in reference to the past, or make a clean break. In editing, *Moving Consciously* (2015a), I define somatics in a spiral path throughout in the first three chapters. Other authors add their own discoveries in the subsequent chapters. The layering of perspectives and practices builds an understanding of somatic movement arts that no one of us could achieve alone.

AMANDA: *Now back to eco-phenomenology.*

SONDRA: Phenomenology has heart. Why wouldn't it, coming as it does out of a concern for embodiment and human experience? The study of ecology also has heart. But how and why, and how does ecology then connect to somatics and phenomenology? This would effect a connection of ecological science to concerns for intersubjective attunement, a not so far-fetched connection. Objectivity is not the culprit in contemporary concerns for human and more-than-human environments; it is actually the hero. Science shows how we are hurting ourselves in ignoring the environment and separating ourselves from non-human nature. Deep ecology is based on science. In tandem with philosophy and the arts, it shows that we need to proceed with heartfelt connectivity to nature. Then we will want to do something about humanity's heartless exploitation of it, which ultimately hurts human nature in the process. Yes, we are natural animals who share the earth and heavens with all other animals and life forms. We all breathe the same air. Trees are friends of air and earth. They are our friends.

It doesn't take rocket science to understand how somatic principles of paying attention and attuning to nature draws the dancing body close to organic life sources. What if it served dance as an art and dance in educational settings to give up 'mastery' of form in favour of 'discovery' of form? This is a phenomenological question that relates us to 'discovery' as a concept and at the same time accounts for the aspect of form in dance. Soma (psyche-soma) is formless until it is discovered in commitment to actions and experienced as able. Dance somatics as a way of attending to ecological concerns is fascinating. Whole theatre works might emerge: dances with wonderful surprising forms, and dances with themes that respect our connections to all of nature. We are part of the life world, and our dances can reflect this. I predict that artists, and dancers as artists, will paint us back into nature as source, envisioning dance and embodiment in the Anthropocene, the epoch that some geologists say characterize our present state, especially the effect of humans on the environment. Human's in having veered off course, need to turn the ship around. Rescue of nature has been a concern for butoh artists, and remains so, especially through the lead of Atsushi Takenouchi.

Through butoh, as through the ecological phenomenology of philosophers Bruce Wilshire and David Abrams, I return the earth its due. Abrams's work, *Spell of the Sensuous*, illuminates the affective in nature, including our own (1996). In his book, *Wild Hunger* (1999), Wilshire, studies addictions through his conviction that addictive dependencies stem from emotional deprivation and an inability to access the regenerative sources inherent in nature. He has also written about theatre and acting as routes toward human development. We met at a conference on phenomenology, and have remained friends. Part of my growth as a writer has been through meeting like-minded scholars at conferences on philosophy, aesthetics and phenomenology, not to mention dance, music and theatre.

AMANDA: *Do you think phenomenology has a spiritual lilt? If so, what would be the debates on spirituality and phenomenology? Where do they meet, diverge …*

SONDRA: Let me speak first of the human drive for power and security. These figure strongly in Heidegger's existential philosophy, which is very critical of technology and the use of earth as 'resource' for human consumption. It seems we humans need to feel secure. Of course we do. I get this, but should this need drive us to seek power over others and dominion over the earth? I am beginning to move away from the word 'empowerment', even as I know feminism needed it initially. Let us feel confident as women, but also let us live in harmony with others and with the earth. Let us seek to know ethnic diversity. Let us live with love as ethic. Failure to love is not ethical, which doesn't mean we can't separate from destructive relationships. The trick is not to live with hate and resentment. Love is life-giving.

Love is spiritual work that requires self-examination, and sometimes forgiveness of self and others. Let our dances come from an open space of love, in loving movement and each other. Dance is prayer and meditation, not competition. Dance is also fun – ecstatic, dramatic, eidetic, and whatever else we make of it. Phenomenology lends us the perspective of intention. If we carry spiritual intentions into our dances, then they are spiritual.

Phenomenology looks deeply into human involvements with the world and into the limits of ego, seeking the large picture. Heidegger shows the importance of allowing all things to be what they are in essence. *Seinlassen* (letting be) was one of his themes in *Being and Time* (1962), almost 100 years ago. Now it returns in the guise of allowing all beings in nature their place in nature. Let the natural world flourish by not interfering. Touch with care. Pick up trash. Recycle. This is spiritual work, and it is somatic work.

In somatic dance contexts, similar concepts appear, like teaching people from where they are, and asking noninvasive questions of movers like 'what is available to you now'. For students in movement somatics, not going beyond what is given would be another way of letting be. 'Doing less to feel more' also allows a perceptual shift away from chronic overdrive. Paying attention, as becoming aware of others and ones surroundings in an allowing frame of mind, expresses a similar idea. This is spiritual work.

No everyone is called to work with ideas in philosophical discourse or through the lens of soma-psyche (the underpinnings of perception and kinesis). I understand this. But for those of us who are, the good news is that we have opportunities to explore aspects of human dignity, and to assist the development of dance studies and performance in this regard, shifting previously marginalized environmental concerns to centre stage and blazing trails for new collaborations between science and art. This is spiritual work, and it is alive in the work of dancers. In our Eastwest Somatics Winter Conference in Zion, Utah (2015), several dancers presented their ecologically inspired projects and dance works.

As to the other part of your question, I seldom encounter debates between phenomenology and spirituality. Some phenomenologists may ignore spirituality simply because they don't understand it, or their questions don't include it. I don't go directly into questions of spirituality, either. Rather I discover spiritual sensibilities by looking underneath cultural cliché concerning dance and embodiment. Early on in my work this morphed into what I called 'body-of-earth and body-of-culture' in *Dance and the Lived Body* (1987). I didn't think my exploration of dance and body would be complete without explaining nature and culture as complementary aspects of embodiment. Admittedly, there is a spiritual component inherent in the concept of the lived body, which holds that the body is not something we have, but who we are. Body, movement and dance shine in this view, and along with this, the body of the earth.

Phenomenology sees earth as 'the living earth', not dead or inert matter. Linguistically, matter comes from *mater, mother*. Of course the earth is alive; it lives in geology and in breath as the entity that bears fruit and holds us. It lives in the wonder of landscape and in the support of our every step and leap. Every microbe of the earth is alive and active in the full orchestra of worlding. Heidegger used this term 'worlding' a lot, and I like it. Everything in the world is part of the worlding of the world. Let our part be supportive of all life, not degrading, heedless, or greedy. Meeting the vibrancy and love of matter is spiritual work. It requires us to make friends with mud and to see the shining beauty of time in the not-so-opulent parts of ageing.

AMANDA: *You are currently publishing a new book on phenomenological traditions within dance studies: can you share your book's themes and the perspectives you hope to offer?*

SONDRA: My essay inspires the new book. I discovered several kinds of phenomenologies in writing it, and there are more than I'm able to explain now. In anticipation of the new book, I have engaged several authors to write from the various perspectives I articulate in this issue, authors who have already contributed to the development of phenomenology and dance, and some who are emerging into the field. The book's themes are declared, but they could shift because phenomenology is about discovery.

We have a chapter on dance improvisation as phenomenological method, and one on Husserl and dance. Dance, phenomenology and epistemology come to the fore in one contribution. Another author takes up place, body, dance and film in urban renewal. Eco-improvisation leads another chapter forward. Ecstatic dance and phenomenology of religion appears as a theme. Body, dance and language are explored in a unique chapter, which is supported by experiential descriptions of dancers. Phenomenology beyond the ordinary makes a pivot toward the super-ordinary in a chapter on dance experiences. So far, my chapter is about living phenomenology. This is not a new theme, but I hope to reinvent it. This perspective opens a clearing where I can learn how to dance all over again, and what this means in my life now.

I hope to write about moving into life and finding centre, even when we are off-balance. Enter somatic processes: We can be in the flow of doing and dancing, not seeming to intend anything when our attention is present centred. We carry aims lightly in what we have learned how to do well; these are the learned abilities that transform how we move into life. Life is not always quite so rational and neat, however. In life as in dreams, we sometimes don't get resolution. Dreams teach us how to live with strangeness and difficulty, as does dancing.

Lateral intentionality and mindfulness occur to me as worth exploring, somatically. I don't actually know where I'll land, however. That's phenomenology.

AMANDA: *You are an American woman in a new century writing in the wake of French and German philosophers from the last century. Most of them were men. You are also a dancer and somatics professor and mentor. How is your work different from the original phenomenologists and from existential philosophy?*

SONDRA: I could write an article on this, but I'll be brief. I have been aware since the publication of *Dance and the Lived Body* (1987) that I would be in uncharted territory in existentialism. I had the feminist example of Simone de Beauvior, of course, but my voice was going to come through dance, a marginalized art in existentialism and philosophy overall. In phenomenology, I eventually discovered Sheets-Johnstone's work, but my orientation was entirely different.

There was madness in me in the beginning. I wanted to see how a woman in dance could write from experience and give new meaning to the concept of 'the lived body'. In *Dancing Identity: Metaphysics in Motion* (2004), I took other chances, expanding into ecological themes, and erasing boundaries between philosophy, poetry and storytelling. Matter, from *mater or mother*, became a new thematic.

My teacher in existential philosophy during my graduate work was Professor Arturo Fallico, author of *Art and Existentialism* (1962). When we studied 'the lived body' through Merleau-Ponty and others in the existentialist movement, I said to Dr Fallico: 'philosophers use lived body concepts in the other arts, but no one writes about dance'. I still remember what he said to me: 'That's your job Sondra'. Little did I know how seriously I would take his challenge to me.

Unlike existential phenomenology of the last century, my themes are feminist, womanist, aesthetic, and now somatic and ecological. I began to write a body-based philosophy through dance. As I continue to update it with current examples and insights, I realize how it has shaped me, and that I am created in my own voice.

The body is the fascinating home for all our dispositions. Spiritual qualities are embodied. We dance and sing them into being.

Contributor details

Amanda Williamson, Visiting Honorary Professor at Coventry University works within the field of somatic movement dance education within the broader context of dance studies, and with a specific specialist focus on Spirituality. She is the founding editor of the peer review journal *The Journal of Dance, Movement and Spiritualities*, which is situated within interdisciplinary frameworks, encouraging debate and promoting an academically rigorous engagement with spirituality. She is editor (with her colleagues Sarah Whately, Glenna Batson and Rebecca Weber) of *Dance, Somatics and Spiritualities: Contemporary Sacred Narratives*, and currently editing the book *Spiritual Herstories: Call of the Soul in Dance Research*. E-mail: ab8863@coventry.ac.uk

REFERENCES

Abram, David (1996), *The Spell of the Sensuous*, New York: Random House.

Barbour, Karen N. (2011), *Dancing Across the Page: Narrative and Embodied Ways of Knowing*, Bristol: Intellect Books.

Braude, Hillel (2015), 'Radical somatics', in S. Fraleigh (ed.), *Moving Consciously: Somatic Transformations through Dance, Yoga, and Touch*, Urbana: University of Illinois Press, pp. 124–34.

Brown, Charles S. and Toadvine, Ted (eds) (2003), *Eco-Phenomenology: Back to the Earth Itself*, Albany: State University of New York Press.

Buber, Martin (1958), *I and Thou* (trans. R. G. Smith), 2nd ed., New York: Charles Scribner's Sons.

Bruzina, Roland (1995), 'Translators introduction', in E. Fink and E. Husserl (eds), *Sixth Cartesian Meditation* (trans. R. Bruzina), Bloomington: Indiana University Press, pp. vii–xcii.

Damasio, Antonio (1994), *Descartes Error: Emotion, Reason, and the Human Brain*, New York: G. P. Putnam's Sons.

Damasio, Antonio (2012), *Self Comes to Mind: Constructing the Conscious Brain*, New York: Vintage Books, Random House Inc.

Fallico, Arturo (1962), *Art and Existentialism*, Englewood Cliffs: Prentice Hall.

Fink, Eugene and Husserl, Edmund (1995a), *Sixth Cartesian Meditation: The Idea of a Transcendental Theory of Method* (trans. and intro. R. Bruzina; textual notations and appendix E. Husserl), Bloomington: Indiana University Press.

Fink, Eugene and Husserl, Edmund (1995b), 'Appendices', in E. Fink (ed.), *Six Cartesian Meditation* (trans. R. Bruzina), Bloomington: Indiana University Press, pp. 163–92.

Fraleigh, Sondra (1987), *Dance and the Lived Body: A Descriptive Aesthetics*, Pittsburgh: University of Pittsburgh Press.

Fraleigh, Sondra (1991), 'A vulnerable glance: Seeing dance through phenomenology', *Dance Research Journal*, 23:1, Spring, pp. 11–16.

Fraleigh, S. (1999a), 'Witnessing the frog pond', in S. Fraleigh and P. Hanstein (eds), *Researching Dance: Evolving Modes of Inquiry*, Pittsburgh: University of Pittsburgh Press, pp. 188–224.

Fraleigh, Sondra (1999b), 'Freedom, gravity, and grace' (Part 1), *Somatics: Journal of Body/Mind Arts and Science*, 12:2, Spring/Summer, pp. 14–18.

Fraleigh, Sondra (1999c), 'Freedom, gravity, and grace' (Part 2), *Somatics: Journal of Body/Mind Arts and Science*, 12:3, Fall/Winter, pp. 8–13.

Fraleigh, Sondra (2000), 'Consciousness matters', *Dance Research Journal*, 32:1, Summer, pp. 54–62.

Fraleigh, Sondra (2002), 'Essay review of Maxine Sheets-Johnstone's the primacy of movement', *Dance Research Journal*, 34:1, Summer, pp. 119–25.

Fraleigh, Sondra (2004), *Dancing Identity: Metaphysics in Motion*, Pittsburgh: University of Pittsburgh Press.

Fraleigh, Sondra (2015a), *Moving Consciously: Somatic Transformations through Dance, Yoga, and Touch*, Urbana: University of Illinois Press.

Fraleigh, Sondra (2015b), 'Images of love and power in Butoh, Bausch, and Streb', in N. George-Graves (ed.), *Oxford Handbook of Dance and Theater*, New York: Oxford University Press, pp. 545–75.

Fraleigh, Sondra (2016), 'Enacting embodiment and blue muffins', in V. Midgelow and J. Bacon (eds), *Choreographic Practices*, vol. 6, 2nd ed., Bristol: Intellect Press, pp. 161–78.

Heidegger, Martin (1962), *Being and Time* (trans. J. Macquarrie and E. Robinson), New York: Harper & Row.

Heidegger, Martin (1971), 'The origin of the work of art', in *Martin Heidegger: Poetry, Language, Thought* (trans. A. Hofstadter), New York: Harper and Row, pp. 15–86.

Heidegger, Martin (1999), *Contributions to Philosophy (From Enowning)* (trans. P. Emad and K. Maly), Bloomington: Indiana University Press.

Husserl, Edmund ([1900–01] 1970), *Logical Investigations* (trans. J. N. Findlay), London: Routledge & Kegan Paul.

SOMATICS IN DANCE, ECOLOGY, AND ETHICS

Husserl, Edmund (1989), *Ideas Pertaining to a Pure Phenomenology and to a Phenomeno-logical Philosophy: Book 2, Ideas II* (trans. R. Rojcewicz and A. Schuwer), Boston: Kluwer Academic Publishers.

Kozel, Susan (2007), *Closer: Performance, Technologies, Phenomenology*, Cambridge: MIT Press.

Lukacs, Georg (1974), *Soul and Form* (trans. A. Bostock), Cambridge: MIT Press.

Marcel, Gabriel (1952), *Metaphysical Journal* (trans. B. Wall), Chicago: Henry Regnery.

McNamara, Joann (1999), 'Dance in the hermeneutic circle', in S. Fraleigh and P. Hanstein (eds), *Researching Dance: Evolving Modes of Inquiry*, Pittsburgh: University of Pittsburgh Press, pp. 162–87.

Merleau-Ponty, Maurice (1962), *Phenomenology of Perception* (trans. C. Smith), London: Routledge & Kegan Paul.

Merleau-Ponty, Maurice (1964a), *Signs* (trans. R. C. McLeary), Chicago: Northwestern University Press.

Merleau-Ponty, Maurice (1964b), *The Primacy of Perception and Other Essays* (ed. J. M. Edie and trans. C. Dallery), Evanston: Northwestern University Press.

Moustakas, Clark (1990), *Heuristic Research: Design, Method, and Applications*, Newbury Park: Sage Publications.

Nagatomo, Shigenori (1992), *Attunement through the Body*, Albany: State University of New York.

Nietzsche, Friedrich (1924), *The Joyful Wisdom* (trans. T. Common), New York: The Macmillan Company.

Nietzsche, Friedrich (1966), *Beyond Good and Evil* (trans. W. Kaufman), New York: Random House.

Pakes, Anna (2011), 'Phenomenology and dance: Husserlian meditations', *Dance Research Journal*, 43:2, Winter, pp. 33–49.

Sheets-Johnstone, Maxine ([1966] 2015), *Phenomenology of Dance*, Madison/Philadelphia: University of Wisconsin Press/Temple University Press.

Tillich, Paul (1952), *The Courage to Be*, New Haven: Yale University Press.

Warburton, Edward C. (2011), 'Of meanings and movements: Re-languaging embodiment in dance, phenomenology, and cognition', *Dance Research Journal*, 43:2, Winter, pp. 65–83.

11

Enacting Embodiment and Blue Muffins

IN THIS ESSAY, a dance of my imagining draws upon topics of embodiment, imperfection and lack of art, political art, implicatedness, boredom and being stupid. Questions of abstraction and records of thought hinge on discussions of disembodied movement, technology and performance. Key choreographic works include Blue Muffins; Bill T. Jones, GHOSTCATCHING; Troika Ranch, and Interactive Installations. Key sources include Susan Kozel's *Closer* (2007); Antonio Damasio's *Self Comes to Mind* (2012); and Francisco Varela's *The Embodied Mind* (1991). The essay explains movement and stillness as bodily enactments that can be arrested and recorded in arts technologies. Such records become part of why we care to make art, and how we make it matter.

Last night I fell asleep choreographing a new dance in my mind. Well I say it came into my mind, but my whole body was involved in the subliminal imagining, as I rolled around, lifted up, churned inside, and pictured dancers I know who might enter into the whole of it. I call the dance 'Blue Muffins'. Will I ever make it? Will anyone perform it? Maybe it will be for digital media, but with its beginnings first in real time – the actual time of first occurrence – with real people moving time–space. Perhaps we will make a video of our dancing and create a collage that would be impossible in real time, enjoying digitally overlapping embodiments once removed from first occurrence, maybe twice, or still more? Maybe a digital occurrence will overlay a first occurrence performance.

For me, the dance of my imagining springs out of nowhere, seemingly from artlessness, and, given its title, might remain there. As I turn around the possibilities, however, I believe 'Blue Muffins' might materialize, and not too badly. The dance will, of course depend on my ingenuity and the willingness of the dancers to trend into Blue Muffins. The budding project raises several questions for me, somewhat related to Heidegger's statement that 'a moment of history that lacks art' can be more genuinely creative than times of abundance, since art is often sustained by 'dominant goal-setting' (1999: 355–56). He implies that art arises not out of

SOMATICS IN DANCE, ECOLOGY, AND ETHICS

surplus but in the face of absence – and that originality, which he often likened to *ursprung*/'original leap', like 'Blue Muffins' (quickly losing their springiness), draws upon a dearth of productivity to set forth treasure in some perceivable form or act. Heidegger speaks of drawing up from the 'closed' ground of consciousness, and 'setting forth in the open' as the process of invention in his article, 'The origin of the work of art' (1971: 74–76). However imperfect and silly my idea, it has potential. For one thing, it does not suggest perfection. More, does it court creative romp through enactments of embodiment – and recycling of these, perhaps, through technological means.

The word 'embodiment' is popular in intellectual writing lately, as though one had to do something to be embodied! Are we not embodied in being born? But I get it! There is more to embodiment than just being here. Embodiment also promises an activity if we are to do it well and not just hang out with it. In dancing we move consciously. Maybe we move in any old way we wish, but more often dancers move with care: delicately, in loops and falls, in tight little balls of fire, in blue dough, or maybe in complex cascades that relate to others in complicated pathways. Dancing can happen quite simply, or be a performance with finish and aplomb. It has so many manifestations, which is one of the reasons I like to dance and to write about it.

Dance, I believe, is fundamental to doing embodiment well, an enactment of energies and forms in a process of actions that fill gaps in time that might otherwise be lacks or absences. When we dance, we can fulfill ourselves, what we might be, what we are, and what we are becoming. Our becoming is not lost or wasted in dancing; indeed, in all creative endeavours we save and record time. If I ever make 'Blue Muffins', the time of its making and performance, will be special, and not lost. Its embodied knowledge will be recorded in memory. I will remember it, as will the dancers, and maybe the audience if there is one.

Will 'Blue Muffins' be an aesthetic or a political dance? Might it be both at once if it is effective in its embodied enactments? As art, dance is political because it calls us to originality. It proffers origins in its workings, the very matter that Heidegger explained. Art wants to fill a lack, and shake up the status quo. Art is non-competitive and non-partisan in its politics. Its arguments are self-contained and *immanent*, or one could also say *heuristic* as discovered in the experience of artists and witnesses. Of course artists have commitments and these show up in what they make, but hopefully not in a slip towards propaganda. Art is not created as a commodity nor aimed towards influence; it cultivates affections of the heart, engaging unique embodied practices that keep us curious and alert. Artists challenge our interpretive capacities. Noting else serves to interrupt and shift perception as art does. If my dance does nothing more than make people think about their assumptions, it will be political. If it baffles them into laughter or smiles, it will be political. If its aesthetic character makes them sense lazuli blueness, it will be unexpectedly political, maybe dimly dark. If it makes them hesitate before saying the thing they usually say, it will be pragmatically political and psychologically useful. We embody aesthetics, sociality and politics at the same time – incorporating affective life and revealing belief. We move our persuasions into being, just as surely as we sometimes falter and fail.

Dancers who practice improvisational methods elicit faltering beauty and the uncertain politics of vanishing moments. At best, they extend themselves to meet nascent circumstances with trust and courage. Wishing circumstances to be different would seem a hindering complaint. Our body of doing and decision is part of the shifting earth and living world. We hesitate and breathe, and in breathing anew, we feel better. Each new day offers potential for inspired renewal. I have this opportunity re-embody if I take it. The act of dancing, in particular, brings favourable chances. When we dance, we develop our capacities for enacting embodiment; this is the material, political ground bass of dance. In dancing with others, we have still more opportunities to experience periods of heightened performance and interpersonal synchrony, enhancing a sense of *togetherness*.

The position of Husserlian phenomenology is that we are not alone, rather we are embedded in the world we see around us, as also people and happenings in the world that may escape our immediate attention. Husserl questioned the empirical view that the world is experienced as objectively already present, prior to any reflection upon it. He called the unquestioned bias that the world pre-exists and is separate from you and me *the natural attitude* (1900–1901, 1970; also Fink 1995: 166). What seems natural may be a habit of thought, an inherited belief, or an ingrained movement. It is the job of phenomenology to question habits that cover something we would benefit from noticing. What seems separate, as objectively other, may not be so very far away or different. What Husserl called 'the flowing live present' (Fink 1995: xiv) includes the human and human history as part of 'the life world'. Existentialism took phenomenology in the direction of psychology, at the same time amplifying Husserl's conceptions. Merleau-Ponty's view of the unity of world and body is presented in 'The World as Perceived', Part II of *The Phenomenology of Perception*, which begins this way:

> Our own body is in the world as the heart is in the organism: it keeps the visible spectacle constantly alive, it breathes life into it and sustains it inwardly, and with it forms a system.
>
> (1962: 235)

We are in every moment enacting embodiment, that of self-becoming, of relational-becoming, and of our belonging to the world's body, which we overlook at our peril. Does it really matter that we grasp relational becoming? Why does it matter that we understand ourselves as implicated in a wider world? I believe it matters in every possible way. It influences how we treat each other, rippling through the continuum of human and more-than-human nature and also the earth as ecological home. Kimerer LaMothe's recent book (2015) develops a similar view of relational becoming in dance from several vantages. My belief that the world's body is not separate from our own is part of the politics of my dancing. The manner of our relational becoming shapes the matter and meaning of our dances; we dance to generate who we can become, indeed to realize more abundant embodiment and world-friendly connectivity.

Then why is the path towards abundance fraught with obstacles, seemingly not of our own choosing? I have observed that when everything is humming along easily, I get bored and trouble the still waters, needing something to do or to create that peaks my attention and carries me past *ennui*. I could be wrong, but I think that most people want a challenge, although I did see a comedian last night whose humour centred on his being dumb and liking it, also on hating exercise or anything remotely physical. I do not think that being stupid and doing nothing, however, motivate most people. Psychologist Mihaly Csikszentmihalyi in his studies of happiness and self-actualization describes a state of 'flow', in which people are so involved in an activity that nothing else seems to matter (1990). His research shows that being in flow, makes people happy. We sometimes speak of such states as 'being in the zone', or 'in the groove'. Daunting to consider that we invite possible happiness in the manner of our daily performances and embodied practices.

Advances in technology pose special questions for considering embodiment, flow and enactment. Contexts for dance bring these into sharp relief. Uses of technology in dance performances are not antithetical to flowing states of consciousness. Indeed, they have the potential to enhance tactile flow of activities, locations and togetherness.

This morning I took photographs with my iPhone and recorded video footage of performances in Snow Canyon in Utah, close to where I live. Robert and I left for the canyon at dawn when the shadows would be long in our dances amidst the petrified sandstone dunes. We felt our way first into the smooth and creviced stones; then finding the dance in bare feet, we paused in between takes to improvise fanciful costumes and exchange cameras. Later we went over all the recorded images at our outdoor breakfast under the burnt-rose mountain of Kayenta. From the explorations, we thought we might have a least five projects to peak our curiosity (an overflow of muffins). The outdoor theatre and possibilities of the camera seemed endless to us, as the day stretched into breath and colour.

Questions about dance and technology, especially possible dehumanization of dance through technology, have been asked at least since Alwin Nikolais'

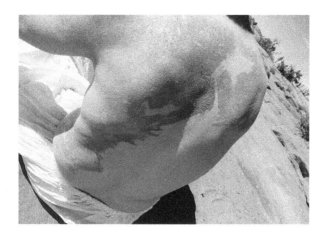

FIGURE 11.1: Robert Bingham in Blue Muffins, a work in process. Photograph by Sondra Fraleigh, 2015.

FIGURE 11.2: Lesly Chamberlain and Roman Morris in 'Magic Egg Butoh', a metamorphic Place-Dance by Sondra Fraleigh. Photograph by Sondra Fraleigh, 2015.

multimedia works of the mid-twentieth century in which he employed an armada of slide projectors. I studied with Nikolais in the early 1960s and felt a great deal of flow in working with props and movement abstractions overlaid with imagistic projections of light and colour. I also enjoyed flowing kinaesthetic moments in witnessing his highly visual multimedia extravaganzas. And he would not be the first to explore methods for shifting perceptions of movement through imagistic manipulations of light and costume. Loie Fuller (1862–1928), a contemporary of Isadora Duncan, extended choreography with light, colour, movement, and prop-extensions of silky fabric.

Electronic music with its own technological means has grown alongside technologies in dance. There is a long history of electronic music in dance performance. Many choreographers rounding the turn into the twenty-first century have borrowed inspiration from Edgard Varese's colliding sound masses in *Poem Electronic* (1958), Karlheinz Stockhausen's orbiting sounds in *Kontakte* (1960), as also the burning embers and naturally occurring statistical distribution of Iannis Xenakis's early work *ConcretPH* (1958). Now with the growth of computer technology, today's electronic music demonstrates many more divergent practices and opportunities for music and dance collaborations. Gordon Mumma, one of Cunningham's collaborators, chronicles developments in cybersonic arts and twentieth-century-music in a recent book about cofounding the Cooperative Studio for Electronic Music (2015).

To trouble myself further with questions of abstraction and technology, I want to know if movement can be disembodied? I first posed this question in an article called 'Soma strokes and second chances', an exhibition essay for 'Digital Incarnate: The Body, Identity and Interactive Media' (Fraleigh 2010b). Now I see other facets of the question. If movement can be disembodied, it would need to be a discrete thing in itself. Can movement be clearly separated from its entanglements with local material embodiments as also the wider world? Movement exists in waves of many kinds, from sound waves to ocean waves. Sound itself has many sources, as musicians will attest, and ocean waves exhibit through water. Dance is often defined as movement, but it is more. As made of movement, stillness, and affect, dance is enacted through human embodiment, and the latter, ongoing and never quite complete, is a process of becoming that entails the whole person.

As a close relative of *enactment, performance* is also more than movement. Both terms suggest the arts, but are not limited to them. The fullest account of *enactment of embodiment* is found in Francisco Varela's studies of cognition, which he relates to phenomenology (and tangentially to Buddhist groundlessness). His focus is an *enactive cognitive science*, not movement as such, but sensorimotor pathways to embodied mind. In completing a cognitive loop, he accounts for doing as knowing, and knowing as doing. Along with Evan Thompson and Eleanor Rosch, he produced a study of embodiment of mind (1991), explaining that human beings enact and bring forth their own domains of knowledge, that the nervous system generates meaningful patterns, and that cognition is not a form of thinking separate from embodiment; rather, it is a form of embodied action. Their work demonstrates how cognitive structures emerge from recurrent sensorimotor patterns of perception and action. Their studies in biology, psychology, and philosophy reveal that what we commonly call 'the world' is not an external fact represented internally by the brain, but arises in relational mode of consciousness. Earlier, we considered the foundational work of Husserl in this regard. Shortly, we turn to Damasio on the same topic. Focusing on dance enaction, Edward Warburton in his article on dance, cognitive enactment and phenomenology, shows how cognitive theories of enaction are relevant to contexts of dancer action and performance (2011).

Considered in light of enactment, perhaps it is impossible to separate human movement from its living source and sensory interconnections? This is the question I want to answer, or at least test. We know the body as presented in dance on film is removed from its living, organic state. In film, the body exists digitally or on celluloid and not as flesh, but the body can also exist as flesh and on film at once, as in the multigenre, multimedia works of Laterna Magika in Prague. I first saw this key group in the development of modern Czech theatre in 1965, seven years after its inception when then Czechoslovakia was under communist rule and I was studying dance with Mary Wigman in a divided Berlin in Germany. As a young American lost in translation, I stumbled upon this fascinating theatre. Travel, more than anything, has taught me about my unquestioned assumptions. In Europe that year, I saw how much I shared with others, and at the same time, how limited my experience was. I wondered how Laterna Magika might have changed when I saw them again in 2005, some 40 years later. The major difference was clearly in technology. The early use of mime and gestural dance, creatively staged mostly in silence, had evolved to panoramic screen, electronic music scores, and mythical stories enveloped in filmic dance, which would be impossible to perform in real time on a traditional proscenium stage. In those 40 years, technology had become an underlying constant in my world, and travels my political teacher.

I am beginning to understand movement as a correlational attribute, part of our entire human becoming, and merely one of the ways we describe happenings in the world and ourselves. If movement is part of sound and vision, part of all sensory perception, and a constant in technologies that help shape perception, can it actually be singular, separable and primary? When I turn my head, my eyes move, as do the potentials of my hearing. Phenomenology through Merleau-Ponty (and others) has held that movement, expression, cognition and body are part of each other, and cannot be separated (1964: 66–67). Human movement is grounded in perception and sensation, or we could also say, 'embodied responsiveness'. It inevitably encompasses modes of memory and consciousness as physical and mental at once. Embodied movement does not contain consciousness; it is consciousness in action. Movement is not merely something we do; more, it is what we are, both volitionally and involuntarily. When I play the piano, I generally do not think of every single note, but rather employ consciousness in a particular way so that my fingers find the keys through attention, memory and practice. What I hear feeds back to me in loops of awareness that sustain the flow. Sound and movement function together with my hands, indeed the whole of me in the music I embody.

But I do get it! We speak about movement and often understand it as a singular phenomenon. Movement is a sign for life – amoebas move as they ooze. Change is another word for movement; we notice qualitative, particular manners of change – smoothness and bumpiness, for instance. Movement does require a home, however. It needs some kind of body – a body of water, a human hand, or a thrown rock – before it 'materializes', that is, before it comes to our attention as an occurrence. *Human movement is concrete through its embodied enactment.* Perceptually, however, it might separate in the abstract: in an image, for instance. Movement cannot be subtracted from embodiment as a singular phenomenon, but it can shift its status from that of immediate enactment to manifestations that are once or more removed from the original source. In such cases, one can have fun with abstraction. I'm talking about 'Blue Muffins' in the digital world. The dance could be taken from the original enactment of the dancers and poured through digital media of several kinds, which would render it, shall we say, 're-embodied' in terms of its original source. But the source, I argue, would remain as part of 'Blue Muffins'. However removed from the original version of the dance, traces of the dancers would remain in the final film or whatever iteration ensued from the source performance. The dancers could in fact see themselves once, or twice, or more times removed. I think the process might in itself prove curiously poignant for the dancers who could see themselves outside of their immediate experience of movement in a semblance of the dance or in digital particles of it. And it could offer the audience a vision of re-embodiments. (On this point, I should be careful, or I'll talk myself into a muffin project.)

Is not one of the functions of the arts to give us ways of seeing ourselves, or of experiencing ourselves once removed? The stage exists for this purpose. It puts life at a distance, while drawing it towards us in more concentration. Advances in technology have extended this function of abstraction still further – extracting movement semblance from its original owner and rendering it 'other' in images and traces. Perhaps it goes without saying but is worth noticing that otherness, even the otherness of our own embodiment, can be an occasion for delight and learning. Otherness, sometimes neighbourly or even threatening modulates consciousness. We can become other to ourselves, where we and our own other each are inversions of the other, not alien, but in proximity and with the ability to turn inside out as well as return. The basic point is phenomenological – a matter of awareness. The Other I'm speaking of is not a fixed entity, but a morphing presence whereby artists get to test their own presence in a game-like fashion. If the game, or dance, proffers excellence, it would require expertise from both sides, that of

FIGURE 11.3: *Other Stories* (2007). Photographed by Devon Cody. Dancer Inka Juslin.

the original enactment, and also that of the technological rendition. I envision an artistic venture of well-matched others (the original enactment and the digital version) bringing out the best in each other.

Susan Kozel provides a good example of this pursuit in her book, *Closer: Performance, Technologies, Phenomenology* (2007), documenting her interactive performances with other dancers and collaborators. Her work explores the politics of bodies as reflected through technology in what she calls 'a poetics of responsivity'. Interactive work asks the audience to meet it, she holds, and not sit in a passive mode. Kozel's very full study in *Closer* (2007), and her performance works, emphasize that technology and embodiment are not opposed, but rather function through 'in-betweenness', the space in between bodies, locations, collaborators, computer-generated images and audiences. Moreover, these spaces are lived poetically. (In Japanese aesthetics, particularly in butoh, the space between is known as 'ma', as I write about extensively in an earlier work, 2010.) Phenomenologically, Kozel speaks in a first-person experiential voice about moving across nebulous regions between locations 'where our images traveled and were transformed' (2007: 113). Wearable computers and cameras often facilitate the art of in-betweens in Kozel's performances. Her performances and writing achieve a coherent philosophy of the relationship of dance and technology honed over many years.

Technology could not be 'Other' as alien in such a view. Artists and their technologies are products of human interrelatedness and world implications. Otherness, in this view is near, even when seemingly far in the distance, or worn on the body. We see up close how technology permeates our lives, when we watch

3-year olds handle iPhones to their delight. The daughter of my niece likes to get the phone to play music for her, and to babble messages out towards imaginary others. Holding to the phenomenology of Husserl and Merleau-Ponty, I understand that creative arts technologists are implicated in an interactive world that is already in them.

Theatre has traditionally provided a 'seeing place', or stage, for societal interaction and testing of identity. Theatre provides the syncretic space between so called 'real life' and fiction, even when based on non-fiction. Dance and visual art reflect human experience, directly through embodied enactment and preverbally, even as language assists movement conceptually in the thinking body. In all of the arts, we get a peek at ourselves as standing outside of our bodies. Dance is perhaps the most problematic in this respect, because it does not or cannot exist outside of the body. Or can it do so in some sense, as we have been asking? Is not one of the deep purposes of dance to help us step outside of our bodies? When we *see*

FIGURE 11.4: *Other Stories* (2007). Photographed by Devon Cody. Dancer Susan Kozel.

FIGURE 11.5: *Whispers* (2004). Photographed by Elisa Gonzalez. Co-directed by Thecla Schiphorst, Susan Kozel, and Sang Mah.

and are *seen* in dance, we understand the aesthetically motivated, psychophysical thinking of the body. It separates in remembered images: visual and felt, kinaesthetically lived as sharp or shadowed, heard, or maybe descriptively interpreted. As a witness, I love to see complicated dance, hard to do movement, virtuoso; and I gravitate to the somatically simple as well. The connective interval in expansive witnessing offers me grounds for optimism; I understand the complexities and beauty of myself in the dance of others. As to be seen and known in dance magnifies my awareness of self in relation to others, I see myself as others do, maybe not exactly, but nearly. Allowing space between provides a perceptual opportunity for *responsive otherness*.

Through speech and social interactions, as also in the arts, we send our bodies away, and they return in our perceptions. We share embodiment interactively and specifically. Technology affords particular discoveries in terms of abstraction and perception. If motion can be abstracted from the body through technological means, it is nevertheless through our living bodies in real time that we will eventually perceive its primal sources and abstracted forms. If we can abstract motion from the body, there is nevertheless someone, a person, who will observe the recorded images, and people have preferences and peculiarities that make them tick. I believe that what exists in perception is a matter of individual consciousness, and I'm not talking about 'the tree in the forest'. I simply want to say, as is the basis of phenomenology, that perception and consciousness matter as the very means of enacting embodiments, and that enacting is more than movement. At the very least, it involves moving as thinking, feeling and knowing. I relate this level of knowing to performance – the ability to act (to perform) and to a reflective self-knowing that Antonio Damasio's *Self Comes to Mind* describes as arising in somatic stages (2012: 24), each stage more conscious of self and other, and consciously related to the living world.

There is something basic behind the question of abstraction, something suggested in the very attempt to extract motion from its source material. All of the arts require bodily enactment in the first instance. They all require performances of some kind. Making is about bringing something into being; Blue Muffins might become a dance or something to eat, but we will never know unless I do something about it. Creativity involves movement, albeit in bodily immanent differing modes and clothed in variables of belief. As part of space and time, movement in the abstract is modification and change. As human, movement is communicative; it is realized in expression and enacted through intention and purpose, unless accidentally. Enactments entail performed interactions – personal and communal – at least enactments in the arts, which are risked and shared in public arenas.

Interactive media art through advanced technology renders embodied immanence (or 'within-ness') more apparent in unique ways, allowing momentary bypass of narrative content, sometimes emotional or expressive in performance. But as we move in towards somatic origins, we might also notice in terms of narrative, that digital iteration may distill and intensify the body's organic threads. This is the power of abstraction. When we remove the muscle of movement in digital tracings, we have the paradoxical opportunity to experience it with more distance while zeroing in on it at the same time. This is what abstraction is about.

To abstract is to draw forth, at least this is a root meaning. Performance is not so much about expression as it is the wellspring of expression, its *ursprung*, if you will. Creativity in performance draws upon preverbal bodily sources, the somatic background of expression. By the time the words or movements are realized in performance, the deep sources are smiling quietly. Do they get any credit? Do they not provide us momentary links to what Damasio calls 'a pulse of core self' (2012: 24)? I would like to point, at least, in this direction. The neuroscience of Damasio explains the somatosensory system and its relationship to movement and emotion as basic to the emergence of thought and eventually to the autobiographical or historical sense of personhood. Damasio states that consciousness, 'the part of mind concerned with apparent sense of self and knowing', begins with the use of body signals when organisms acquire the ability to tell stories without words. Knowledge of what the organism is living through emerges (Damasio 1999: 30–31). We could say that dances are stories without words, even though they do not always tell stories. If a dance is simply about moving, or being, or morphing, as many dances are, the mode of 'aboutness' is the wordless story.

Part of Damasio's project in neuroscience is concerned with embodied creativity – to show how, as he says, 'the ability to transform and combine images of actions and scenarios is the wellspring of creativity' (1999: 24). In making dances, as in all of the arts, the *subliminal soma* which is the preverbal basis for affectivity, specifically the ability to feel and be moved, can be coaxed to awareness through attention – triggering feelings, images, and ideas in consciousness. Damasio develops a view of the somatic basis and totality of the minded body, explaining how the deep layers of the soma, the proto self and core self, underlie life, quietly and automatically (1999: 170–74). I have observed wordless stories coming to the surface of consciousness through direction of intention in meditation, somatic movement facilitation, and in dancing – in both the doing and witnessing, especially through the improvisations where we let go of any conscious effort to control or remember the movement. Letting go of excess effort can be beneficial, as hopefully in 'Blue Muffins' and perhaps a blue muffin video attempt.

Technology enables distinct ways into the subliminal soma, as we see this surfacing in the computer-generated strokes of such works as Bill T. Jones's *GHOSTCATCHING*, distilling emotional traces of capture and breaking free. His work is made possible through advances in 'motion capture', a technology that tracks motion through sensors attached to a body. The resulting record captures forms of motion, without preserving the body, at least the material physical body. Such captured phrases then become the basis for virtual composition, as they are edited, rechoreographed, and staged for a digital performance in the 3D space of the computer. As a result, we witness a virtual dance that can recall its organic source. I think of these forms as 'soma strokes' somewhat like painters' marks that nevertheless bear the imprint of their origin. The human body is implied, implicate in the explicate order.

Another question that interests me is how collaborative interactive installations such as those of Troika Ranch engage contemporary society. What is their particular relevance in our world today? On first glance, one might say that their very interactivity speaks to our times, as cultural borders disappear in part and the globe becomes more interactive through technology. Troika Ranch combines traditional aspects of live performance, interactive installations and digital film with advanced technologies. The hybrid triad dance/theatre/media in cooperative interaction is Troika. Ranch is a homey sprawling word that seems to designate a place of meeting and working together. Dawn Stoppiello and Mark Coniglio with their team of collaborators have developed much of the technology they employ in their art, allowing works such as *Loop Diver* (2009) to answer questions about the influence of technology on contemporary life. More particular to physical and emotional experience their relentless examination of the moving body in a digital age enquires into fundamental shifts of embodiment in relation to technology. The repetition of short phases of movement in *Loop Diver* using atomic loop structures shows perfection of computer renditions against the imperfection of human performance in the moment. Human movement is full of flaws in contrast, but to my mind more interesting in 'noise'. Mechanical perfection gets boring after a while, but not in juxtaposition with live dance.

The work I encountered in writing for 'Digital Incarnate' (Fraleigh 2010b) shows that digitized art rooted in live dance and performance can have its own integrity as a form and achieve independent value. Electronic media can excavate and extend the live performance of dance, as Merce Cunningham proved more than a decade ago with *Biped*, made in collaboration with two digital artists: Marc Downie and Paul Kaiser. The innovative approach of Downie and Kaiser frequently combines non-photorealistic 3D rendering, the incorporation of body movement by motion-capture and other means, and the autonomy of artworks assisted by artificial intelligence. Since *Biped*, developments in technology have crossed disciplinary boundaries of art and performance, responding to an expanding range of materials in visual drawings, film, motion capture, photography, music, and architecture's invention of interactive science museums.

This brings me back to my question, but from the perspective of values, the 'why' of it all. Why try to capture movement or remove it from its bodily source in the arts? On one level, it gives us the ability to capture and observe consciousness in action, especially enactments of embodiment in making and doing. Such observations of consciousness have the potential value of extending perception in the larger field of human awareness. It is significant that through awareness, we can learn to direct and focus our thoughts. Electronic, digitized works can make us more consciously aware of our creative image-making abilities. Technology need not divide us from organic life; it can reveal it imagistically and creatively.

Images (patterns, forms, gestalts) are basic materials in the arts, be they revealed in forms of movement, sound images, visual, digitally distilled or the thought images of writing. They give us pause to see ourselves from outside (spatially) and glancing back (in time). All art is abstract in this sense. Performances stop time

FIGURE 11.6: Sondra Fraleigh in 'Visiting Butch Cassidy's Cabin', 2015. Place-Performance collaboration with Robert Bingham. Video and computer generated music by Sondra Fraleigh. YouTube: https://youtu.be/lkpnErW5eQ8.

and space, making it stand out and saving it at the same time. Books save forms of thought in writing, dances preserve gestalts of the thinking body. When works dive inward to show the will to do and make in action, they capture something of the somatic background of imagery in a glance and feeling. We commonly assume that what we call 'the outside world' is the basis of images, but in Damasio's refusal to separate body and mind, he teaches that 'a vast proportion of the images the ever arise in the brain are shaped by signals from the body-proper' (2003: 214). The brain-body maps images that are experienced in the body-proper, while the body-proper informs brain maps.

Because digital technologies can stop minute slices of movement, they have a chance to draw up somatic backgrounds of embodiment. Advances in technology give us myriad interesting reasons to go to all the trouble of dancing, and of making video installations, and computer-generated interactive art. Engaging such troubles, we have a chance to glimpse our experiential entwinement in the world, signalling from deeply embodied sources. Technology need not divide us from the organic and natural world, it can remind us of our belonging and promise individuation at the same time. My 'digital twin' (a term coined by Kozel) might not be me in the flesh, but it certainly is not anyone else. It reminds me of myself dancing in a slice of time. It talks to me of where I was and now am. In the image, I grasp moments of who I am – immanently and interactively.

Humans are curious. We like to make marks whereby we identify our world and imagine ourselves anew, engaging each other in the processes and the results. We call these marks art. As specifically marking the tenor of contemporary life, technology helps us extend these marks, extending our possible-selves and possible-world in the process. We create histories and politics in such marks, inscribing belief. Damasio shows that records of events and things we once perceived include the original motor adjustments we made, how we moved and also our emotional reactions, which are themselves responsive movements. Mind and memory are made of motor adjustments and emotional responses. 'You simply cannot escape the affectation of your organism, motor and emotional most of all, that is part and parcel of having a mind' (Damasio 1999: 148).

Technology can render human and other embodiments in abstracted forms, removing traces, forms and indicating feelings of movement, but it does rely on original occurrences – bodily enactments. And if the world is in us through our implicatedness as phenomenology teaches, then technology is not an alien-other sci-fi character, but increasingly part of the evolving world that is part of us. We have choices, however, and can use technology for good or for ill. Sometimes, we need to stop everything in order to see and hear more clearly. This is a necessary caesura in the ongoing flow. Meditation can do this, stillness in dance can, and so can photography. Photography is a basic technology that has selected and captured movement since the mid-nineteenth century, but it does require an embodied subject – a dancer, or a melting mountaintop. Movement and stillness are bodily enactments that can be arrested and recorded in arts technologies. They become part of why we care to make art, and how we make it matter. The marriage of art and technology is of great value when we use it to extend human capacities for caring, which is after all the goal of being aware and awake to the flowing live present, the politics of filling a lack with art.

REFERENCES

Csikszentmihalyi, Mihaly (1990), *Flow: The Psychology of Optimal Experience*, New York: Harper and Row.

Damasio, Antonio (1999), *The Feeling of What Happens: Body and Emotion in the Making of Consciousness*, New York: Harcourt Brace and Co.

Damasio, Antonio (2003), *Looking for Spinoza: Joy, Sorrow, and the Feeling Brain*, New York: Harcourt Inc.

Damasio, Antonio (2012), *Self Comes to Mind: Constructing the Conscious Brain*, New York: Vintage Books, Random House Inc.

Fink, Eugen (1995), *Sixth Cartesian Meditation: The Idea of a Transcendental Theory of Method, with Textual Notations by Edmund Husserl* (trans. R. Bruzina), Bloomington: Indiana University Press.

Fraleigh, Sondra (2010a), *BUTOH: Metamorphic Dance and Global Alchemy*, Urbana: University of Illinois Press.

Fraleigh, Sondra (2010b), 'Soma strokes and second chances', exhibition essay, *Digital Incarnate: The Body, Identity, and Interactive Media* (curated by Alycia Scott and Sara Slawnik), Columbia College Chicago, 8 February–2 April.

Heidegger, Martin (1971), *'The origin of the work of art'*, in Heidegger, *Poetry, Language, Thought* (trans. and intro. A. Hofstadter), New York: Harper and Row, pp. 15–86.

Heidegger, Martin (1999), *Contributions to Philosophy (From Enowning)* (trans. P. Emad and K. Maly), Bloomington: Indiana University Press.

Husserl, Edmund ([1900–01] 1970), *Logical Investigations* (trans. J. N. Findlay), 1st ed., London: Routledge & Kegan Paul.

Kozel, Susan (2007), *Closer: Performance, Technologies, Phenomenology*, Cambridge: MIT Press.

LaMothe, Kimerer (2015), *Why We Dance: A Philosophy of Bodily Becoming*, New York: Columbia University Press.

Merleau-Ponty, Maurice (1962), *Phenomenology of Perception* (trans. C. Smith), London: Routledge & Kegan Paul.

Merleau-Ponty, Maurice (1964), *Signs* (trans. R. C. McLeary), Chicago: Northwestern University Press.

SOMATICS IN DANCE, ECOLOGY, AND ETHICS

Mumma, Gordon (2015), *Cybersonic Arts: Adventures in New Music* (ed. F. Michelle), Champaign: University of Illinois Press.

Varela, Francisco J., Thompson, E. and Rosch, E. (1991), *The Embodied Mind: Cognitive Science and Human Experience*, Cambridge: MIT Press.

Warburton, Edwaard C. (2011), 'Of meanings and movements: Re-languaging embodiment in dance, phenomenology, and cognition', *Dance Research Journal*, 43:2, Winter, pp. 65–83.

12

Attunement and Evanescence

THE FOLLOWING ESSAY is both subjective and theoretic, based on personal conviction, and also an enduring fascination with the potentials of dancing relative to Buddhist philosophy. Butoh, the postmodern dance of Japan, appears in context, especially where it relates to the terms of the title. Zen poetry in the form of haiku dots the essay throughout. We also note that in Japan, last names come first.

Mono no aware

Experiences of Zen emptiness are individuated in a variety of ways and understood circumstantially. We also grasp them existentially through the lens of poetry, movement and dance, as in this Zen haiku of Nakagawa Soen (quoted in Kazuaki and Tensho 1996: 30):

> Inside the zendo also
> dancing
> evening maple leaves

I like the ease and simplicity of Nakagawa's poem. It speaks of season, place and time, and also contains a conundrum or surprise. Zen haiku should do all of this in a few syllables. The setting of this poem is a zendo where maple leaves blow in the wind. If the leaves *also* dance, what else is dancing that we don't see? The poetic whole inspires Zen emptiness without naming it, while setting dance apart and giving it significance through nature. In a few words, Nakagawa visions sensitivity to ephemera and fleeting time appreciated in Japanese literature as *mono no aware* (impermanence). Zen focuses on the evanescence of being itself, the coming and going of everything. Death as part of life is understood in Zen, particularly in the generation/extinction principle of Dōgen (later we take a closer look at the lasting significance of this thirteenth-century reformer of Buddhism in Japan).

SOMATICS IN DANCE, ECOLOGY, AND ETHICS

I don't believe butoh dancer Ashikawa Yoko ever professed such Zen influences, but I nevertheless gathered them from her dancing, as I do from much of butoh. I remember her morph through disappearance in dance. Melting, she could float to the floor ostensibly boneless and dry – like a drifting leaf. Ashikawa was the primary protégé of Hijikata Tatsumi who founded butoh, the postmodern dance of Japan, now global in participation, and arising slowly in the latter twentieth century amid the ashes of the Second World War. It seemed to me that Ashikawa expressed Zen single pointedness when she danced. Zen and butoh are not the same, of course, but in my experiences of both, they often share similarities. I took classes with Ashikawa when I lived in Tokyo in 1991, and saw her dance at the Joyce Theater in New York on 22 October 1992. She danced in *Nagareru Kubi* (*Floating Visage*) that I mention above. There were others in the dance, but her self-erasure etched in my memory, as she emptied towards nothingness.

FIGURE 12.1: Sondra Fraleigh at age 75 near her home in Southwest (Color Country) Utah. Photo by Kay Nelson © 2014, used with permission.

One month after seeing Ashikawa perform in New York, I woke in the mountains near Tokyo very early on a November morning at the Maple Leaf Monastery in Yumoto Hakone. I had come to meditate at the small wooden temple on the grounds. My friend Akane Akiko and I walked to the temple in the morning dark and stillness. After shuffling through damp maple leaves in preparation for meditation, we were alone in the chilly temple, except for the officiating monk. I can still smell the dark sweetness of the temple, the dew on the leaves, and will always carry the memory of Akiko's father Shodo Akane-sensei, whom I acknowledge as my Zen teacher. He is noted for helping Japanese businessmen integrate Zen into their work, and smiles when he says his other student is an American dancer.

Akane-sensei gave me only two pieces of advice: 'Every day be beautiful', and 'empty yourself and dance'. That was more than twenty years ago, and to this day, I attune to his advice. He gave me my Zen name of 'Bright Road Friend', which also means 'gathering beings together in learning', he told me. Sometimes I question that he didn't say, 'teach'. Rather he said, 'be a friend'. My life had been caught up in study and teaching, mostly teaching and writing about dance, art and philosophy. Now I have finally graduated, and can just be a friend.

Non-possession and just dancing

Emptiness and evanescence relate to the Zen principle of non-possession. Let me explain in personal terms and then through dance. I know I'm a possessive person. I hold onto things, which dispose me to worry. So a big part of my work in the world has been to learn how to let go and trust that everything will work out well. When I can do this, it does, and I become beautiful. When I interject my worries and expectations, they turn back on me, and I get tangled up in the ugliness of control. I totter. When I let go and practice patience, I can see a way through perceived problems. I dance. I dance to know myself, my capabilities and potentials, my shadows and fears. I dance to be free of ownership, free of egotism and to feel my human continuity with other beings and also with the environmental world of rivers and rocks, animals and plants. Dance provides a means of enquiry, the movement of which reaches in – and in crisis may totter – the movement of which cannot be held as mine. In Zen, non-possession is an attainment. In dance, non-possession manifests as guilelessness.

Zen emphasizes right livelihood as a way towards non-possession. Here 'right' is not so much a moral edict, but rather a pragmatic one. To be happy, we need to know how to integrate discrete acts of doing with larger purposes of living. I have had pause many times to reflect on dance as a career, dance as theatre and also as a profession in education. I have often questioned my relationship to dance, since it would seem a great deal of my livelihood has been through what I call in various guises 'dance', which really has no existence beyond the definitions and manifestations at hand (art, therapy, fun, freeze, and much more). Dance fades and falters; it soars and breathes, and then it goes away when we lose track of it. When we attune to some aspect of what we know as dance, it magically reappears. This I know: that even as I hold dance dear, it slips through my fingers.

Looking back, I see that dance has never been my livelihood, nor has it been my profession or career. Having ways to dance has given me self-sustaining work and play. As work, art, ritual and play, dance can be undertaken in a Zen frame of mind. One can dance for intrinsic purposes, for the value contained in the act itself, and not for end gaining, as one might say somatically. On a metaphysical level, I have danced through my understandings of yoga and Zen to transform my attitude towards work and everyday rituals.

In the largest sense, I dance to live towards light and peace. I have been a university teacher of dance, so it would seem my livelihood. But 'right living', as 'just living', is more than making money. Money can be made through wrong conduct, and we have plenty of examples of this in our current world, but money can also flow from working with love and trust in the outcomes. When I reach for some desired goal, something unforeseen and often better arrives. Letting go of desire (as dominant goal setting) creates more room for what one can become. I recognize that not all dance is life giving. Dancing can reflect greed when it serves egotistical goals. I don't want to say that performing for others, or in theatrical contexts, is necessarily ego-driven, but it can be. Dancing for others can also occasion community. *Intention* makes the difference, as phenomenologists like to say.

Regarding intention, dancing for the sake of dancing imbues trust, and through this, it teaches non-possession. When we dance purely for the dance, and not to please an audience, or to make money, we can touch the world lightly, even in stamping dances. I call this approach to dance, 'just dancing', as a way to associate it with the values of 'just sitting' in meditation. In 'just dancing', we practice release of 'me' and 'mine', and have a chance to experience a pure relationship to dance and to others in the dance. When we dance together in the spirit of just dancing, we move interdependently as one and for no other reason but the dance.

Non-possession is one of the primary tasks of old age. This implies letting go, not holding on, eventually letting go to whatever binds you to life itself. The unsettling eventuality of non-possession is that we all at some point will let go of everything, releasing our body and our loves – all our fleeting dances. Many people believe that in the process, we will gain something else, even if we have no perfect knowledge of this. The mystery of what is to come inheres in the beauty of present time.

My dance mentor Ohno Kazuo-sensei died in 2010 at the age of 103. In his butoh dance classes, he sometimes spoke of a river that connects this life and the next, where souls both living and dead commingle in peace on the shore. He asked students to dance this comingling as *Konpaku*. Ohno-sensei along with Hijikata Tatsumi is considered one of the primary founders of butoh. His use of *Konpaku* startles even the Japanese; it is such an old Buddhist word and concept. If I see the whole, I understand that death may not be a purely personal experience – that I will have help crossing the river. This belief in transcendent community, eases my aloneness, as does poetry. It often keeps me company in a magical frame of mind where emotions flow and the heart has wings. Poetry even more than dance attunes to the moral life and ultimate questions. Dance seems more immediately on fire and flung into time.

Japan has had a tradition of death poems. Emptiness and non-possession enter the Zen suchness, or everyday quality of these poems. Here is one I like from Michikaza, a man greedy for wealth and fame who denounced his vanities later in life. He wrote this simple poem near his death (1709). I like its straightforward ordinary tone:

Today I put on summer
clothes and Journey
to a world I haven't seen yet.

Masumi Kato's death poem (1796) is more florid, and I'm drawn to it also. This haiku appears on the poet's gravestone. He died during plum blossom season. His poem suggests that this life and the next have congruence through flowers:

The path to paradise
is paved with bright
plumb petals.

Stilling and falling

And here is a haiku that I arrange from a popular song that Ohno Kazuo-sensei often used as the finale for his dance concerts:

Wise men say, only
Fools rush in, but I can't help
Falling in love with you.

Certainly we recognize this as Elvis Presley. I think it has Zen elements – especially in its simplicity and foolish acceptance. Nothing seems more wisely foolish than Ohno Kazuo, a centenarian and Japanese veteran of the Second World War, dancing to this popular American icon. Well into his 90s, unable to stand and sitting in

FIGURE 12.2: Ohno Kazuo in his 90s. Photography by Koko Kiyama, 2001, Tokyo's Shinjuku Park Tower Hall. Used with permission of Ohno Kazuo archives.

a chair, Ohno lifted his arms and gestured with his large expressive hands, sometimes closing his eyes to the music of Elvis.

In Zen, wisdom arises unbidden and can't be forced, just as it does in love. Should we not be foolish and fall in love?

The wise fall in love with every new day, because they know that love heals. Giving up control heals, and can bring unexpected rewards. Early modern dancers gave up the control of uprightness, plying the ecstasy of spiraling downward into the floor-earth, only to throw themselves into the air with gangly abandon in the next moment. In falling down, we give up the desire to be perfect; in letting go, we let things be as they are – already perfect. We find ease in balancing control with freedom. In letting go, we need less and listen better.

I have taught dance in several forms for more than 40 years. Now I teach nothing, because in a very Zen sense, there is nothing anyone needs to learn. Realization of self in relation to others and an objective world is where learning lies, and teachers can't do this for us. They are, at best, catalyzers who help us fall in love with a subject or activity. Joanna Macy, scholar of Buddhism and deep ecology, tells us we are not here on earth primarily to learn from the world but to fall in love with it and take care of it (1991). We are already complete, as I have realized in studying Zen and its close relative, yoga. And we are not alone. What we do and how we live ripples out into the world and returns back to us. We are connected with each other and a part of the perfection of the world. This understanding is present in the deep doctrines of the East, and also has precedent in Plato and Greek classicism, where it is believed that learning is about realizing what is already present in the perfection of form, and that the artist elaborates the intelligence of the world of forms. In his *Timaeus*, Plato calls these perfect forms 'ideas in the mind of God' (Plato in Cairns 1961: xviii–xix).

Such perfection is intrinsic, or already always in us. The task of the teacher is to stimulate in the student what he already knows and can access, those potentials that reside in sleeping and dreaming, in tending plants and animals, in taking care of others, in service, and most certainly in dancing, painting, music, math, story and poetry. The teacher pays attention to the talents or natural proclivities of her students and encourages these. That is all. Teaching is not about stuffing information; it is about paying attention to emergent possibilities with trust. Martin Heidegger wrote in his phenomenology, *Being and Time*: 'What is essential in phenomenology does not lie in its actuality as a philosophical 'movement' ('Richtung'). Higher than actuality stands possibility' (1962: 62–63).

Stepping into the unknown, like falling in love, is risky and open to the moment. When we are in the flow of doing, the end result is learning. We progress naturally through paying attention to the work at hand. When work is done for its own sake – not in a goal-driven way but for the work itself – working is *just working*, like dancing is *just dancing*, and the incomprehensible reveals its simple parts. *Being lacks nothing.* In the whirlwind of her dance, the dancer loses self-limitations and becomes present to her freedom. She releases her great doubt and moves with faith instead.

Out of being, nothing becomes possible. We fall into stillness, empty of ambition in meditation. A main ingredient of sitting *Zazen* is posture, sometimes called 'right posture'. In my experiences of sitting Zazen in Zen temples in Japan and in Zen centres in the United States, sitting upright is a major component. If one can do this, one can meditate. In fact getting into the 'right' posture is considered enlightenment (Suzuki Shunryu in Kazuaki and Tensho 1996: 29). I like to think somatically of feeling right, breathing and feeling good in the posture. Then I can be light, with my back long and my head floating lightly upward.

In my somatics perspective, I prefer to think of 'just posture', the singularity of sitting alone or with others, and in silence. 'Just Posture' is somewhat like the

Zen practice of 'Just Sitting', where there is nothing else but the sitting, no images to focus on, no counting, just sitting, stilling the body and quieting the mind. In preparing posture for meditation, there is nothing but the posture. One can dwell in it, as in a poem on nothingness. Does it have to be right? Perhaps I depart from the formality of Zen, when I say 'no'. I don't think posture has to be right. Rather, let it be poetic. Well, maybe it needs to feel right, and this can vary from person to person, conditionally. Not everyone can sit easily upright. In fact it can be a struggle, as I have witnessed in my teaching (or non-teaching). Becoming adept at meditation has a lot to do with learning how to sit more easily upright, and this is a process that continues throughout life. Somatic practices and gentle yoga help with this. We can find rightness in the posture available to us in the moment. I like to ask students in somatic explorations, 'what is available to you now'? Rituals need to be adaptable to be put into practice.

To enlighten is to make lighter. Dance lightens as well. It can also produce heavy feelings, strong or weak aspects, and is alive with expression. I teach (or don't teach) that the very act of paying attention to our movement in any kind of dance is enlightening. Like just sitting and just walking, the purity of just dancing, engenders wholeness. In multiplying moments of wholeness, we need less, and can become lighter. One cannot command easy uprightness, but one can remember and rehearse it in dance and in somatic movement processes, including gentle yoga, which can support practices of meditation. At night, I practice the Zen of just walking and looking at the moon, turning towards the light while being turned by it. In the day I just dance, and the mood might be yogic-baroque and twining, or as Zen-simple and wabi-sabi as a forgotten sunflower leaning on a weathered shed. When I breathe easily and sit with presence and self-forgiveness, I meditate, clear my nervous system and shine my attention.

The mind of the dance

My quest for silence and true nature enters into my dance, and provides an anchor for my life. Being silent fosters resilience, clear thinking, and increases capacity for compassionate listening. The latter has helped me understand the importance of being inclusive – and in mindfulness terms – not ever giving up on a friend or student. Being transparent in my butoh awkwardness also seems to help.

I have asked myself whether the somatic field might include meditational practices, since somatics is a field that claims to develop perceptual awareness. The silence and stillness of meditation clears attention, thus presenting a special case of affectivity through the somatic readiness of *tabula rasa* erasure, which I develop more fully later. Being present to the moment and suspending judgment is one of the narratives I develop in my work in somatic movement education and therapy. It is a meditative practice and philosophical ideal, both east and west. When Heidegger writes about 'the ecstasy of time', where past and future meet in the present, he might as well have been describing the temporal experience of meditation (1962: 401–03). He admired Buddhist and Taoist teachings and learned from them, as we observe in *Heidegger's Hidden Sources* (May 1996).

The East has not been lost on western thought, including the philosophy of Nietzsche and his teacher Schopenhauer, who was one of the first western theorists to take inspiration from eastern philosophies. How could any philosopher miss the metaphysics of time expressed in Zen and Taoism, as also in Indian yoga? In all of these, time is lived and can be experienced as psychophysical oneness, as we will take up soon with Dōgen. Present time is oneness, lived in flow and stillness, as difficult to grasp as our own being here and now. When we still ourselves and dance, we can be present with our attention, not looking back with regret or worrying the future. When we are in contact with others in stillness, we can attune to them in the moment. My Zen teacher, Akane-sensei, puts the importance of this simply: '*Kyo Ikiru*'/'Live Today'. I wrote the core chapter of *Dancing into Darkness* as an existential leap from his exhortation (1999: 180–85).

Holding Presence is a point of view that I develop in my somatics work related to meditation and present time consciousness. It is simply about being present without prejudice, and thus it also speaks to relationships between people. The quest is how to be present to the concerns and dances of others. Neuroscientist Daniel Siegel, in *The Mindful Brain*, says: 'When we become our own best friend, we become open to connecting deeply with others' (2007: 322). Compassion and empathy are possible outcomes of structured explorations (or somatic choreographies) of body consciousness. Indeed, movement and dance produce feelings and prompt images of self-awareness. Dance, it is commonly thought, is about self-expression, but I believe it is more potent in its aspects of self-generation and body image: our existential becoming through movement expression, if you will. What we dance also dances us.

Dance, yoga, and somatic bodywork have together given me ways to explore consciousness, even as I understand that not all dancers or yoginis seek this. My forays into philosophy, especially phenomenology, took me towards 'moving consciously' and the study of movement somatics as such. Now I don't look so much for expertise in dance as I do for a beginner's mind, as I understand this through Zen. This doesn't mean I don't appreciate excellence in performance, but what if dancers could achieve excellence with attentional expansion? Yes, but attention to what? In a Zen sense, attention to the 'mind' of the dance or its intrinsic power. The mind of the dance might even encourage and inspire, or as in the case of some butoh, help us empathize with illness and death like Hijikata

Tatsumi's *Leprosy* (1973) and *Story of Small Pox* (1972). The mind of the dance is its nature or disposition, none other than the nature of the dancer, thus dancers cultivate themselves in both personal and physical attributes to deserve to dance for others.

I have known dancers whose daily practice of dance is a form of prayer. My practice of dance is less religious, but I do think of it as spiritually renewing. Zen meditation helps me with this. Everyday I dance, both literally and symbolically, with gratitude for the ground under my feet and awe for the sky that draws me upward. I dance to pay attention to the seasons, attuning to the people dear to me, as also those to come. When I cast my attention widely, I sometimes make music from the dance that flows through me with the help of my midi-keyboard and computer. I love infusing somatic yoga with dancelike flow, as I practice a friendly adaptability in my weekly volunteer work with seniors. They teach me resilience, patience and surrender. I practice dance as an improvisational art, but I appreciate dance in many forms, modern, postmodern, contemporary (in various guises), butoh, folk and ballet. I don't think it makes sense to claim superiority for any particular form of dance, or to claim that Zen belongs to a particular dance form like butoh. I have seen a lot of butoh that didn't resonate with Zen. I have also experienced elements of Zen mind in much dance. Audiences find themselves in their interpretations. We turn towards the dance, and sometimes it returns us to ourselves.

Dancing is essentially an action, and it is also an autotelic action, one that accomplishes nothing and goes nowhere. Dance serves no practical purpose in the world. We dance because we want to, not because we have to. And yet dancing of any kind seems most practical as consciously undertaken cultivation of embodiment. In dancing, we can feel whole and free, exuberant and alive, just as we can also feel splits of attention or we can lack awareness. Humans experience whole stretches of attentional lull and sometimes depression and existential turmoil. These can also motivate dance. The trick is to be able to pay attention to the mind of the dance, and to consciously direct it in influencing self and other.

Nothing is more cloying than complete sweetness. Dances that I like have undertows and darkness as well as light. But in general, I sense the importance of finding joy and peace in dancing as an activity for personal development. We can dance towards wholeness. Embodiment is an everyday eventuality. We attune to the world through work and play, and especially through art and dance. We can embody dance as a conscious act and for the same reason we practice Zen, to feel at one with the beneficence of the world.

The Zen oneness of the world is offered to us when we attune to it. This is not a given, but rather a choice. We can attune and become attentive in stilling and moving mindfully. Conversely we can practice negativity and criticism. I am not suggesting that we ignore social problems and cultural strife, but we have a better chance of doing something about them if we ourselves are well. It doesn't make sense to become sick with the supposed sickness of the world, or even to envision the world as problematic. We can see conformity around us without question, injustice and corruption. Certainly these are rife. But they do not define the world. The question is how to keep alive the inner attitudes that make a better world, and this begins with the self, as spiritual teachers continue to emphasize. Gandhi put it most famously and best: 'Be the change you want to see in the world'.

Zen is applicable to all dances, most basically it is about moving mindfully, and this is a matter of intention and attitude. Ballet can be as mindfully whole as butoh, and folk dances around the world are given away with abandon, performed for love of community and tribe. Some of my most memorable early experiences with dance came through ballroom dance – tango and cha cha, especially. I could easily abandon myself to the rhythm and vital essence of these dances, especially with a good partner. Improvisation in ballroom dance is a skillful infinite art. Mindfulness in tango, as in butoh, is about full presence and participation, not withholding awkwardness when it occurs. The skillful tango dancer can transform mistakes into curious innovations, as can a skilled jazz musician or concert dancer. Improvisation in dance and life shines the present centered moment, the same vital moment of art and Zen. It is not just that anything goes; everything appears both coming and going. We can't capture moonlight, but we can experience its beauty for a time. The same is true of all dancing, when we just dance.

At zero: Tabula rasa *Dōgen*

I digress for a moment to look back and take stock: Beginning in 1985, I became acquainted with butoh, the postmodern dance of Japan, which expanded my understanding of the East and eastern concepts of the body. I learned through butoh and Japanese phenomenology that the body doesn't end with the skin but extends throughout time–space. When we breathe, nature breathes. When we bleed, nature bleeds. Subsequently, I studied butoh in Japan, Canada and the United States. It was not my intention to write about butoh in the beginning, but Shodo Akane-sensei, my Zen teacher in Japan, encouraged me to write about dance and Zen. In the process, I discerned relationships between Zen and butoh, and once more invented myself, now in the guise of the East with *Dancing into Darkness: Butoh, Zen, and Japan* (1999).

Later I wrote two more books about this globally responsive dance form, which is still evolving – *Hijikata Tatsumi and Ohno Kazuo* (2006) and *BUTOH:*

Metamorphic Dance and Global Alchemy (2010). Through study with butoh artists and writing about butoh, I became a butoh teacher (not-teaching). I have already mentioned my inspiration and mentor in this art, Ohno Kazuo-sensei (27 October 1906–1 June 2010), who provided a resounding example of dancing into old age that sustains me still. My association with him continues through his son Ohno Yoshito, who is a year older than I. Once while dancing an improvised duet with Yoshito, I asked him to marry me, and he promised he would (next life I guess). The Ohnos' approach to dance, both spiritual and somatic, continues its global influence.

Dance is body poetry, a special kind of body language and wordless communication. The poetry changes with the style of the dance and the performers. Mindfulness, being awake to the present, reinforces all matters of somatic sensibility and thus all dances and bodily poeisis. I sometimes interpret this state of naked aliveness as zero, or the state of nothingness that precedes the birth of new ideas and dances. Sometimes I say, 'zero yourself', to my students. 'Disappear' is not the same, nor is 'now yourself'. Zero is the place we start from before we are aware of anything at all. Zero is emptiness of a certain kind. Now is present time, and disappearance is a visual phenomenon. Stillness and silence bring answers of themselves. Like many, my personal quest has been to silence the chatter of my mind and to transform my pain body. When I dance into healing, I seek the still centres of movement. I like to disappear and cover myself with imaginary wings, so no one can see me, and I especially like the emptiness of dancing zero. Zero is a feeling, however fleeting, a feeling of release and effortlessness. Zero is light. From zero one might move to plus or minus. Zero is an empty middle that floats. In butoh explorations, I ask my students to dance zero, and they do. The human faces of zero are incredible, anti-gravity, evanescent, attuned and unburdened.

Intuitive understanding and pleasure are the happy results of realizing effortless ease in movement. Healing can arise from ease as a sense of well-being enters consciousness. Jon Kabat-Zinn, the author of books and scientific papers on mindfulness and its clinical applications, refers readers to the capacity of the brain to change according to whole body responses (1991, 1994). In my own background, The Feldenkrais Method of Somatic Education is based on the same principle. It is no secret that we feel better when we can lower somatic thresholds. We breathe better. We are not in a struggle or stress mode, but rather at ease with the world and ourselves. When we embody movement effortlessly and with love, we can heal if only for a time. Healing, it seems to me, is a daily practice. When we multiply the times of feeling good, we create momentum and change in a positive direction.

Ease in doing entails doing less to feel more, and building confidence through listening better. These are aspects of being present with awareness and knowing about the potentials of zero. I have learned present centered awareness from three studies and practices – phenomenology, somatics and Zen. These three seemingly disparate practices teach non-judgment and *tabula rasa* thinking, developing a consciousness of not knowing, just as we can aim to dance every day into existence without expectations and with appreciation for the chance to start afresh. Phenomenology teaches one not to assume anything in advance, to suspend what one already knows, and to let go of prejudice by questioning presuppositions. The goal of this kind of thinking is to wipe the slate clean, so to speak, as one aims to see things (phenomena) for the first time.

Non-judgment in somatics may be compared to the suspension of bias in phenomenology, but it also takes on a Zen aspect, that of waiting and patience, finding stillness within movement and in the moment. I learned the most about this from sitting Zazen. In practicing Zen meditation, the very erasure of thought, or at least the attempt, releases the known. To be at rest in meditation is to be cleansed if even for moments of silence. In silence and not-knowing, there is no judge. Thoughts can be unpacked and seen simply as thoughts, coming and going, as they fade.

Phenomenology, somatics and Zen allow me to be in the moment, and to forgive myself when I fall into worry or fear. I can always recover and start peacefully at zero. I adhere to Zen as a practice in silent sitting – in laughter, composure and compassion. Sitting Zazen engenders forbearance and respect for suffering. I practice yoga to lengthen, to flow and to unify. I have had several gurus in Zen, yoga and phenomenology. For that I am grateful, and I will probably have more.

Zen emphasizes emptiness. Phenomenology and somatics do this in related ways, especially by erasing expectations. Nothing existing rests undisturbed in its original pure state, and yet I can envision a clear place and consciousness in my dance. From there, the possible is a beacon.

I zero myself in phenomenology, Zen and somatics. A phenomenologist doesn't assume a ready-made answer. In this one breaks the mold, and asks consciousness to speak anew. This way of seeing and understanding doesn't depend on accepted theories. This doesn't mean that one disrespects disciplined bodies of knowledge, but one does not depend on them. What new knowledge might come from not-knowing? This is my question. What new knowledge might come from experience if I'm paying attention? This is my next question.

Like phenomenology somatics may seem too involved with the self, but its aim of integrating experience and connecting to others and nature are as important as its focus on self-awareness. Care of self comes first because it is basic to the ability to connect. In excavating possible-selves, we understand that consciousness is vast, welling up through psychic life, and that it has somatosensory sources in movement, touch and stillness. We find precedent for this in both the East and the West, through phenomenology, yoga and Zen.

During my 1990 Japan visit, my Zen teacher, Akane-sensei, introduced me in a few strokes to a calligraphy that continues to guide my path in the world: *Shin Shin Ichinyo*, meaning *Body and Mind are One*. This expression of nondual realization is essential to the teachings of Eihei Dōgen (1200–53), the historic reformer of Buddhism in Japan, and a prolific author and teacher of Zen who founded the Sōtō School. My teacher is in Dōgen's lineage. In this path, the body is to be cultivated, not abused or neglected. Cleansing is important, as is the use of beautiful aromatic oils. Wellness is the way. Wholeness is an aspiration. Oneness of body and mind is an ultimate achievement of wholeness, of 'self returning to self' and 'return to the source' (Dōgen in Tanahashi and Levitt 2013: 17). Through my studies in Japan and association with Zen and butoh, I now use the term *Shin* to identify my work, more fully expressed through movement as *Shin Somatics*.

Return to source is whole in its return to nature Dōgen tells us: 'Saying that the self returns to the self is not contradicted by saying that the self is mountains, rivers, and the great earth. All Buddhas are wind and rain, water and fire' (in Tanahashi and Levitt 2013: 177). Dōgen teaches that water, mountains and grass, like tiles and walls practice together with one who meditates. Water is also realizing its way to the source. The entire world of phenomena unfolds in our dancing, because we dance as nature does, maybe not as Isadora did, but each in his/her own way returns to what Dōgen called 'source'. Physicist Carl Sagan also put it famously: 'We are a way for the universe to know itself'. Heidegger characterized source as origins, poetically as *ursprung, original leap*. In dancing, we return to the cosmos, and the stars are already and always in us.

Paradoxically, in such achievement, the body and mind 'drop off' or 'fall away' in Dōgen's poeisis. Such non-doing is also an achievement, just as non-teaching is. The means is silent sitting and conscious dancing. Our sitting is mindful, as is our dancing, and people find the way to dance that is theirs. I believe we have individual dispositions, just as rocks and rivers do, and still we are all tending towards a common source. Mind includes body, and body includes mind. Both include nature. This perspective has been stated for centuries in Dōgen's Zen, and is now borne out in the findings of neuroscience, especially through the work of Antonio Damasio and others who study consciousness. Damasio's view is beautifully expressed in several volumes, first in *The Feeling of What Happens* (1999), and more recently in *Self Comes to Mind* (2012). One can realize seamless body-mind oneness in meditation and in mindful cultivations of dance. I have experienced that the values of meditation can be translated to dance and our human belonging to the natural world; our moving as nature is part of such mindful wholeness.

For this reason, I develop dances in the environment, using the camera as witness; since film also belongs to the world of phenomena and can help us

FIGURE 12.3: Sondra Fraleigh in *Ancient Body Butoh* (2014), Snow Canyon, Utah. Photo by Kay Nelson, 2014. Used with permission.

remember our belonging to nature. Here is a dance of bonding with soft sandstone, brush and lava rock in Snow Canyon, near where I live in Utah.

Zen maintains that the human being must be understood as a being rooted in nature as a 'being-in-nature', to use Yuasa Yasuo's phrase. His work appeals to me as a synthesis of Zen with phenomenology and the somatics of personal development. I met him at a conference in Tsukuba, Japan in 1986, where I became acquainted with his very adept explanations of eastern philosophy through the western lens of phenomenology. I continue to study Yuasa through Shigenori Nagatomo's writings and translations of eastern philosophies of the body, including Yuasa's phenomenology of depth psychology and perspectives of Dōgen Zen.

For Dōgen, the body is developed from studying the way and becomes the true human body through cultivation:

> The concept of the true human body may be understood to be the body that has been transformed through personal self-cultivation, which is a type of habit-formation, and which is accompanied by a change in the body image, since the nature of the body image is shaped by the kind of training or cultivation that one goes through [...]. This personal self-cultivation meant for Dōgen the practice of just sitting.
>
> (Yuasa in Nagatomo 1992: 165)

Shin shin ichi nyo, in Dōgen's scheme and more generally in Buddhism, indicates that through meditation and in self-cultivation, the body and mind arise as one, functioning as an integrated whole (Nagatomo 1992: 126–27). The common sense dualistic notions and experiences of physical and mental phenomena are 'cast off' in oneness and deepened states of meditation. I would add that meditation in motion is also about 'casting off the body and mind' (*shinjin totsuraku*). The latter is an achievement that eventuality marked Dōgen's authentication of oneness (Nagatomo 1992: 129). Something common to both body and mind provides the ground for samadhic awareness. Modern neuroscience is showing that there is no way to separate physical and mental processes. As also in Dōgen's philosophy of Zen, generation and extinction are constant. We are coming into being at the very moment of disappearance, as we do in *just dancing*. The arrival of the leap is present in its beginning. In Zen and in dancing, time as lived is relative and seamless, as indicated in the haiku of Vietnamese Buddhist monk Thich Nhat Hanh:

Don't say I will depart tomorrow –
even today, I'm still arriving.

(Thich Nhat Hanh)

Dōgen's metaphysical influence on Buddhist thought is unmistakable: oneness is not an abstract concept for him. For me, oneness is symbolized in *Shin* and realized in Dōgen's frame of reference through cultivation of the body-mind, casting off the mental and physical in a *tabula rasa* process of self-erasure. We can leave the clutter of mental and physical self-constructions behind and dance towards self-renewal and source. I have observed that purposeful cultivation of wholeness manifests in the everyday as peace, health, foresight, trust, creativity, compassion and hope (to name a few qualities). In wholeness, we can speak our truth with power and love and let go of outcomes. Purposeful cultivation of the body-mind (or body-self) is a matter of paying attention, bringing awareness to ones acts and words: dancing oneness, dancing zero with abundance.

Being awkward

One spot, alone,
Left glowing in the dark:
My snotty nose.

(Gaki)

This is Gaki's death poem, and I think it is meant to be more existentially absurd than funny. Gaki, a haiku poet who died on the 24th day of July, 1927 at the age of 36, is better known by his given name, Akutagawa Ryunosuke. He was a celebrated writer in his day, well known in Japan's literary scene. His mother became insane shortly after his birth, casting a great pall over his life. He killed himself by drinking poison shortly after asking his aunt to deliver his death poem to his doctor.

Gaki was apparently not afraid to embarrass himself, even in death. Most of us push away the unpleasantly awkward. Butoh dancers are the only ones I know who consistently explore clumsy registers of movement and affect, though not to the exclusion of other expressions. I have learned a lot from them about self-acceptance and the beauty of my awkward moments.

My puppy is never awkward, even when she falls and tumbles, or turns her belly up for 'rubbing' – her legs akimbo. Unfortunately humans are sometimes awkward and get embarrassed because they lose control, or seem to say the wrong thing. Puppies are very Zen creatures, I think, because they never worry about barking too much, and they don't judge their own cavorting. When I was young, I worried a lot about what I said and how people would see me through my words or actions. Now I'm gratefully awkward, not needing to please anyone. This is part of the gift of growing older, not that you just don't care, but that you can see power in awkwardness. Grace is not a better state, especially when achieved at the cost of stress. When you can simply be yourself, there is no distinction between grace and gracelessness, only a beginner's mind.

I learned the power of awkwardness through Zen and butoh. In Zen one can cover oneself in silence, not hiding necessarily, but rather taking a break from judgment, including self-judgment. One can be happy in silence and stillness, not needing to impress anyone, to speak or to dance. Nothing to teach or learn can be comforting; nothing becomes something in math when we discover the value of zero. Nothing is the blank page of *tabula rasa*, the clean slate out of which creativity and intuition can flow.

Early on in my study of butoh, I realized I was practicing a form of phenomenology in self-erasure and non-judgment, letting go of the need to be adept, clever or accomplished. Letting go the desire to connect with expectations, I practiced uncomfortable positions and facial expressions, twisting my face into ugly shapes, rubbery and rusty. Eventually, I practiced a butoh technique that plys the edge of falling. This is similar to risky leaning positions and movements in modern/postmodern dance, and also akin to difficult balances in ballet, except that edgy butoh moves clumsily on and on, staying off-balance, hanging awry whenever possible.

There could be several reasons for interrupting the grace and perfection that is typically sought in dance, and instead choosing the emotional upheaval of the notably uncool. One reason I see is that life itself brings unexpected interruptions of couth, and if we get a chance to practice awkwardness in dance, we can more easily smile at our own faux pas. I have observed over the years of knowing many people in varied circumstances that no one gets away without social blunders (and movements) they regret or transform and make use of – hopefully the latter.

Another reason to court awkwardness inheres in the metaphysics of *artlessness*, *emptiness* and *lack*, lest we remember that in lack lies every potential. *Shoshin* or the Zen concept of *Beginners Mind* expands this idea as process, explored in the spiritual classic of Suzuki Shunryu, *Beginner's Mind* (1970). In an act of *tabula rasa* writing, Suzuki sees that beginners have many possibilities, while experts have few. We can set aside what we think we know in order to approach a topic or activity innocently. Then we can learn.

The founder of butoh, Hijikata Tatsumi, takes awkwardness towards a surrealist turn when he says, 'I'd like to be caught smack in the middle of a mistake'

FIGURE 12.4: Sondra Fraleigh dances *Ancient Body Butoh* (2014) in a burned out trailer home. Photo by Kay Nelson © 2014, used with permission.

([1961] 2000). In his admission I find bald permission to acknowledge mistakes and use them. Let me stumble, fall apart, burn and recover, so I can begin again – each new day and each new dance. Let me live with lack, and not the dominant goals of art.

I say I don't give advice, but I do have some advice about awkwardness relative to pain. Get lost and clumsy, and get a little foolish when you dance. Get crazy, and give up perfection and opulence in order to find a little friendly inelegance. Then you can listen to your pain, not needing to hide it. Invite your pain to tea, and you will learn a lot. Its lessons vary according to individual situations. I learned from my back pain that I couldn't please everyone. I also learned this simply from growing older. I'm 75 as of this writing, and every year requires more resilience. I have grown beyond many of the childhood memories that haunted me, and I continue to transform my physical pain. I no longer seek my worth through that of men. I see my own worth. I'm happy. I know that whatever comes, I can morph and move through it, not correcting myself, twisting into absurdity my foolish butoh face.

REFERENCES

Cairns, Huntington and Hamilton, Edith (eds) (1961), *Collected Dialogues of Plato*, Princeton: Princeton University Press.

Damasio, Antonio (1999), *The Feeling of What Happens: Body, Emotion and the Making of Consciousness*, London: Heinemann.

Damasio, Antonio (2012), *Self Comes to Mind: Constructing the Conscious Brain*, New York: Vintage Books, Random House Inc.

Fraleigh, Sondra (1999), *Dancing into Darkness: Butoh, Zen, and Japan*, Pittsburgh: University of Pittsburgh Press.

Fraleigh, Sondra (2010), *BUTOH: Metamorphic Dance and Global Alchemy*, Champaign, Urbana: University of Illinois Press.

Fraleigh, Sondra and Nakamura, Tamah (2006), *Hijikata Tatsumi and Ohno Kazuo*, London: Routledge.

Heidegger, Martin (1962), *Being and Time* (trans. J. Macquarrie and E. Robinson), New York: Harper & Row.

Kabit-Zin, Jon (1991), *Full Catastrophe Living: Using the Wisdom of Your Body and Mind to Face Stress, Pain, and Illness*, New York: Delta.

Kabit-Zin, Jon (1994), *Wherever You Go, There You Are: Mindfulness Meditation in Everyday Life*, New York: Hyperion.

Kazuaki, Tanahashi and Levitt, Peter (eds) (2013), *The Essential Dōgen: Writings of the Great Zen Master*, Boston, London: Shambhala.

Kazuaki, Tanahashi and Tensho, Schneider (eds) (1996), *Essential Zen*, Edison: Castel Books.

Macy, Joanna (1991), *World as Lover, World as Self*, Berkley: Parallax Press.

May, Reinhard (1996), *Heidegger's Hidden Sources: East Asian Influences on his Work*, Oxon: Routledge.

Nagatomo, Shigenori (1992), *Attunement through the Body*, Albany: State University of New York Press.

Siegel, Daniel (2007), *The Mindful Brain: Reflection and Attunement in the Cultivation of Well-Being*, New York: W. W. Norton & Company.

Suzuki, Shunryu (1970), *Zen Mind: Beginner's Mind* (eds T. Dixon and R. Baker), New York, Tokyo: Weatherhill.

Tatsumi, Hijikata (1961/2000), '*Keimusho e*'/'To prison', *The Drama Review*, 44:1, Spring, pp. 43–48, in *Hijikata Tatsumi: The Words of Butoh* (trans. J. S. Ruyak and K. Nanako), *The Drama Review*, 44:1, pp. 10–28.

Postscript Notes to Self

If I could interview myself concerning the project of this book of essays – ranging from *Ethical World Gaze* to *Attunement and Evanesce* – I would continue my attempt to engage readers in somatic quests of values and practices. Could I carry this work forward into future projects? They might read something like this:

o   Addressing Oppression
o   Revaluing Aesthetics
o   Revaluing Nature
o   Cultivating Hope
o   Fairness as Intrinsic Value in Somatics
o   Acting on Ecological Regeneration
o   Engaging Multicultural and Multiracial Community Building
o   Practicing Civil Discourse through Somatic Methods
o   Practicing Dynamics of Power-Sharing
o   Promoting Pluralistic Ecosomatic Geographies

Bodies of knowledge and geographies gain resilience through change – the migration of new ideas, methods and power-sharing. Dependence on mastery and masters is oppressive and a dead-end; instead, a field of practices survives on innovation and renewal, and I advocate for this. In understanding the body as part of and known through nature, we might hope to understand better the latent potentials for decentering the self and the human – somatically – as we foreground current ecological crises. Likewise, the developing work of somatic movement and performance can and should advocate for planetary resilience and build networks that sustain multicultural and multiracial flourishing. *Ethics are mind matters of life and breath*. In somatic endeavors, let us be mindful that we belong to the earth, all life, and each other. I want to remember these two things in particular, that the flourishing of all people is a somatic issue, and the flourishing of all life is a somatic imperative.

Milton Keynes UK
Ingram Content Group UK Ltd.
UKHW051057211123
432914UK00059B/92